DEVOTION

DEVOTION

A MEMOIR | MIRIAM LEVINE

The University of Georgia Press • Athens and London

© 1993 by Miriam Levine
All rights reserved
Published by the University of Georgia Press
Athens, Georgia 30602

Designed by Louise OFarrell
Set in 10/14 Aldus by Tseng Information Systems, Inc.
Printed and bound by Thomson-Shore, Inc.
The paper in this book meets the guidelines for permanence
and durability of the Committee on Production Guidelines
for Book Longevity of the Council on Library Resources.

Printed in the United States of America

97 96 95 94 93   C   5 4 3 2 1

Library of Congress Cataloging in Publication Data
Levine, Miriam, 1939–
Devotion : a memoir / Miriam Levine.
p.   cm.
ISBN 0-8203-1555-9 (alk. paper)
1. Levine, Miriam, 1939– —Biography.   2. Women poets,
American—20th century—Biography.   1. Title.
PS3562.E898Z465   1993
811'.54—dc20
                                        [B]   92-44781

British Library Cataloging in Publication Data available

Excerpt from "Already the ripening barberries" by Rainer Maria Rilke, from
Selected Poems of Rainer Maria Rilke, translated by Robert Bly. Copyright
1981 by Robert Bly. Reprinted by permission of HarperCollins Publishers.
Excerpt from "Richard Cory" from *The Children of the Night* by Edwin
Arlington Robinson (New York: Charles Scribner's Sons, 1897). Excerpt from
"During Fever" from *Life Studies* by Robert Lowell. Copyright 1956, 1959 by
Robert Lowell. Renewal copyright 1981, 1986, 1987 by Harriet W. Lowell,
Caroline Lowell, and Sheridan Lowell. Reprinted by permission of Farrar,
Straus and Giroux, Inc. and Faber and Faber, Ltd.

For John and for Gert

Contents

Acknowledgments

Affectionate thanks to readers of the manuscript who offered advice and encouragement: John Lane, Patsy Vigderman, Patricia Hampl, Alan Feldman, Marilyn Harter, Stephen Love, Linda Bamber, Sharon O'Brien, Linda Julian, and Madelon Hope. Abiding gratitude to my editor, Karen Orchard, to Alan Feldman, who suggested that I write this book, and to Helen Heineman, who gave me the opportunity to do so.

Thanks also to the Artists Foundation of Massachusetts for a finalist grant in nonfiction, to Sam Galvagna for technical assistance in preparing the manuscript, to Marcia Brubeck, my diligent copyeditor, and to Kelly Caudle, David Des Jardines, and Gene Adair at the University of Georgia Press.

Thanks, finally, to the editors of the following journals in which parts of *Devotion* were published in slightly different form: the *Emrys Journal*, "Angelo Bertocci at Boston University" and "Passaic Junction"; the *Hawaii Review*, "Sam."

SOURCE

Sam

My uncle Sam, my mother's brother, was blind. When I asked her how it happened, Gert vaguely answered, "In the war." She and I were in the dark back kitchen overlooking a courtyard, which let in muted gray light. The light was not dreary; although a visitor might believe the room was always *one* dull gray, I was used to watching white light very slowly darken, as the day went on, to shade after shade of gray. The light came down into the brick funnel of the courtyard and through the two windows from such a great height it seemed a small wonder that, without turning on the electric light, I could see the sink, the big set tub, the green and pale brown stove on legs, the metal-topped table, my plate, my mother at the stove. "What war?" I persisted. At seven I was already a righteous interrogator, enjoying my victim's discomfort. Gert hesitated. "The first," she finally replied, as if she had trouble remembering.

Her answer seemed to make sense. We still saw wounded veterans from the first war begging on the streets near our house: a man with one leg, a man with no legs. Before every Saturday matinee we watched news of the current war. There were white and gold satin banners hanging in the windows of Gold Star Mothers; their sons had died in the war, and they had been made mothers in perpetuity, symbols of grief and sacrifice. There was no doubt: war meant maiming and death.

For a time after my conversation with my mother, everytime I saw my uncle, I would search his head for scars. I could stare and stare without any risk of offending, yet although unchallenged, I felt like a sneak and a spy. I would examine his temples. In war movies it was always a wound to the temples that caused blindness. Uncle's were perfectly smooth, incurved, unmarked. I had also heard of veterans with steel plates in their skulls. Maybe that's what Uncle had. If I could find the secret door, which I thought had to be concealed under the scalp, I might, I believed, touch this damaged place, put my fingers over the cool metal conductor, and feel some deep vibration from within, which would strangely reassure me. But Uncle's grizzled close-cropped hair grew smoothly in undisturbed whorls.

Perhaps it wasn't a scar from a stitched-up wound, I began to think, but a half-moon-shaped dent like the kind you're likely to leave in wood if you hammer a nail in too far. I knew a boy with such a dent in his forehead. Uncle's forehead was lined, not dented.

I was a small girl, not more than seven or eight. He must have been close to fifty. His head seemed enormous, perhaps, because so nakedly unprotected. He would turn and raise his head at the sound of my voice, but he would not smile, or frown, or look sulky in response to anything anyone did or said, yet he was not expressionless. He could look angry, but mostly his face had the appearance of raw still weariness.

His eyes were somewhat sunken, the lids slightly sore-looking. When I called to him, the lids would raise, and I could see his clouded eyes. Sometimes there seemed to be movement in the pupils. He would close his eyes almost immediately, as if the light hurt him. Because he looked, at such times, like an ordinary person blinking at a sudden harsh light, I would begin to imagine he could see—a beam of light was somehow getting in! But at the same time I realized that the movement I thought I saw was only reflected light, a yellowish marbly gleam, and the opening and closing of his eyes only a reflex that went with the turning of his head. This reflex gripped me more than if he had stared into my eyes. His eyes became—weirdly—like ears, a second set of blind cockles turned on me.

Unlike my fine-featured, smooth-faced Levine relatives—my father's side of the family—Uncle had rough grayish skin like that of a frozen potato. His features were deeply cut, angular yet drooping. There were deep lines on either side of his mouth; his cheeks sagged. The upper part of his face, the sensitive eyes, the large domed Jacobs forehead, just barely lifted his face to grandeur. I contemplated a wrecked colossus, but he wasn't completely broken.

He had a harsh resonating laugh with an edge of irony and an undercurrent of joy. It was a laugh in conflict with itself. Whenever I heard it, I felt as if I were being taught something, but I didn't then know what, though I sensed that Uncle's laugh was truth. The sound of his voice, the look on his face, were exposed and intelligent, unlike the prissy conventional manner of some grownups as they lowered their voices so I wouldn't hear them talking about sex and whatever else they thought I shouldn't know. Their eyebrows would be lifted, their fingers raised to their mouths, their mouths opened as if for the dentist, their eyes wide: a slow-motion pantomime for fools. I became contemptuous. I made believe that I knew everything about sex and about everything else in the world. I was afraid of appearing stupid.

I didn't find out what had caused Uncle's blindness all at once: I pieced it together over the years. As a small child I noticed how my relatives always lowered their voices when they mentioned my mother's family. Once—and once was all it took to hook me—I saw one of my aunts make the crazy sign to punctuate a whispered conversation with her sister-in-law. She raised her left hand to hide the gesture from me, but I saw her twirl her right index finger at her temple as if she were winding up string. In the way of all children, I felt afraid and ashamed, as if somehow I was at fault along with the rest of the Jacobses, but at the same time her gesture had galvanized me: there is a secret, I thought, and I'm going to find out what it is.

One afternoon, while my parents were at work, and the house was silent, I searched through their drawers. Most of their things—my mother's seemingly immense pink bloomers, my father's ironed-flat boxer shorts—gave off the heavy seriousness of middle age in the postwar years, the mystery of concealed sex. There was hardly anything new or fresh. The top drawer smelled of bitter lavender from a bottle of Yardley's so old that the few remaining drops of scent had turned brown as whiskey. Next to the round box of loose floury face powder were pairs of sad unused gloves like pressed and shrunken corsages. Among my mother's costume jewelry was a brassy bristling brooch-and-earring set with Life Saver green stones. I fingered my father's cheap "Swank" tiepin shaped like a fish, his worn Liberty Head dollar—1902, the year of his birth, almost obliterated. I found his gray suede dress gloves. They were still clean and soft, and their backs were stitched with black lines, which looked like cat's whiskers. He never wore the long white silk scarf, which I unfolded from its slippery layers and kept wrapped around my neck as I worked. The silk was heavy and cool. When I looked up from my search, I would see my intent face in the mirror. (In early adolescence this scarf became part of my "spy" costume: wearing a tightly belted black sateen raincoat, the scarf wound around my neck and thrown over a shoulder, lips bright red, I would stand in front of this mirror and stare into my serious daring eyes, into myself.)

Pushed in the back of the middle drawer was a black wooden box that I knew had belonged to my grandfather. Finally—I don't know whether it was on this day or one soon after—I found the cold stubby key. In the box were my grandparents' immigration papers, worn thin and separated at the folds. There were also documents concerning my mother's sister Rose and her brother Meyer. They had been put in Greystone Park mental hospital. The papers said "committed." In the space after "diagnosis" were the words "congenital syphilis." I got out the dictionary and looked up "syphilis." Then I had to look up more words: venereal, spirochete. I didn't completely understand, but at least I learned there was a disease. The meaning of "venereal" wasn't interesting. I wasn't exactly sure what "sexual" meant. I couldn't picture "intercourse." There was the male sex and the female sex: I knew about that. But the word "congenital" was important, mysterious—a fate.

Eventually, certainly by the time I was ten or eleven, I understood, and somehow my parents came to understand that I knew. My mother, with a look of calm but eager distinction, told me the family story. My grandfather had become infected in a brothel in Poland, in Lodz, and had unwittingly passed on the disease to my grandmother. Three of their children—Rose, Sam, and Meyer—had been born incurably infected. My mother told me that by the time she and her brother Louie were born, the family illness had been diagnosed. Both were examined and pronounced free of disease. (Ironically, the ill children were large, and for some time robust looking, while my mother and Louie were tiny, under five feet, yet energetic, driven.) Meyer and Rose went mad and were put in Greystone Park in New Jersey. Sam's eyes were damaged at birth. He eventually went blind, my mother said, "when he became a man." Puberty had never sounded so biblical. This was something to rival the Bar Mitzvah's celebration, a blow that descended with more force than the little bags of candy we threw down at the Bar Mitzvah boy from the women's gallery of the shul.

If knowledge is sanity, Uncle was sane. In a terrible scene he accused his father; he lifted his head and turned it toward the old man's pleading voice: "You did this to me!" My mother said that her father ran from the room, his hands pressed to his ears. His face was lit up with tragic light, lifted also like his son's but to heaven.

Much later in college I found myself bored with discussions about whether or not Willy Loman was a tragic hero. I was a ferocious snob—worse than any Yankee with her family's export china. The Lomans simply did not measure up to the Jacobses, whose frequent bread was pity and fear. Willy and my Uncle Sam both had been helpless to prevent the fate that rolled over them, but Uncle, unlike Willy, had understood what happened to him and in that knowledge had become powerful. Power and helplessness was the truth I grew up with, the truth I heard in Uncle's voice.

After my parents married, they lived with Sam and Rose (Meyer was already in Greystone) in the family house on Twelfth Street in Paterson. Sam and Rose had the attic apartment. Rose, once a tireless weaver who worked with manic energy, was fired from her job at the silk mill; she was becoming more and more violent.

The progressing syphilis intensified Rose's already madly despotic nature. Since childhood she had ruled the household. If she didn't like the food, she would fling her plate to the floor. She and my mother, who was five years younger, shared the same bed. If my mother did not do what Rose wanted, Rose would wait for her to fall asleep and then throw her out of bed with a violent shove. My grandmother, who wanted peace, would tell my mother to do what Rose wanted, "Such a small thing," she would say, "what difference does it make?" Gert told me that Rose, in her early teens, began to "torture" my grandfather. She could not stand to see him resting. If he sat in the kitchen reading the paper, she would taunt him. She knew how to pick on those who could not fight back. My grandfather was a quiet man; he'd leave the house and spend his evenings at the library on Broadway, a few blocks from home.

By the time I was born, Rose was at her violent worst. She would creep down the stairs, sneak up on my mother—"while I was trying to give you the bottle," Gert says—and, with a ghastly shriek, hit her from behind. Even now when I read Blake's, "How the youthful Harlots curse / Blasts the new born Infant's tear," I substitute "Rose's" for "Harlots."

My mother was not strong enough to fight Rose. For too many years my grandmother had soothed and manipulated her into giving in. Only my uncle could control Rose. Once, after she had tried to hurt him, he told my mother that it was either Rose's life or his own, and, blind as he was, he ran after her, caught her, and shook her hard; his mouth close to her ear he told her he would kill her if she did not stop. From then on she was afraid of him. His voice meant business. He was strong enough to stop her; he wasn't afraid; he did what had to be done. He protected us, my mother and me—my father worked long hours—but eventually it was too much for all of them. My mother stopped eating and sleeping; she broke down completely. In February when I was three months old we moved in with my grandmother Molly in Passaic. She and my uncle Dave took care of me and my mother. For most of the first year of my life my mother was not there for me. She had been sacrificed to Rose and in turn had sacrificed me. In the spring we moved into the apartment next door to my grandmother. Rose had finally been committed, a life sentence.

When I knew Uncle, he spoke about people with tough authority in the third person, his voice rough with affection or sarcasm or both. Sam's English was accentless, but the inflection, and the ironic, intelligent, zinging pauses were foreign. East European without the shmaltz. He was a storyteller—who won, who lost, who hit it big, who lived, who died. Everyone in his world was lifted out of his or her given name to an appellative, which rang with the truth of a fable: The Kid, The Sister, The Old Lady, The Dope, The Big Mouth, The Big Shot, The Thief— no saints or nice little girls. I was The Kid: cheeky, rude, and stubborn but admirable. Sam would defend me. "Leave The Kid alone," he would say when my stubbornness would madden my parents. He sounded like the Romanian-born actor Edward G. Robinson—he played gangsters—rescuing a smart protégée.

Sam had a girlfriend. My mother told me that, when they had all lived together in Paterson, Sam had hired Jessie to help with the housework. Jessie was Irish. She had a lighthearted smile. One day my mother came back early from her trip to the store— she would usually leave Jessie to her work and be gone for a few hours. She paused on the porch; something looked different, but she wasn't sure what. Then she realized that the living room shades were pulled down. "They were having a party," my mother said. Gert was proud of Sam's affair: the Blind Man was getting some pleasure, stealing from the gods the way my family would steal from the boss. Jessie did not cancel Sam's fate; she was the proof of his courage—this man who should have been paralyzed by shame but wasn't. "Would you rather be Socrates unsatisfied or a pig satisfied?" asked my sophomore philosophy professor, fancying himself a gadfly. What a choice! I snickered. Now I think of Sam *occasionally* satisfied. Good for Sam.

Like all the Jacobses, he loved to give away money. He lived off his pension and what he could make playing the numbers and the horses. When he won, we all won. He always seemed to have money, seemed to be ahead. Sam was in the action. Early I found myself siding with the disreputable. I imagined him on the downtown Paterson streets, on the way to the bookie, in the delicatessens and cafeterias where he loved to eat corned beef sandwiches and apple pie with ice cream. I imagined his swiftly lifting face, his thick brown wavy hair, which rose from his high forehead in one dense smooth mass, his white cane, like beacons. He'd thrust bills at my mother, "Here, get The Kid an ice cream. . . . Here, get yourself a coat, a good one." I heard just recently that he used to give money to my grandmother Molly and that years before, after her husband had died, when she had very little, he had given her a bundle of army surplus underwear, which he had probably gotten from some charity for the blind. They were her first underpants, soldiers' drawers! Before that she had worn only peasant petticoats under her skirts. With money from a big hit he bought the solid maple three-quarter bed I slept in. I don't know exactly how much he gave my parents, but in our unlucky household one big hit made you a winner—forever. I realize now that my mother needed to create Sam for herself, and for me, to reimagine him: she had the ability to select a person's gift—or flaw—and make it count in the telling of a story. What do I know? He won big at least once. After all, how many times does a person need to win? I slept on his winnings. A three-quarter bed was a good one—better than a single.

All of my relatives were judges of a good thing, especially of fruits and vegetables. They could discuss the provenance of an apple the way a collector traced the origin of a painting. They were connoisseurs. It was their gift, not a gift of their poverty. They would note the differences between California oranges and Florida oranges; between California carrots and Florida carrots; between local Jersey cultivated "True Blues" and wild blueberries; between Long Island potatoes and Maine potatoes. They waited for freestone peaches, for winesap apples, for the first spinach, for sweet corn, for greengage plums, for black bing cherries—the big ones. A ripe melon would be an occasion for celebration. As they would bite into the orange meat, a look of almost nasty, discerning pleasure would come over their faces. They would bite into a whole tomato, as if it were a hard-boiled egg, adding a small pinch of salt before each bite. "Good tuh-mayta," my uncle Louie, who was in the fruit and produce business, would say. "Jersey." And they would all nod. I thought of America as a country of gardens, pockets of good stuff, linked by roads that brought the harvest to us.

Most other supposedly good things in the forties were disap-

pointing, ugly, and sometimes frightening. The Dionne Quin-
tuplets were kept in a nursery that was supposed to be happy but
that looked to me on the newsreels like a hospital, a prison. The
Quints themselves were supposed to be cute, but in their identical ruffled dresses and identical lavish hairbows, they looked
like freaks, although I couldn't have used that word then. Instead my face would burn with shock and embarrassment. I don't
know where a child like me got an idea of beauty at five years
old, but I had one. I knew there had to be something better.
The women's rough boxy suits literally rubbed me the wrong
way; their stiff pointed hats, like lifted visors, poked against my
forehead when they tried to kiss me. The sickening smell of gas
seeped into the prickly dark car interior and made me sick. The
square, overstuffed furniture hulked against the walls. It was an
underlit world, as if an air-raid darkness still hung over us.

Many names during those times, particularly the names
of institutions, sounded unconsciously satiric. I puzzled over
"Lighthouse," the name of a foundation for the blind, which
sounded like a lie, a trick. It also sounded like a product name.
Lighthouse: Lifebuoy Soap. Advertising, not metaphor. When
I heard of a theater called the Palace, I became uneasy. I never
figured out the Church of Christ Scientist, which I passed as I
walked up Passaic Avenue. Einstein was a scientist, so was Robert
Oppenheimer. They had made the bomb, but Christ! How could
he be a scientist? My confusion was not caused by anything
peculiar to those times. The literal-mindedness of children makes
them turn a word over and over, as they try to match it to an
actual thing. The product names that came flooding out of the
radio didn't seem to mean anything, like the names of dead and
forgotten gods: Lux, Oxydol, Clorox.

But the most disturbing name had nothing to do with the
radio: Camp Happiness, a retreat for the blind where my uncle
spent part of the summer. My parents took me to Camp Happiness and to Greystone Park mental hospital without, I guess, a
thought to my nerves.

My father and I usually waited outside, sitting on a bench over-looking Greystone's sloping green lawns, while my mother went inside to see Rose. Inmates would pass us, heavy hunched figures dragging themselves down the neat paths that crisscrossed the "park" lawns. My father would read the paper. I would watch the sleepwalkers. Their slow steps and stunned faces made me feel unbearably awake. I have memories of being taken inside to see Rose. She too seemed to be sleepwalking. A heavy woman with a helmet of dark brown hair, she always wore, like the other women in the ward, a cotton housedress and slippers. An ironic costume: they were always at home but never at home. The in-mates' look of stunned blankness could not conceal their misery. It thickened under their skin. I know now that their eyes were dark and ripe with shame. My friends talk about being terrified by Walt Disney's *Bambi*. After visits to Greystone and Happi-ness, I watched *Bambi* calmly, and not just because I knew it was an illusion. Bambi's fate—his losing his mother—wasn't as bad as I knew things could be.

At Camp Happiness my father took Sam and me out in a boat. My father rowed. My uncle stiffly held onto the gunnels. I must have been sitting between my father's knees, facing my uncle. As my father effortlessly pulled on the oars, as effortlessly as he swam with me on his back, I gazed into my uncle's face— this was before my mother's lie about the war wound—and was frightened by its heavy blind weariness looming above me. All day among these pale, sensitive-fingered men and women, I felt too innocent, too seeing, too quick, too alive. The lake on which we rowed was too blue, the sun too golden, the grass too green, like the grass that grew at Greystone, and on this green, under this green, broken platoons of the blind and mad walked with their dragging gait. Later when I read about the Greek heroes' descent into the underworld, I thought of Camp Happiness.

When I was in the seventh or eighth grade, my uncle came to live with us in Passaic. He had had a heart attack. He also had diabetes. He brought with him a heavy suitcase of strange black bumpy leather. It was "textured" to look like rhinoceros hide. Like my father's heavy gray Plymouth, it seemed to come from a distant world where things were made for eternity. The suitcase, and all of Uncle's things, smelled of Lifebuoy soap: sharp and medicinally sweet. The radio ads for Lifebuoy mentioned B.O. When I thought that Uncle was afraid of having B.O., I felt a stab of pity. Why else would anyone use a soap that smelled like medicine?

Sam's restless Paterson life had been free. When he came to live with us, he was forbidden the rich heavy food he loved. He didn't know the Passaic streets, and the kind of friends he had—storekeepers, waiters, newsmen, bookies, gamblers, hustlers—could not find their way to him. He was cut off, left with women.

My grandmother Molly would sometimes visit him in the afternoons, if my mother went out. She liked to use our bathroom because hers was so cold. When she told me this I saw her bare, shivering behind on the toilet seat.

My mother devoted herself to making Sam well. I watched her put slices of white meat of chicken into the shallow cup of the newly bought kitchen scale. She weighed his bread. She steamed his vegetables. She would lean down to her low worktable and scrutinize the numbers on the scale, once, twice, just to make sure. I sensed it was already too late. The kitchen air was thick with the intimacy of their bond. Family. Their life together had begun long before I was born, and continued now. He sat at the table, heartbreakingly patient. I had never seen her so concentrated.

She wore a cotton housedress. Her slightly bowed chunky legs were bare—she had rolled her stockings down to her ankles. As usual she wore high wedgees. Of course, I've always known my mother was small, but only recently, when I watched a nurse measure her height, did I learn how small. Then I realized that for as long as I've known her she had slipped on her heels as she got out of bed. Even at the lake she would wear heels—these with ankle straps. I had no recollections of ever having seen her barefoot, except in that brief moment when she swung her legs out of bed.

Uncle had lost weight, and his pants rode loosely around his waist. I thought of the pictures I had seen of clowns wearing barrels held up by suspenders. Uncle was soft and wasted; he had never worked. Everyone else in my family—except for uncle Louie, Sam's brother—was hard, carved by work. When they got old or sick, they got scrawny. My father's hands looked as if they had been broken and barely put back together; his forearms bulged; my mother's arms were sinewy from scrubbing clothes. She also worked as a salesperson. She was brilliant and cunning in her job. Her mobile mouth was shaped by the passion of her intention: she would make that sale. Her customers did not "walk." My aunt Jennie, my father's sister, had a crooked shoulder from sewing ties for thirty years. She would lead the fabric through the machine with her right hand, and the repeated motion had knotted and raised her right shoulder. She led like a boxer. If my relatives were ruined, they were hard and ruined.

Every nice day that spring, on my way back to school after lunch, I would take Sam to the park. First I would help him with his shoes, slipping them on and tying the black laces. The shoes were heavy and black and always well polished. He got them from the army-navy store. My mother had instructed me: "Never lead a blind person; let them take your arm." So with Uncle's cool light hand on my elbow I would adjust my step, and we would walk together down Madison Street and across busy Myrtle Avenue.

Unlike most other adults, he was very careful of me; he did not clutch or grab or press his lips in big smacking greedy kisses against my cheeks. He had the practiced finesse of a longtime patient who must court his caretaker. He was a graceful seducer. But he could not hide his body. He was naked: his blindness, his frailty. All the old and the sick were pleading, exposed. They were like the lover who uncovers his stiff penis and asks—except that they did not uncover, did not ask. Their infirmity did it for them.

On hot days I liked walking in his shadow. I barely came to his shoulder. I would lead him to a bench under the trees. Once seated, he would reach deep into his pants pocket and finger the loose change, reading the coins. When he found a dime, he would press it into my palm. Uncle's money was ripe. Each coin he gave me had weight and heat; each coin had been read.

I wasn't brave, although I talked big. Mostly I wanted to be liked. Yet somehow I was never ashamed of walking with him or worried about what my friends would say. When I remember this slow walk, I see the two of us alone; there was a space around us, as if we were on the mound of a baseball field, with all the people far away at the edges of the field. No one came close to us.

I would leave Uncle and race to find my friends. We would play wild games of ring-a-lareo in the short time left before the bell rang. Only a few girls played: Carol, the hard-faced Polish kid with piss-off eyes; Camille, whose parents told her they'd break her legs if they ever saw her with a boy. She didn't listen. We'd careen around the yard in a swirling pack, which looked as if it was blown and separated by the wind. A tingling heat would shoot into my legs and arms, right out to the tips of my fingers and toes. I felt as if I were flying. We'd run until we were breathless; then we'd run again. If you were caught, you went to "prison" to wait for the next round.

When the bell rang, we straggled to the doors, boys on one side, girls on the other. My braids were undone, my socks muddy, my Oxfords scuffed. My blouse was usually pulled out of my skirt, and my face flushed. The teachers disapproved. I was wild; I talked too much.

At three-thirty I gathered up my books and went to pick up Uncle. I would watch his face for the first sign of recognition. He knew who it was before I spoke. I loved that look. Everyone in my family had this kind of lit-up look of recognition. I went for it. Most of them were so pure in their modesty, they took any sign of love as an unheard-of gift, and so they beamed. And Uncle's look was the best, because his joy—because The Kid had not forgotten—was tethered to an inescapable harsh gravity and vulnerability. He who had so much weakness to guard went unarmed.

As always, I felt a kind of distinction, which he, the giver, conferred on me. Uncle, through his gifts of money, and my mother, by her instructions, were training me, perhaps too well. My mother was proud of her ability to be natural with afflicted people. She certainly had had enough practice. Only recently she had told me about a relative who had stopped calling a deaf cousin because she was tired of yelling into the phone. "I still call her," my mother said without a trace of irony; "I know how to talk to deaf people."

Uncle slept on a daybed in the small doorless foyer where he was on view to anyone who passed through. Leaning slightly forward, his shoulders hunched, he would sit on the edge of the bed, his long-fingered graceful hands curved over the mattress edge. He would be in shirtsleeves, pants, and suspenders. In the evenings, as he sat there on his bed in the middle of our apartment, he'd listen to the radio. His favorite program was "Gangbusters."

I would usually be in the small crowded living room just off the foyer doing my homework. Memorial School was "progressive." We were studying Greek myths by turning them into plays. As I wrote dialogue for the story of Ariadne, which fascinated me, the strident sounds of "Gangbusters" and the clatter of dishes would disappear. I was inside my head. I couldn't hear my father's loud snoring. He usually fell asleep in his chair after dinner with the newspaper in his lap; he wore only his pajama bottoms, which he would put on as soon as he got home from work. He would have one leg slung over the arm of the chair, a toothpick in the corner of his mouth, and—the way I sleep now—one arm raised and curled over his head in the gesture of the orangutan.

One night, after I had finished my homework early, Uncle and I argued. He was listening to "Gangbusters," and I wanted another program. His voice rose and cracked with all the bitterness of his life, "The Kid wants . . . I want one lousy program." For a moment my rebellion was exhilarating, like grabbing something I wasn't supposed to eat and quickly biting into it.

The next day he did not give me the usual dime when I took him to the park. Once I backed him up to his favorite bench, he just sat down abruptly and said nothing. I felt terrible. As usual I picked him up at three-thirty on my way home from school. Later I wished him goodnight. The next day we walked together to the park again, and without any reproach he gave me the dime.

It was my grandmother who found him. I was due home from school on the afternoon my uncle died. If my grandmother had not come in, I would have found him, since my mother was away at work. When I recently thought about Uncle's death, I was sure that, when I got home, the ambulance was just pulling away. I remembered a crowd of people, but now I realize that I'm not sure about what I saw, so there are two versions. I also remember him lying on the bathroom floor in the narrow space between the tub and the radiator. I could see the shape of his frail legs through his pants. The long black shoelaces were untied and lay loosely across his white cotton socks like wilted stems.

At the funeral I bent over to kiss him in his coffin. He was wrapped in a white shroud with a blue Star of David stamped on the forehead. The shroud came down almost to his brows like a Greek priest's headdress. His face was arranged in a faint, somewhat silly smile. A thin layer of rouge gave him a pink tinge. They had composed him, given him a peaceful conventional look he had never had in life: I hated it. I grew more and more furious as the rabbi spoke his pious platitudes. You don't know anything, I thought; how could you? I had heard the truth from Sam. Wounded, blind, he had understood his life and had stayed in the action. He was helpless and powerful. He had had his pleasures; he had served the god of gamblers and thieves, not the God of Abraham. He had lived in the action on the streets of Paterson. "He knew everyone," Gert said. Sam had named me. I was The Kid, the wild brat who had found out the family secret. I knew what was what. The wounded stayed wounded, but recognition—like Sam's self-recognition—was a kind of grace, which lived alongside pain. The forbidden, "the feast of fat things full of life," the juiciness of Sam's racetrack money, was good. Nothing could cancel out that savor. I could say, along with my Jacobs relatives, "I have news for you," shrugging my shoulders and laughing with their characteristic rough cackle, and the news would be bad and glorious.

Molly

I wonder if I ever really knew my grandmother Molly, my father's mother who helped bring me up, when my parents and my brother and I lived in the apartment next to hers at 3 Lucille Place in Passaic. When I took hold of her arm and carefully, between my small index finger and thumb, lifted the crepe-like, crosshatched skin, as if I were lifting fine fabric or stretching out a bird's wing to reveal the underweb, she looked into my eyes and laughed a bit foolishly. Her thick cataract glasses gave her a startled yet dopey funhouse look. There was no conscious cruelty in my gesture. I found her loose, sallow skin beautiful, more beautiful and interesting than the poreless angel skin of my child friends. When, years later, I saw fine church candles of pure beeswax, I was reminded of the color and cleanliness of my grandmother's skin. Perhaps she laughed to hide her embarrassment.

Like the Victorian domestic ideal, she never complained or raised her voice, never argued, never was cruel. Her calm seemed universal, not something reserved for grandchildren. Her daughters-in-law, their voices full of wonder, still praise her for not having meddled—they all have daughters-in-law of their own now. But even as they praise, their eyes narrow in unacknowledged anger, as if Molly's serenity had been calculated to rob them of someone to blame for their marital troubles. Her calm silence, which now continues from the grave, also seems to them a triumphal comment on their own rivalries with "those bitches," their daughters-in-law. "I get more affection from the dog," one of them said.

The memory of Molly's serenity does not interest me: there are no quirky bumps, no sticky places, and certainly no passion. If she had a personality, her clothes did not reflect it. They were like a habit: old woman's costume. She wore cotton self-belted housedresses, sometimes a white linen babushka, blue felt slippers, and toast-colored cotton stockings. She twisted her hair into a bun and secured it with large tortoiseshell pins. Only these pins seemed exotic to me. She never wore jewelry. Molly was as unadorned as a nun—even more so: she had given her wide gold wedding band—it had come from Europe—to a daughter-in-law. Thinking of Molly's bare hands disturbs me. I wish I could have given her a ring—two rings. She never knew the exact date of her birthday. Sometime in the spring, I believe. Peasants don't keep those kinds of records.

No one ever imagined that she could mind getting old. I am only forty-seven, but like most modern women, I notice every sign of aging. I've decided to adopt Colette's appreciation of her own decay, the one she expresses in print, that is. In *La naissance du jour*, she praises her "good little hand, slightly blackened, the skin wrinkled . . . around the knuckles." She accepts the scars and burns, and the thumb, which "bends back like a scorpion's tail." I doubt if my grandmother ever had Colette's verve. Few do. Will I ever know what was in Molly's heart?

Sometimes my memories of her appear like a book of illuminated pictures, beautiful still and distant. After school I would usually find her in one of the calm scenes of her life. The morning cooking and baking would be done, the covered pots would be on the stove, and the loaves of challah and the apple cake laid out on a clean white cloth. The odors of food would have subsided. If it were early enough on a Friday afternoon, I would find her with a large white linen babushka wrapped around her head. "You've washed your hair," I would say, and she would smile her gentle smile. Yellow-white wisps of wavy hair would escape over her temples. If I came in at sunset, she'd be lighting Sabbath candles, silently moving her lips, moving her hands over the flames, through the smoke, seeming to pull the smoke and fire toward her. As far as I know, she never went to shul. The women who attended services did not look like peasants. They had their hair done; they wore makeup; they had aspirations. She didn't fit in.

Often when I came in, Molly would be watering her plants. They were outlined on the windowsill—in that dark purplish eye-smarting backlight—a row of snake plants, their flat stiff painted leaves bordered with yellow. As she tilted the clear jar of water, I could see the exact angle of the water; the difference in color and form between the clear glass and the clear water would stand out so sharply as she poured; the gray line, which separated air and water, moved and yet held its liquid shape. With her strong naked hands she would hold a little cloth at the lip of the jar like a wine steward.

Along with my own pictures, I've inherited Molly's last incarnation to my father. When he was dying, he dreamed of his mother, who had been dead for many years. In the dream, he was back in their old forsaken neighborhood in the Dundee section of Passaic, "the wrong side of the tracks," near the river where he had, as a boy, taken off his shoes to wade across to a small island loaded with blackberry bushes. (He was always losing his shoes, Grandma had told me.) In the dream, his mother came toward him carrying a white umbrella, which, like a lamp, illuminated her face while the heavy dark rain fell around them. "Ma, what are you doing here?" he asked. He was shocked. She had come to take him home.

When Molly had become old and weak, my father returned

to our apartment after a short visit next door and said to my mother, "When she holds on to me, her hands shake; you go in, I can't take it." He was used to a mother who into her eighties went out without a hat on the coldest days, her head lifted, her white hair flying in the wind.

Recently I saw a film about Mother Teresa and the Sisters of Charity that made me think of Molly again. The nuns had been asked to care for a group of spastic patients in a hospital that had been abandoned by the regular staff during a war in the Middle East. One of the sisters, an Indian, lifted the twitching, contorted body of a child, or a man, or a boy; there was no way at that point to tell how old he was, since he was folded up like a crab on its back and like a crab seemed hardly to have any head at all. The nun, with spread fingers, put her left hand on his back and her palm between the shoulder blades and lifted him away from the pillow. With her right hand, she stroked his chest, from the collarbone down across the sternum, patting over and over, firmly. His limbs relaxed little by little, and he lay back for a moment, uncontorted, his young man's face smooth and alert under its ruff of coarse black hair. The rhythm of the nun's hand on his chest was like the fall of an animal's paw, hot with intimacy yet artfully ruthless—my grandmother's touch. The nun did not speak.

Molly had taken care of me when I was a baby and then, as I got older, on Saturday nights when my parents and my aunt Jennie would go to the movies. On one of those nights I was sick with a painful stomachache. I must have been around six or seven. My grandmother pulled me toward her so that my head was in her ample lap and with her strong hand rubbed my stomach until the pain went away. Round and round her hand went, pressing in with a firm but soothing pressure. The heat from her hand seemed to penetrate to my backbone. There was nothing tentative in her gesture. Unlike my mother, she didn't seem afraid to touch me. I can't remember what we did on most of those Saturday nights. She couldn't read to me—something my mother did beautifully. We just sat together and grew sleepy. It was a little boring but comforting.

My grandmother said very little about life, hardly ever expressed an idea, but she did tell me two very short stories. The first was actually a joke, about Jesus Christ of all people. "You know, they say he walked on water," Molly told me in her heavy Russian-Yiddish accent—her maiden name was Kaganovitch. "But he pished, that was the water." I had seen pictures of Christ in the bedroom of my friend Lois Burke. He had blond curls, a blue robe, a red heart that jumped out of his smooth chest. His head was surrounded by white clouds. He was in heaven. As my grandmother told her joke, I saw Christ lift his blue robe and piss on the earth. In my grandmother's view, Christ was a pisher. She must have had many peasant jokes and stories, but I heard only two. Her second story had to do with a memory of Europe. She had been sitting on the porch of her family's farmhouse— this was in a small village outside of Bialystok—when a man pulled up in a horse and wagon. He spoke to her, he touched her breast. End of story. She touched her breast, as she told what had happened so long ago. I understood that something important and exciting had happened to her, but I wasn't sure what it meant. I was too small to know what questions to ask her. Now it seems that she was telling me who she was: a woman who had had an adventure. As far as I remember, that was the only time she mentioned Europe to me.

Her English was poor, as was my spoken Yiddish. Yet I could understand almost everything she said in Yiddish. I would have listened to her stories, but she had good reason to be shy, even perhaps a little afraid of me. Once I had asked her if she could read English; she said yes. I wanted to test her. I asked her to read something to me. She held the English paper in her lap, making believe she could read it. Her face was hot and red—

never mind that she could speak and read Yiddish, recite the Hebrew prayers—I don't know if she could read Hebrew—speak Russian and Polish. Finally I shut up. I had gotten more than I bargained for. A small hook had caught a big fish, a hot shocking fact, my grandmother's fear and shame, and my power as an English-speaking American. No matter how much time I spent in Molly's house, no matter how much I loved her, I was assimilated into American life and separated from her.

Family life was rich in these secrets, these revelations of shame, and sometimes had the same effect on me as the language of the psalms we read every morning in school. I had no trouble with simile. The hills could "skip *like* rams." "Like" made all the difference. Metaphor was the problem. I didn't know what to do with the heavy blessing of "my cup runneth over." How could you drink it? How did you get your lips around that slippery rim, when the water, or wine, or honey, or oil, or milk, or whatever it was—not a Coke or a malted, though—was flowing over the sides onto the table, your clothes, the ground? It was making a mess. It didn't stop: that gift of too much, "like"—I was back to the safe ground of simile—the mystery in my family; there was always something more.

My grandmother's shame and her children's desire to be modern and American robbed her of some authority, even within her own family, which adored her. Her son Ben and his wife, Judith, came to live with my grandmother. Judith soon had a baby boy—my cousin Leo—whom she bottle-fed. I would stand at her side while she carefully mixed the formula and water. Her efficiency fascinated me. She'd dip a measuring spoon into the Dextri-Maltose or powdered milk and then level off the heaping tablespoons with a metal spatula, which made a faint scraping sound against the spoon. (I would use the same measuring technique years later when following Julia Child's recipes for *biscuit au beurre, gateau à l'orange,* and *le marquis,* a light chocolate sponge with a dense soft center.) The bottles came steaming and

clouded from the big white sterilizer on the stove; except for
the color, it was exactly the same as a canning kettle. The rubber nipples exuded a sweet gummy smell. Judith looked like a
chemist.

During one of these formula-making rituals, I turned sideways
and caught a glimpse of my grandmother. She, who usually stood
so straight, was now bent over, half-turned, like the hunchbacked
old woman in one of my fairy-tale books. She was standing in
such a peculiar way, looking over her shoulder. Her face stood
out like a mask, like the face of a snowy owl, white skin, white
hair, black black eyes. Now I remember that I had seen this look
of hers before, when she was saying something about the way
my mother treated me; she was whispering in Yiddish to an aunt,
thinking I would not understand, "Sie koyft ihr gornisht." (She
buys nothing for her.) So my grandmother did notice things.
I wore mostly hand-me-downs. "Gornischt." It was true. As
Molly stared at the bottles, she had a look of a woman who
knew what she knew, an uncanny, shrewd witch look that said,
"This is piss." She had no authority to speak. She understood
that Judith could not now nurse the baby. But she also knew that
the formula disagreed with the child. Leo screamed after every
feeding.

My grandmother had kept six children alive on her own milk.
Ben, her youngest son, was already walking when she weaned
him. He would pull her behind a door and beg "for a suck."
Bella, the youngest daughter, who was born after Ben, told me
that by the time she came along, my grandmother was tired of
children and had very little to give. Bella would later consult a
psychiatrist. My grandmother had a saying that was quoted to
me when I was in my early twenties and she was dead: "Children
grow up by themselves." When I first heard it, I was baffled: did
she mean that children grow up lonely? Later I realized what
she meant: relax; we are powerless over our children. We get
them started, but life itself is the force that moves them; we are

not in control. But at least my grandmother's children had not screamed after they were fed.

My aunt Jennie, the eldest daughter, had never married. She lived with my grandmother, along with Ben and Judith and the baby Leo. (As I've said, my parents, my brother, and I were in the apartment next door.) My grandmother had three of her five surviving children still living close to her as well as two daughters-in-law and three grandchildren.

Except for my brother, we all helped her. Jennie did most of the cleaning and washing and ironing. It was she who taught me how to iron a blouse: first the collar on both sides, then the yoke, the cuffs, the sleeves, and finally the body, along with the buttonhole and button facings. The cotton crisped under the hot heavy iron, which had been steel-wooled to a slippery smooth finish. At the end of the summer she would wash the cotton net curtains. She'd add a shot of bleach to the soapy water in the deep set tub in the kitchen, plunge in her arm up to the elbow, then swirl the water. The curtains would go in a pair or two at a time to be squeezed, not rubbed. She would gently wring out the soap and pile the curtains on the drain board. She was a scrupulous rinser: three times at least, until the rinse water was clear. For years she held off buying a washing machine because it only rinsed once. She would get down on her hands and knees and wash the floors with steaming water. Her passion was to get every speck of dust and dirt. She couldn't stand the least suggestion of grease. Later when I had my own house, I found her in the kitchen staring at my black-topped Chambers gas stove. "Isn't it wonderful!" I said. "It's as heavy as a car." She looked puzzled. "You *like* a black stove?" she asked with amazement. "How do you know when it's clean?" Jennie was happy when she and Molly finally got the longed-for white stove. She also loved the vacuum cleaner. "When you sweep," she said to me during a pause in her weekly cleaning, "where does the dirt go?" She was philosophical: "It goes back into the air; that's where it goes."

The vacuum cleaner could be emptied into the trash; it would then be taken away, gone forever. Like most city dwellers she did not imagine the journey of the dirt once it had left 3 Lucille Place. When she was in her eighties, she was still scrubbing on her hands and knees. She would tell me stories of her victories over dirt. She had removed the old wax from the kitchen floor of a new apartment. "For a week, I lay on that floor and scraped with a razor blade." Her lips would curl with disgust and triumph.

Jennie was constipated. When she was visiting me a few years ago, she noticed my dog Daisy squatting in the backyard and pointed it out to me, "Look, she just does it." "She's only pee-ing," I said. "No matter what, she just squats down and does it," she repeated with envy. They all talked about their bowels. Uncle Nathan said he had no problem "going" because he drank hot water mixed with lemon juice every morning. My grandmother and the men didn't seem to be affected, only the daughters.

Judith, who knew how to guide people through the perilous work of keeping kosher, would clean the sink, the drain board, the wooden koshering board; the places where food touched had to be scalded with boiling water. She would know which rags to use, which soap. Keeping kosher did not interest me, but I loved the look of the kosher soap, the size of a Japanese ink block, but white—of course—the pink Hebrew letters spreading to a blur then disappearing as the soap became hollowed in the center where the rag was rubbed, the edges worn to a raised thinness.

Years later in a stifling Bronx apartment I watched Judith close the windows before she said a Hebrew prayer. "What are you doing?" I asked. She had a furtive expression on her face. "I don't want the neighbors to hear; I don't want to draw attention or make it seem that I'm showing off or intruding." "Let them hear," I said. Judith was an educated woman. She had gone to the Jewish Theological Seminary in Manhattan. She had been born in this country. But she had reason to be afraid. She had her own history, as I had mine. I remembered that she had been closed out of jobs when employers found out that her name was Richman, not Richmond. One man even had the nerve to sarcastically point out the difference. Judith had blue eyes and red hair, but the "Richman" gave her away. She had refused to change her name.

My mother and I shopped for Molly. I would be sent to the bakery for fresh rolls sprinkled with poppy seeds, to Gutkin the Butcher for hamburg—I was instructed to order lean chuck, examine the meat after it was trimmed, judge its degree of leanness, and—if it met my grandmother's exacting standards—ask that it be ground. I was not yet considered experienced enough to choose more expensive cuts of meat like "baby" lambchops and rib steaks; that job was entrusted to my mother. Gutkin, who was short and fat and pink as a pig, had made a lot of money in the black market during the war. He had kept the stacks of bills—thousands and thousands—in a large black safe the size of a home refrigerator. One day, his young wife, who people said looked like a showgirl—she was famous for her red platform shoes—cleaned out the safe and disappeared. "There was nothing Gutkin could do," my father said with admiration. He was in awe of people who got away with things. In fact, most of my family admired criminals who made money—thieves, not murderers—as long as they weren't politicians or bosses. As I waited for my grandmother's order, I would think of Gutkin's wife. I would turn my head from the sight of the butcher's red plump hands trimming a pound of chuck down to the muscle, and stare at the black safe, which I could see through the half-opened door of the back room.

I would go to Mr. Weil, the grocer, for dairy: sweet and bland cream cheese, sour pot cheese, cottage cheese, a pound of "loose" sweet butter cut from a large rough block that bore the marks of the knife. (The butter I buy now always seems too smooth and waxy.) I went to the A&P for Red Circle coffee, which the clerk would grind to order. The Levines drank their coffee with scalded milk, like Europeans. The milk had to be brought to the point of steaming, but on no account could it be allowed to bubble and form a skin. I would also be sent to the A&P for gallons of prune juice when they were on special sale. I'd lug them back one at a time.

Jennie would turn over part of her paycheck to Molly. Jennie had whispered to me that she wanted "Ma to feel in charge." Jennie would give her the money and then ask for whatever she needed, as she needed it. My grandmother kept the money in a three-compartment leather change purse: all three compartments snapped closed in the same bowlike clasp. How many times had I watched her open and close that purse! The sound of the snap was loud and serious. Three split-second notes that could sound like one: it rang. Jennie needed to hear it ring.

My grandmother's household revolved around rituals. Gone was the hardship of her earlier domestic life, when she had had to take care of her husband's parents, her young children, and her daughter Etta, who slowly died of heart disease as well as to mind the fruit-and-vegetable store while her husband peddled produce from door to door from a horse-drawn wagon. The business did not prosper. My grandfather, I've been told, blamed it on his two "roughneck" sons, Nathan and Joe. Ben was the quiet obedient one, who would eventually win a scholarship to Cooper Union. Nathan and Joe would run through the store grabbing handfuls of cherries, the story went. But how many cherries can two boys eat? My mother told me that my grandfather's sarcasm drove away customers. Sometimes Molly was so tired she lay down on the sacks of potatoes and slept. Now, in her later years within a few square blocks—the size of her village in Europe—she bought groceries, went to the yarn shop, cooked dinner, tended her plants, knit and crocheted.

She became both a master of form and a creator—with some help from her son Joe, my father, the eater of cherries—of intense flavor. She cut beets for borscht into perfect matchsticks, braided dough into loaves of challah, whose egg glaze would turn the color of mahogany but would not burn. She made large loaves and small loaves; the braiding grew intricate. Sometimes she shaped the challah dough into snakelike coils. Making blintzes, she would hold the paper-covered end of a piece of butter in one hand, quickly rub the unwrapped end over a hot surface of a small blackened frying pan, pour in just the right amount of batter, quickly tilt the pan until the batter formed a lacy edge, and then knock out the almost transparent silky blintz onto a clean cloth.

The kugel would be browned; the noodles cut; the tsimes baked; the soup skimmed; the brisket potted until the grain of the meat had a pale delicate pastel rainbow tint; the mushroom and barley soup, which she made with dried imported wild mushrooms—they cost a fortune now—thickened; the spaghetti sauce simmered—she got the recipe from an Italian neighbor—the strong sweet and sour cabbage soup with its floating island of fatty shoulder steak given its final tasting; the kreplach cut and plumped with ground meat; the stinging subtle tschav, a summer soup made with sorrel—they called it "sour grass"—cooled; the prunes stewed.

At Passover she would make a huge sponge cake. The pan, which had a ring fastened to it at one end, was larger than the drainboard. I saw her beat at least a dozen egg whites with a wire whip. The weak foam turned into high glistening peaks in what seemed like an instant.

Especially during these holidays, as she performed the most extravagant pieces from her repertoire, she would be attended by her children. They were geniuses of protocol and decorum. They had the seriousness of the men at shul, who assisted the rabbi by pointing to the place in the text. They would hand her a spoon; they would hold the bowl as she mixed. They would remind me of my art teacher Mrs. French assisting a talented student by deftly handing her a stick of pastel and watching with calm appreciative attention. They were given over to her; they forgot themselves. Their faces were attentive, absorbed, and contented like the students in my poetry workshop who are able to appreciate fine work and assist. They were not like the transported audiences at rock concerts, clapping and raising their hands, swaying to the music: they never confused their roles with the queen's, yet somehow they shared the gift.

At the end of my grandmother's culinary feats, my father would usually be called in. He was thought to have the best palate in the family. He would stand quietly poised before the pot on the stove, holding the clean tablespoon his mother had just handed him, collecting himself, gearing down as if he were still a basketball player about to shoot from the foul line.

By that time, I had probably formed my ideas about men. There were those like my father, who had a palate, who when they smelled their wife's or mother's food would ask, "What smells so good?" and those like Harry Melinkoff, the upstairs neighbor, who, home from work with one foot in the door, would call out, his nose wrinkling with disgust, "What's that *smell?*"

Joe and his brother Nathan used to have to fight off the "Polack thugs" every Saturday morning as they walked their grandfather to shul through the tough Dundee streets. They went as bodyguards, the two broad-shouldered football players who looked like Americans, their thick black hair cropped above their ears, one boy on each side of the old man, who had a long untrimmed beard and hair like the Maharishi Yogi's.

Neither Joe nor Nathan seemed to think of themselves as Jews. (Joe's football nickname was "Cowboy.") They hadn't even gone through the Bar Mitzvah ceremony. But I was to feel the violent passion of my father's Jewish identity formed in opposition to his enemies. He became enraged when in high school I became friends with an Italian boy who lived in our neighborhood. "They hate us," he shouted at me. "You should hear what they say." It was the only time I would ever hear him use the word "us" to mean Jews. As a truck driver he did not work with Jews, and he was seldom taken for a Jew; people said things in front of him. Nathan, who married an Italian, appeared to be as assimilated as Joe. Yet, like Joe, he must have, in the deepest part of himself, felt that he was a Jew. But I never had any proof of it.

During Prohibition, Nathan had led a shady life, working for a Mafia bootlegger, Willie Marietta. Nathan hadn't liked the job; he and the other men had been locked in the back of a truck with the cases of bootleg rye. "If anything goes wrong," Nathan had said, "there's no way to get out." He switched to running numbers for Marietta and got arrested. It was one of those periodic "crackdowns" that was supposed to convince the public that the police were doing their job. Marietta wasn't touched. Nathan did what he was supposed to; he pleaded guilty and went to prison. He was sent to the "country club," where he spent most of his six-month sentence strolling around the prison grounds. He was well fed. The guards were paid off by Marietta. Later Nathan went semilegit, opening a bar called The Crystal Spa. His lean good looks, his expression, a hair away from a scowl but without any sulkiness, had a tough self-contained charm. He was a remarkable dancer, sure and graceful but somehow in the shadow, untheatrical. Women would come to the bar to dance with him. That's how he met Carmen, whom he later married.

In those postwar years both he and my father seemed to have much more physical power than they could actually use.

I'd watch my father as he carefully dipped the spoon into the pot, bending forward from the waist. He'd throw back his head and roll the broth across his tongue. They'd all wait for his advice. The most difficult flavor to achieve was the complicated balance of sweet and sour of the cabbage soup. So they'd add and add and get it right.

I usually did not eat at my grandmother's table. She would send in a jar of soup or a plate of kugel to round out the separate meal my mother cooked for us. My brother would stare into the steaming soup and extract a hair, which he would hold up triumphantly, a long white hair, a judgment. He'd push his bowl away. I would go on spooning up the rich soup, whose concentrated essence was like veal demiglace. I would taste layer after layer of flavor. I've never been able to reproduce her mushroom soup.

Sarah Orne Jewett posted Flaubert's advice over her desk: "Write about ordinary life as if you were writing history." The motto above my grandmother's stove might have read: Reduction is the essence of taste. And form was the cup that held flavor. None of Molly's creations outlived her. She never thought about whether they would or not. Molly created; we feasted until nothing was left. Jewett's and Flaubert's work will also disappear, but, of course, more slowly.

Many times after school I would find Molly in the large comfortable barrel chair in a corner of the living room. She'd be knitting or crocheting, sometimes darning. Her darning was faultless. She would string a little loom over the tear, which she had stretched over a shiny black darning egg, and weave a perfect patch of new cloth. Her cable-stitched sweaters seemed as miraculous to me, as unattainable, as the fabulous braids that crowned the heads of my Polish and Ukranian schoolmates.

Molly knitted vests and pullovers for her sons and grandsons out of oatmeal-colored wool; for her daughters and granddaughters, pale yellow or white cardigans for spring, dark green or navy for fall and winter. Jennie would block the sweaters between the mattress and box spring of her bed. The weight of the mattress and her body were thought essential to give the garment its final shape. For two weeks, in her sleep, Jennie would turn from side to stomach to back, pressing down over her mother's creation.

Molly made a purse for me. She bought a small round basket, which formed the bottom of the purse, and crocheted the top, which closed by drawstrings. I can still remember the summery smell of the straw. I loved the purse because she had chosen a multicolored thread divided into segments of color along its length. It produced a random pattern impossible to untangle: blacks, reds, violets, yellows. It swung on my arm, her favor.

For so many years in remembering Molly, I had made myself comfortable again with her body. I had put my head in her lap again. In nursing my own child, I felt that I was following her example, getting strength from her to keep a child alive. She did it; I could do it. A good thing—certainly! But I had not realized that by watching her I had learned art. I never found out how to create Molly's witchy cable stitch. You can't learn that just by watching. I found out how to work, how to be.

Hers was the passion to get things right, to shape, to plump, to reduce, to dazzle, to thicken, to boil, to clarify and complicate and create. Her art was not separated from the life of the body; she made beauty to taste, to wear, to wear out. While her children tended her, she whirled her needles, counting stitches with a rapidity that I could not follow.

She cut, she carved, she shaped. Even her throwaways were beautiful. The long, unbroken coil of red apple skin lined with the thinnest layer of white flesh fell from her small sharp knife.

After
Jen's Death

*J*en had worked most of her life at a modest job sewing neckties, but she had managed to accumulate a small estate that was to be divided among her six nieces and nephews. She had never married. I was the executor of her will.

Because she lived alone, the apartment was "sealed" right after her death and the locks changed. The keys would remain in the police station until the will was registered and the necessary papers processed.

Two weeks later, after all these legal matters had been taken care of, I picked up the key at the police station and drove up Passaic Avenue to her apartment. Her reading glasses were still on the table next to the lamp where she had always kept them. Her things were in order, as they had been all her life. Nothing was out of place, from the dozens of pairs of almost new shoes, each in its compartment in a plastic zippered shoe case, to the clean rags, which she kept neatly folded in the bottom of the bathroom hamper. Her few pieces of dirty laundry never filled the hamper; she'd lay them over the immaculate rags.

I worked steadily, emptying drawers, filling large plastic trash bags, putting aside the things I wanted, among them a peach-colored sweater Jennie's sister had brought back from China—

Jennie never wore it—my grandmother's black wood darning egg, and her battered tin thimbles with no tops like tiny hats without crowns.

The next morning I went to see the lawyer. The offices of the brothers Riskin—Joel and Jay—were in downtown Passaic. Although the town's tallest building was getting shabby, the halls still smelled of pine soap and wax, from years of night mopping and rubbing. The floors were black marble. Each heavy wooden office door had a panel of vintage smoked glass. The light was dim. Dentists, lawyers, accountants: you went to meet them through dark passages that seemed to tunnel through deep underground stone even though you were on the fourteenth floor. I was told that William Carlos Williams once had an office there. It was the highest you could go in Passaic; brains, not physical bravery, got you here; the height had become a figure of speech; the height was social; you weren't actually supposed to feel it; it might make you dizzy.

The Riskins had once been our neighbors in Second Ward, a mostly blue-collar section of small apartment houses and wooden two-family houses that leaned toward each other over the dark narrow side yards barely separating them.

The lawyer's father had been the "linoleum man." My family always called him by his last name. "I got Riskin," they'd say, or "I'll get Riskin." In this context, they pronounced the words "get" and "got" with a forceful uncharacteristic determination, as if managing to secure such service was like catching a prize bride or a groom or a lion. They used the word in other ways: "What can I *get* for you?" they'd ask, with a magisterial intimacy that seemed to promise kingdoms even if they were only preparing to open the refrigerator door.

"Inlaid" was for kitchens; linoleum "rugs" for living rooms. Mr. Riskin put down "inlaid" on expertly swirled and scraped syrupy brown gum that held the tooth marks of the spreader; I'd watch him on his hands and knees. He'd unhook the wicked-looking curved linoleum knife from his wide leather belt and cut without faltering: the material would fit smoothly around the radiator pipe, against the gouged and painted-over baseboards, around the grooved doorway moldings.

He never said much. His almost bald head was perfectly barbered. He seemed to me a wise person—calm meant wisdom—and for some reason, he treated me as if I too were wise. There were certain people in that neighborhood—like Riskin—who granted a child an identity long before the untested child had one. It was a form of entitlement, but it made us ripe for guilt and confusion, especially if what they insisted on believing about us was different from what we were.

Joel Riskin was expecting me. He looked like his father, but in Joel, the old man's vigorous features had sagged into flaccid, froglike folds. His weak brown eyes bulged; his skin was pale and unhealthy looking. I wondered if his thyroid had slowed him down to a walking hibernation. Taking in his extraordinary pallor, I chatted insincerely about the old neighborhood. He sat behind his cluttered desk. When we got to business, which was mostly my showing him Jennie's various accounts, he got up to sit next to me. He waddled; his sloping shoulders looked weak; his loosely buckled pants belt rode over the crest of his large bobbing stomach like an apron band on a pregnant woman.

"Let's see what you have," he said, as he sank with a heavy sigh into the chair next to me. I showed him the checkbook, the certificate of deposit, and a savings account passbook. There was also some cash. He noticed a five-thousand-dollar withdrawal from the savings account made in May, a few weeks before Jennie died. "What's this?" he asked roughly. "Someone got an extra share." His face had turned red. In the same accusatory tone he told me that the estate was to be divided equally among the six nephews and nieces. "You know, she changed the will and then she changed it back again," he added.

I did know. A month before she died, I had taken her to lunch.

She wanted to eat fish, not deli, so we went to Caughey's on the Paterson Plank Road. I ordered fish and chips; she chose sole Florentine. After we began eating, she jerked her head toward my plate and said, "I should have ordered that." It was her last meal out. After she had had some beer, she forgot about her disappointment with the fish. She leaned across the bright red table with its red candle—Caughey's always looked like Christmas. "I did something I shouldn't have," she said, as she frequently did, usually about buying the wrong thing, a pair of shoes, a coat she would come to hate. She had cut one of her nephews out of the will, and now she was going to put him back in. Perhaps long ago she had made other changes besides excluding the inattentive nephew; why else would the lawyer now so strongly emphasize "equal shares"?

Joel kept repeating that the will had been changed before the withdrawal, implying somehow that the withdrawal was unethical or in some way violated the will. I told him that the five thousand dollars had been withdrawn on May 7 and the will had been changed on June 7. "She wrote you a check for seventy-five dollars on June 7," I said. I had the record, and I knew she had taken a cab to his office a week before she died. "It was for a hundred," he answered peevishly. I didn't respond; I was sure of the amount. He was unsatisfied with the seventy-five; he should have asked for more; he had regrets. He needed—what exactly I didn't know.

Why was I getting into this discussion about dates? They meant nothing. Jen had been alive then, taking care of her own business. "It was her money," I said. "She could do what she wanted, before the will or after the will. I don't know who got the five thousand, though I have an idea; it was a gift." Riskin lifted his weak hands, palms out, "Of course, of course." I believed that she had given the money to one of her nephews, whom she felt hadn't gotten his fair share in life, but I didn't know for sure. She had kept it from me, her favorite niece, and now I was being badgered by a lawyer who felt he had to be a watchdog and thereby justify his fee, even though he hadn't had the nerve to charge enough.

We added up the figures. His mood softened; his face returned to its habitual paleness. "You don't make a fortune sewing ties," I observed. He nodded. "Bindelglass," he said, "was my father-in-law; he owned the tie factory." Joel was holding Jen's bankbooks. She had taken them out of the gray metal strongbox months before and held them like a deck of cards: "If anything happens, they're here." She knew she was on her way out.

Joel smiled guiltily but without warmth. "You look like your father," I said too quickly, immediately blaming myself for trying to put him at ease. But I still didn't stop, "He was an easygoing man." "He was," Joel answered, relieved. We were in the tame waters of cliché. "He hit me only once. I'll never forget it. I beat up my brother; you know him, Jay. My father ran down stairs and hit me. 'Don't you ever fight with your brother,' my father said. I never did." "And now you're partners," I said obviously. Jay had charm. He went to court. Joel stayed in the office. Joel smiled sadly; he didn't realize that he was sad; he didn't know he had described one episode in the long death of his spirit.

"I'll make copies," Joel said, with surprising self-importance, stressing the word "copies," as he held up the bankbooks. In Passaic, any person who had a copying machine or access to a copying machine might feel important. I had spent a whole morning trying to find one and had failed. The Indian owner of the variety store where I bought the paper—most of the downtown shops once owned by Jews were now owned by East Indians—had sent me to the public library. It was closed on Saturday like most public libraries in the Northeast. Budget cuts. The one in the bank lobby was broken. A man in the street told me to try the print shop; it was closed. I wondered if Joel would charge me for the service. With the same emphasis he told me that he would have to send *copies* of the will to the heirs.

When he came back, Joel asked me about my brother. Len worked as a supervisor, Sup Two, in the crisis center for abused children for all the five boroughs in New York. "I suppose you heard about my secretary," Joel said. "She was arrested for beating her kid." I hadn't heard. "I fired her; it gave me a reason; she was a lousy typist, couldn't get out a letter. Stupid, a very stupid woman." His voice was cold and tired.

"If you're going to take care of the tombstone," Joel said, handing me a card, "call Barry Fisher; he's gone into business for himself." I took the card. "You can call him from here." The voice on the phone sounded too young. Barry talked a lot; he was already selling. Finally I managed to make an appointment for him to meet me at Jen's apartment. "A stone for a single woman; I'll bring the brochure" was the last thing he said.

Barry Fisher arrived promptly at two. He was a trim man with a new haircut and the new look of middle age, a hard body. He went to the gym. As soon as I cleared a place for him, he took out his papers and began selling. There were no choices: a stone with a menorah for a single woman, a stone with a star of David for a single man. I forget what a couple got. He tried to make it seem as if he were doing something special. He would eliminate a curve that he felt would mess up the design. He took out the stone samples; there were two, dark polished and light unpolished. I chose the light gray and gave him the dates.

He looked up Jen's Hebrew name in his book: "Shaynah bas Lazar," Barry said. I first heard this name at the funeral. Shaynah meant pretty. She was. It was the only reason I agreed to have her Hebrew name on the stone, even though I couldn't read it.

"We have to get the name right," Barry said nervously, as if this were a matter of greatest difficulty, and his book of names a cabalistic mystery. Who knew? Maybe they did get the names wrong.

After Barry had been there for about a half an hour, my

mother came by. She brought some tea bags and fruit. "Did you eat?" she asked. It was the family's most important question. Barry was relieved to see her, an old customer. When he looked at her, he smiled less nervously, as if she reminded him that yes, he had made a sale, he was a salesman, he could do it again. "Gertie," he said with a friendliness that made her jump, "I left Rock of Ages; I'm on my own." He had had a heart attack; he blamed it on his rotten former boss. "I gave them everything; it doesn't pay."

Gert looked at the samples and asked him if it was the "same" stone, the "real" Rock of Ages. She knew how to play the game. Barry relaxed a little. "The same stone, from Vermont." He told us he had seen the quarry; it had frightened him, looking down into the enormous dark hole—the tombstone salesman.

Barry said my mother's name so often, he seemed to be calling her. He wanted to talk. He skipped into the chaotic kitchen— dishes, pots and pans, silver, bottle openers, all Jen's saved jars were piled on the countertops. Barry was oblivious. He spread out his arms; he could almost touch both walls. He was de-lighted. "The kitchen in our first apartment was as small as this. Smaller. I could touch the wall easy. You could hardly move in that place." Gert and I exchanged a look. Barry did a little dance.

I told him to send me the contract. My brother and I both had to sign it. His shoulders sagged. "It's only a formality," I reassured him; "you've made the sale." He didn't believe me. Where else would I go, to his former boss? There were only two places in town to buy tombstones. I wasn't going to shop around for bargains; I wondered if anyone did. The price seemed fair. For once, I wasn't looking for an unusual design. I would take what Barry ordered. "The stone will last forever," Barry pleaded. "That's what the Egyptians thought," I joked. Barry looked stricken. "The pyramids—that stone was soft, this won't flake; you have my promise." He looked longingly at the kitchen; he opened his mouth.

"Barry, we've got all this to do." Now I spread my arms. "O.K. O.K., I'm going." He packed up his brochure, the two stone samples, and the book of Hebrew names, and hurried down the small apartment hall, looking over his shoulder as he went. His eyes kept asking for reassurance. "You'll hear from me." He shrugged. He had heard that before. I repeated myself. It made no difference. Whatever loss Barry had experienced in the past was still with him. He looked wounded. He had got what he wanted; he had made a sale, which he had never had any chance of losing, and he didn't believe it, so sure was he in his stricken heart that at the last minute he would be cheated.

"When you're alive, you need every little thing; when you're dead, you need nothing," Jen's cousin Dora had told me. There was a lot to give away. Whatever the neighbors wouldn't take would go to the Salvation Army. Jen lived in subsidized housing for the elderly. She was well off compared with many of her neighbors, some of whom came to the Boulevard after being burned out of their apartments.

All that afternoon, I carried things down the long hall and stacked them near the elevator. Glasses went down that hall, pots—quart pots, two-quart pots, three-quart pots—fry pans, six-inch, eight-inch, an electric defroster—that a man took after he asked me if it worked; it was still in its original box—cups, stacks of saucers, teaspoons, tablespoons, dull knives, and always more shoes.

An old woman with a thick-skinned handsome face and a wig suitable for the opera stage lent me a shopping cart, which made the job easier. The squeaking wheels alerted people. As I repeatedly returned to load up again, I would hear apartment doors opening behind me.

I saw a woman take Jen's broom and a few minutes later carry her old broom to the trash; it was worn to an inch stub, good for nothing.

At one point, while I was in the apartment, loading up the cart, a woman barged in. She looked around the living room and asked me how much I wanted for the paintings. The woman's face was hard and appraising. "Fifty dollars." "I'd like the plants," she said. I told her to take them and hurried her out, letting her know that anything to be given away would be on the table in the hall.

On my next trip down, a woman who lived just across the hall followed me. She had had a stroke and her right foot dragged. For the rest of the afternoon she followed me. I'd meet her coming and going. As I put the stuff down, I would hear her in back of me, and when I returned with another load, I'd meet her coming back with her hands full. She wanted me to bring the stuff directly into her apartment, but I wanted to give everyone a chance; there were people worse off than she.

She had left her apartment door open. The walls were painted a bright sky blue. Every surface held a vase full of neon pink and acid yellow plastic flowers. On the wall just over the TV were pictures of her son in marine uniform, the dress hat set squarely above his serious young face. The Iran-gate hearings were on. Ollie North was testifying. The marine's mother was beaming at the screen. She asked me if I had an ironing board. I brought it to her along with a tray of silverware. She was wearing me down. One of her sons came to visit. "When did she pass?" he asked me. His pregnant wife was standing in back of him. "She was my buddy. I used to talk to her all the time. Isn't that so?" He turned to his wife; she didn't answer; her lips tightened. The man appraised me. He was nervy and timid at the same time. "When can I get in there?" he asked, meaning the apartment. "It's for the relatives," I said and left.

As I looked down the hall, I could see three or four women in housedresses bending over the boxes. They all seemed to be wearing wigs. Below their enlarged symmetrical heads, their shrinking bodies seemed even more wispy and fragile; they looked ghostlike, extraterrestrial.

The next morning I started on Jen's clothes. By noon the dozen or so pale tan pocketbooks and white pocketbooks were gone. On Memorial Day Jen would begin wearing light shoes and light bags. The boxes of dress gloves, most of them from her sister Bella, the piles of dainty handkerchiefs: they were gone too. I discovered she had lined her knitted hats with layers of heavy material, which made them feel like pillows: she couldn't stand the cold.

The knitted hats were child-sized. When she'd see me wearing a scarf on my head, tied under the chin, she'd invariably say, "You can wear a scarf like that; I can't; my head is too small." She'd complain about her thin hair, her sallow skin, her shallow ankles—she always had to put a pad in her shoe so her ankle wouldn't rub—her nearsightedness, she who was so pretty. Her black arched eyebrows, each hair stroked in, contrasted with her white hair, which had turned while she was still in her early forties. She could not bear to put a naked foot into a shoe or slipper and always wore either peds or stockings. Her legs were shapely and slender, her body full, until the final six months of her life.

Despite her self-made catalog of faults, she dressed and undressed in front of me without shame, talking as she did so. At those times, she was unselfconscious and graceful and still looked as she did in a picture I have of her taken when she was less than twenty, which I've just interrupted my writing to find. It's a small sepia-toned snapshot, three and a half inches by two and three fifths—I've just measured it. I have it here next to me under a magnifying glass. As I move the glass toward me, her face becomes clearer, larger. A hair closer and the face begins to blur. Moving the glass over the picture is as mysterious as memory dropping away from me, leaving its shadows and questions. Everytime I look at the snapshot I see something different and lose what I've seen before. The sun is shining over her left shoulder; the left side of her face is bright, the right eyebrow paler. Her right eye disappears in a neat round shadow. Her dark hair is swept up loosely from her high square forehead. She seems to be smiling with such natural ease and delight! Where is she? Leaning back, half reclining against the bow of a rowboat. Or perhaps she's in the corner of a porch. Then why is there such a tangle of woods and weeds behind her? It must be a boat pushed against a riverbank. When I take the magnifying glass away and look at the picture from a distance, I see a pattern of browns and whites. Leaning back—the white of her skirt and blouse and face against the dark triangle of the boat, against the darker tangled bank—her arms spread and bent, her head directly in the center, small-waisted, dolman-sleeved, she looks like a wasp or a kind of insect on its back. Under the glass, the cushion she's leaning against seems to be falling apart; perhaps it's just out of focus. There are four large buttons—two and two—on the luxuriantly full middy blouse tucked into a high waistband. The buttons are fading. Her widely spread arms and her hands rest on the gunnels. The fingers of her right hand curl as if she were about to strike a chord. They are firm. The fingers of her left hand are also curled but more loosely. Under the glass I can see an object in the foreground with three letters: HAP. It's not a newspaper, but a thing with writing on it. Jen looks so welcoming, leaning back, her knees open under the long skirt.

Although she was never a great kisser and hugger, she wasn't cold. One time when I was having lunch with her at her apartment, she stopped—I was seated—leaned over me, and, with a quick graceful gesture, cupped my chin and lifted my face to her gaze. Her head and lips moved with such gentle relish and delight. Her gesture of love left me free.

When I was small, I used to love to watch her get dressed. She'd pull her dress over her head and smooth down the hips. Her dresser was near the window. She would roll the ivory-colored shade all the way up rather than turn on the light. Holding an oval mirror in one hand, she would put on her lipstick, smoothing the color into the corners of her lips with her pinky, then blotting her lips with a small square of tissue. Then she would comb her hair with a comb that seemed much too large. The last thing she would do was put on her watch and, with her right hand, cup and move it back and forth into her wrist so that it found its groove between the bones.

In the afternoon my cousin Claudia came to help me. I had put aside all of the pictures of her father taken when he was young and sober; in most of them he was in a World War I uniform with tunic and puttees. Nathan had died before he was sixty; he had sobered up the last year of his life, but by then his health was shot. Claudia touched the pictures gingerly. As she bent over the bed, her heavy rope of pearls swung away from her firm small breasts and hung straight as a plumb line; a lock of thick hair broke loose. I asked her if she had any pictures of her father. "Not one. My mother has them all." She rolled the "r" in mother, making it sound like a growl.

Claudia noticed a picture of our grandmother Molly on Jen's bureau, where it had been since we were children. The picture had been tinted; the pale pink on Grandma's cheeks still looked like a flush, as it had when I stared at the picture as a child. Claudia and I had rubbed our toothless infant gums against Grandma's jutting chin. "Take it," I insisted.

Claudia told me she had nothing from the Levines. I had also put aside the best of Jen's china. Claudia liked good stuff. She hesitated, not wanting to seem greedy. Again I told her to take what she wanted; there was pale green depression glass, some Staffordshire. We wrapped it together. Claudia told me that her mother had promised her an Austrian chocolate set. I had seen it in my aunt Carmen's china cabinet. It was splendid, gold-swirled court china, which had found its way to Carmen's credenza—

one of my relatives called it a "crescendo"—in the Barry Garden
Apartments in Passaic. "She still hasn't given it to me," Claudia
said with bitterness. The family pronouncement on Carmen was:
"She gives with her mouth." They said this with equanimity because they didn't need anything from her. Carmen's stinginess
seemed as much a part of her as her blue eyes, and she was as
stingy with herself as she was with other people, but Claudia still
wanted something from her mother.

Carmen needed too. Claudia said, "She wants me to tuck her
in and kiss her goodnight. I can't do that. She needs a man." Apparently women weren't supposed to touch each other. Claudia
held our grandmother's pressed glass fruitbowl in her hand. Old
pressed glass had become important, "collectible." She was getting something.

Carmen had once bragged about how she had taken the children to Florida on the train. Claudia had been dressed in starched
white cotton. She had been a ravishing kid, her dark blond hair
streaked with lighter blond, so pale it looked white. Her eyes
were dark brown. Next to her, blue-eyed blonds looked insipid.
"I told her to sit there and not move," Carmen said. "She didn't,
not for hours, not even to go to the bathroom."

We started to empty the hall closet. Claudia suddenly took
off her dress, reached down and pulled it over her head—she
didn't want to get it dirty—then the high heels. I looked at her
hard body, the beige lace, the pearls. "The neighbors will wonder what's going on here," she said. I laughed falsely, suddenly
embarrassed. She filled the cart; I pulled it down the hall.

When it was time for her to go, I kissed her tight unyield-
ing face. We would see each other in a few days: her brother's
daughter was getting married.

The marriage ceremony and reception would be at The
Crystal Palace in Livingston—apparently aspirations and images
of the ideal hadn't changed since the twenties, when my uncle

Nathan had called his bar The Crystal Spa. Livingston was a wealthy suburb where many of the people I had gone to high school with had bought homes and raised their children. My former classmates wanted nothing to do with Passaic. Driving home from work or from the vast malls, they entered the streets of Livingston, which seemed to say, with their leisurely conspicuous curves like nineteenth-century park roads or cemetery lanes, You don't have to go anywhere, you don't have to hurry. I liked to think that the foul Passaic River, the black asphalted playgrounds, the broken curbstones, the chaotic shop windows jammed with cheap flimsy clothes, the furious roses in the church gardens surrounded by chain link, the blacks, the Puerto Ricans—chalked on a wall: "Mr. Gringo Starr sez your chances are you don't go far, white trash sez jump on the wood, or bugaloo down Broadway"—had all entered their unconscious and lay there, shrouded but not dead. I liked to think that suburban transcendence could not work completely.

But when I walked into The Crystal Palace, I could see how it might. The mirror-lined foyer gleamed like a star's dressing room. Everything was done up in shades of pink and mauve. The double staircase, which rose from the lobby, was carpeted in pale pink. The air was discreetly perfumed. I liked the show.

Claudia had told me that there would be a brunch before the ceremony and then dinner. "Can that be true?" I asked my husband. I had gotten used to New England restraint. Brunch was laid out. A chef was cooking omelets to order. There were bagels and lox and caviar, pastries, trays and trays of hot hors d'oeuvres, champagne, anything you wanted to drink, anything at all.

Aunt Carmen was swathed in pink chiffon; an immense corsage of pink orchids covered half her chest. "I can't walk straight," she confided. She was taking cortisone to prevent a stroke. "I look like a chipmunk." Her once perfectly oval face was puffy and soft. I speared a marinated mushroom with a frill-tipped toothpick. Carmen said, "There was a waiter at the Ritz—

you remember the Ritz, it was downtown. They took him to the hospital with terrible pain, they cut out his appendix, sent him home. The pain came back—worse. They opened him up. Guess. A toothpick. He had swallowed it eating a club sandwich. If you swallow anything, it's better to swallow a penny or a button, it's the same shape as your asshole." She bounced against me as we laughed, her still firm hip against mine.

At two, we all went up the pink staircase to the chapel, which was also carpeted in pink. The guests were feeling good. They leaned back in their upholstered theater seats, laughing and chatting until the wedding began.

Under the canopy, the wedding couple were flanked by their parents who, except for my cousin Frank, seemed about to burst into tears. The bride and groom were calm and smiling. The rabbi, who looked like a college student, married them after an irrational lecture about the significance of the breaking of the glass—the groom stamped on it at the end of the ceremony. It symbolized, he said, the persecuted Jews in Russia and the miraculous passage across the Red Sea. I had heard a similar discourse at another wedding: they must be getting it from the same how-to book.

Finally the rabbi stopped talking. The groom lifted his foot and came down hard; the glass shattered with a loud crack that sounded like a gunshot. An action, a sound that survived rabbinical emasculation. Cheers, clapping, laughter, release. Goodbye to the old life.

It was time to eat again. I had another glass of champagne at the table where we sat with my cousins and their husbands and wives. My cousin Leo was there, the one whose infant formula I had watched being prepared in my grandmother Molly's house. Leo had flown up from Atlanta, where he had just taken a new job; he was making money. He had recently shaved off his beard and replaced his hated glasses with contacts. "You look great," I said. "So you didn't know I had blue eyes?" he answered. He was drinking his champagne quickly.

We began talking about Passaic. "What did I do there?" he asked the table rhetorically. His head tilted back. "I went into the backyard—what do I mean?—the alley, and I took a screwdriver, and I hit an old rotting pole; I hit and hit it. With that red screwdriver. That was the summer."

The music picked up. Leo and I got up to dance. He was good; he was fast. He had a way of pointing his foot as he brought it forward while at the same time raising his chin. He didn't miss a beat. Light, graceful, high but controlling his high, he whirled, and I whirled with him. Claudia joined us. "Are you sure he's a Levine?" she asked, laughing. "He's from the South," I answered. We kept it up. Claudia and I broke into a lindy. I led. She danced like a Passaic kid. We had the same steps. I twirled her in and out; we came back to the center and broke again; she went under my lifted arm and swung out as far as she could go without breaking my hold. Leo danced around us. Then Claudia and I dropped hands, and the three of us stepped and rocked together. We stamped, we glided, we whirled and jumped. The music rose and fell, and we, the heirs, let it carry us, as our feet worked against the polished floor.

Louie

From time to time, I would get news from my mother about her brother Louie. Gert would visit him and his second wife, Bessie, at the couple's Florida condominium in Boca Raton. "How did it go?" I asked her when she returned from her last trip south. "All right," she answered, drawling out the word. She looked angry and thoughtful. She was sitting on the couch between a basket of torn clothes and her sewing box. When these mending fits come upon her, she sews for days. Her mending holds. She looked up from a pair of my son's jeans, which she was patching at the knee, "They took me out a lot. We went everywhere. It was nice." "Nice?" I asked, waiting. "Well, you know," Gert hesitated, "he has Al Heimer's disease." She pushed the needle through the tough denim, "He can't play cards anymore, and he doesn't drive the car."

Louie would begin a poker game with his old enthusiasm and then sit quietly, holding the cards, looking like a person who had rushed into a room and then stopped, unable to remember what he had come for. He would have gone on sitting at the umbrella-shaded table in the soft Florida air, waiting to remember, if one of his cronies hadn't led him off to play shuffleboard, a game that he could still manage. "But it's not too bad yet," Gert continued. "He still knows who I am."

My family grudgingly admitted each other's inevitable mortal decline with statements, which, no matter how often they had said them about various people in the past, still sounded like mysterious news from a distant country when applied to the new arrivals at the gates of decrepitude: "He doesn't drive the car anymore," and "She can't push the vacuum." These were the decisive markers in the slow progress of aging. The tone in which the news was conveyed was a mixture of certainty, irony, wonder, and incomprehension, as if they knew and didn't know what was going on. They seemed to be buying time for themselves by savoring the mystery, and holding off the recognition scene, when the truth—stroke, heart attack—would finally make past, present, and future clear. But the admission of death would last only for a short while. After all, *they* were still living.

Last week I heard "Aunt Carmen can't take the bus anymore." On the way to her weekly doctor's appointment, she had stood in the hot afternoon sun, waiting for the Passaic Avenue bus, which was slow in coming. Feeling faint, she walked back to her apartment and passed out in the hall with her key in her hand. "If that's what death is like," she told my mother, "it's not so bad." No one had found her; she came to by herself, her head under the mailboxes and her feet against the bottom step. Everyone in the family wondered how she would get downtown by herself. None of them liked to depend on their children, and like Carmen, they refused to take taxis. They got angry at the mention of the word; they'd rather die. It wasn't so much a question of money as an article of belief. They fought giving in. Even though Carmen tottered, she refused to "walk with a cane." As the story of Carmen went around, her direct reference to death got lost in the telling. The recognition, "Carmen can't take the bus anymore," was as far as they would go. Only my mother continued to tell the whole story. " 'It's not so bad,' " she would repeat.

In Florida, Gert would spend a lot of time alone with her brother, when Bessie went to get her hair done or to her mahjongg game. They'd walk arm in arm around the shuffleboard courts. Louie still looked well. Gert was thin. She had not yet been diagnosed for a glandular problem, the condition responsible for her weight loss. The doctors said she was shrinking—and she was so small to begin with!—because of old age, but we could all see that she wasn't shrinking slowly. She was burning up, while at the same time continuing to shop and cook with great energy. Louie would urge her to eat more and suggested vitamins. Gert assessed Louie's reasoning abilities, "He tells me to eat and her not to eat." She meant Bessie. "She tells him she went in the pool. He says, 'So how come your suit ain't wet?' He's smart enough," Gert insisted. She had once defended my dog in the same way. When my son had made fun of the pet, Gert had shot back, "She's as smart as she has to be."

Louie had always loved the water. When people said, "He lives in the water," they meant it. There he was most alive. Still a strong swimmer, and now slim and sleek in one of those blooming returns of youth that sometimes happens before a disease really takes hold, he had led Gert into the pool. Emotionally reckless, she was physically timid. He had lured her, talked her in, his dripping small hands outstretched. Gert followed his voice, forgetting about her feet, about falling. Perhaps, he had watched, as I had done in Florida in the same role, Gert's changing look as the water touched her shoulders—fear, calm, shock, and finally glee.

"I got along with him," Gert continued. "It's her; she's the one; she has no patience." "Well, Bessie's with him all the time, Ma. It must be hard," I replied. "But she didn't have to do what she did. That yenta, she called the police on him. While I was there. They woke me up in the middle of the night." Gert told me that she had stood behind the door of the guest room and listened to Bessie tell the policeman that Louie was trying to have sex with her. Bessie had first locked herself in the bathroom, and then run out, and called the police. "I'm an old woman," Gert heard her say, "I have high blood pressure." The police-

man asked if Louie had hit her or threatened her in any way.
He hadn't. "To do such a thing while I was there . . . ," Gert
mused. "There are other ways to handle it," I said reasonably.
"She could just have said no. But who knows what's been going
on between them. Too bad that you had to listen to all that."
If there was anything Gert Jacobs coming from a family with a
history of sexual shame didn't need, it was to have her diminu-
tive brother portrayed to the police as a satyr. Though maybe
he was, not dark, hairy, hooved, but a water satyr, white-blond,
stepping out of the pool with a hard-on.

Gert wanted to leave the next morning, but Bessie persuaded
her to stay for the remainder of her vacation. So for another
week the three of them tried to ignore—actually Louie may
have forgotten—what had happened. Every morning they sat at
the glass-topped breakfast table under the rattan-shaded light.
Bottles of vitamin pills and other pills were clustered like condi-
ments on the orange plastic doily. Although the cut glass sugar
bowl stuffed with bright pink envelopes of Sweet and Low was
still on the table, my mother said that Bessie did not put out the
Light n' Lively Lowfat Cottage Cheese and rye toast. Instead, as
if to make up for her behavior or perhaps to solace herself, she
offered fresh bagels, cream cheese, sturgeon, sweet butter, and
wedges cut from a melon as big as a bowling ball.

Louie was again urging Gert to eat more. Bessie chatted about
her children, but her voice had a raw edge. "She was aggravated,"
Gert said, relishing the word "aggravated," which my English
teachers had told me never to use to describe feeling. "A wound
is aggravated, not a person." Little did they know. Finally, when
Louie had left the table to go to the bathroom, Bessie turned
to Gert, "You don't know," she said. "Your brother is a little
Napoleon."

When Gert told me this part of the story, I wondered if Bessie
hadn't confused "Little Caesar" (the character in the film of that
title) with Napoleon. "Little Napoleon?" I asked Gert. "Napoleon

is 'little' already. Are you sure she didn't say 'Little Caesar?' " I was thinking to myself, Caesar? Who knows how tall he was, but certainly taller than Louie, taller than Edward G. Robinson. Gert shot me one of her scornful this-is-what-I-sent-you-to-college-for? looks.

I didn't think to ask Gert where Louie was when the police came. Gert was behind the door. Bessie was talking to the policeman. Had Louie run away? Was he standing there in his yellow pajamas? Was he confused? Was he ashamed? I hope that Alzheimer's had weakened the shame center of the brain—probably not. I hope he was still able to get angry, but I can't say I minded Louis Jacobs's being stopped. I was familiar with the Jacobses' will. Tiny Louie and tiny Gert never gave up on anything, seldom admitted, despite appeals to reason or justice, that they might be wrong. They had to be beaten back. I had had to stop my own mother, who at one time thought she knew what kind of person I should be, nice. Yet I did not enjoy the thought of the Jacobses' humiliation.

Bessie's calling the police clinched Gert's view of her. She had always thought the woman was a brute and a yenta. Gert couldn't help comparing her to Louie's first wife, who had died of cancer in her early forties.

Lillian, Lily, we called her, never Lil. She had been born in London. She had a brother Harry, whom we met. No one seemed to know much more about her family. I remember asking about her parents. Where were they? In England? No answers. My family always got nervous when asked a direct question. Lily's family weren't killed by the Nazis, but it seemed they had just disappeared "over there" somewhere. Actually, as I've just recently learned, they were all here, the Beresfords, living on Holsman Street in Paterson, but so alone did Aunt Lily seem to me, and still does, that the distance separating her from her parents seemed oceanic, unbridgeable. It was marriage that had orphaned her. When she came to our house, she brought no antecedents.

I believed that she and Harry were twins. It was something I made up. Their coloring matched. I sensed they were a couple in a way she and Louie were not. Louie was fair; Lily was dark. His short whitish spiked hair and her coarse black hair, which she usually wore shoulder length and pulled off her face with a black or white band, seemed like intractable elements that could never mingle.

Aunt Lily's voice was low, husky, intense. I would call it breathless, except for the rasp that gave it depth and substance. She had a firm heart-shaped face, high cheekbones, and merry eyes. They dumbfounded me—the glee. The plodding Levines had the sad-dog eyes of people whose spirit was trapped by muteness and shame; the Jacobses had ironic eyes. Aunt Lily looked out at the world and laughed.

Only about feeding children was she desperate. She would have been happy to have been surrounded by squawking children who constantly had their mouths open like baby birds. "They don't eat," she would say about Audrey and Marsha, my thin cousins. I thought they looked fine. When I stayed with Aunt Lily and my cousins in their rented apartment at Far Rockaway Beach, I would stare at my cousins' eyes where the Beresford-Jacobs marriage seemed to have produced an alchemy: blond Audrey had dark eyes like her mother; brown-haired Marsha had blue eyes like her father.

Aunt Lily welcomed me as a kid who would eat. At first her approval was wonderful. My own mother, who had once devoted herself to overfeeding me and had finally won the battle—I had become a chubby kid—now felt I ate too much. Aunt Lily would mix up chocolate malteds. The Jacobses had their own machine, heavy chrome and pale green metal, exactly like the one in the candy stores. I'd drink my malted to the dregs. There were no malteds in my mother's kitchen in Passaic. After a few days of this, I was beginning to feel stuffed. One day, Aunt Lily asked me if I liked cucumbers. She was packing a lunch for the beach.

I told her I did. Later, after we had all come out of the water, she produced our lunch. There were tuna sandwiches, fruit, and the cucumbers. She unwrapped a bundle of cucumbers as large as a roast. I ate a few pieces. She kept urging me. Finally I refused. Staring at the vegetables with a look of anger—the look of most mothers I knew whose bounty was refused—she said, "I thought you liked cucumbers." "I do but not this many," I answered, pointing to the moist seedy pile, "there's enough here for ten people."

We children were supposed to relieve our parents of the glut of America. "What am I going to do with this?" they would moan and implore, staring down at the plates in their hands full of lamb chops, baked potato, and spinach, at bowls of cereal large enough to keep a miner going. "What am I going to do with this?" they would cry most desperately, when they lifted the heavy half-full tumblers of milk. "Drink your milk," Estelle Slutsky Green, our upstairs neighbor, would scream at her tiny daughter, Susy, who looked as if she should be lapping a few tablespoons from a delicate pink saucer, "or I'll kill you." Estelle's window would fly open with a bang. Susy had won. "Greenberg, Greenberg," Estelle would call across the courtyard, "take her, take her; I can't stand it anymore." Greenberg was a Russian-born older woman relied upon for her ability to relieve parents and rescue children. We all called her by her last name—like Einstein.

"What am I going to do with these?" Aunt Lily asked tragically, as she pointed to the cucumbers, which were now gritty with sand. The vegetables lay there all afternoon, turning into garbage.

One weekend, when Louie had joined us, we went to see the water ballet. Stuffed into my tight sundress, I watched the sleek swimmers in their iridescent bathing suits. In the moving spotlights—the brightest, whitest light I had ever seen, brighter than the light at Ebbets Field where my father took me to night games—the shallow waves made by the swimmers seemed unreal, seemed to be moving in a sculpted pattern. On their backs, on their sides, treading water, only briefly on their stomachs, the swimmers seemed always to be lifting from the surface of the water, like half-completed beings. What were the legs doing? I wondered. When the swimmers turned on their backs, forming a circle with their feet pointing to the center, their legs appeared as if newly unsheathed, and their breasts threatened to float out of the tight suits. Their hair was hidden under petaled blue, pink, yellow, and green rubber bathing caps. When we ten-year-olds put on bathing caps, we looked hydrocephalic, our compressed foreheads wrinkled. Not these swimmers. From a distance, they seemed glorious, perfect.

I sensed Aunt Lily belonged to their party, as I did not. She looked only a little older than she had when she first got married. In her Florida honeymoon picture, taken on the beach and sent back to my mother in Passaic, she's wearing a two-piece white bathing suit, high-heeled white sandals; her thick black hair is smoothed and coiled, this time under a white headband. Beautifully calm, looking, in white trunks, more naked than if he had been naked, Louie glides against her side. There's the slightest plumpness about her glossy shoulders, and she's smiling at the camera with a look of complete happiness. She had no kids to feed.

Aunt Lily never dieted, never put on a pound, except when she was pregnant. Her sexiness was contained by her trim body.

When Louie remarried, the family looked away in embarrassment. Jack Sprat—he was still slim then—had married a fateater. Bessie had hips, large breasts, a real stomach. She was in her forties, and perhaps reminded the uncles of their frighteningly sexy corseted mothers. They whispered and snickered.

After Lou and Bessie retired to Florida, Gert would come back from visits with new stories of Bessie's eating. "They took me to an Italian restaurant. The food! I couldn't finish it. They gave me a doggie bag. Bessie got up in the middle of the night and ate it all—after that big meal! There was nothing left the next day. Veal parmigiano, loaded with cheese, that thick." Here Gert measured with her thumb and index finger, then paused for a second, looking off into the distance. "She ate it," Gert said with awe and disgust.

By this time, both Louie and Bessie were struggling with food. They'd starve themselves for weeks before going on a cruise. On shipboard, they'd gorge themselves. Bessie would return angry and defeated. Her dramatic oversized opera-singer-like face— big eyes, big curving mouth and nose—would sag under its new weight of flesh; her balabosta's bosom would push out with authority. Louie would come back with a round gut, which would sit between his hips like a ball. The rest of him was intact, even elegant. Soon the gut would shrink—he swam every day.

Louie liked pastel outfits: yellow pants matching a knitted yellow shirt, which he would wear unbuttoned to show his gold chains—a thick one and a thinner one. Sometimes he'd wear all blue, the shirt collar trimmed with the thinnest white line. His shoes were like slippers—soft, white leather. He dressed like a baby, a sophisticated baby, for his new life in Florida.

Louie had made his money in the fruit and produce market in New York. He had worked himself up until he owned his own business, The Washington Market. "I didn't have a nickel when I started," he was fond of saying. I loved his figure of speech. I could hear the flourish, the exaggeration, the lie. It seemed so daring. How could he not have a nickel? I asked myself, as I thought of my own few coins. I was a little girl and I had a nickel. I had even found money in the street. "I didn't have a pot to piss in," he would continue. "All I had was these." He'd hold up his small hands. "I lugged." How I loved that word. There was no suggestion of dragging. Louie was not a schlepper; he lugged. Somehow the work had not ruined his beautiful skin. Although he was very fair, his skin was thick; it did not crack or burn.

He liked being in the market at three o'clock in the morning, drinking coffee with his friends. He had a good "mouthpiece," the family expression for people who had the gift of quick speech. He spoke to his customers, to everyone, with an intimacy that bound both listener and speaker in mutual need. He always had news to tell, and after a minute with him, you felt you had as much desire to listen to his story as he had to tell it. He always knew when to pause, to nail you with his eyes, to put the quick hand on your arm, to call you by your first name, but unlike the con man, the hustler, he was in it too; he gave himself away, the lugger.

When frozen and processed potatoes came in—french fries, instant mashed—he was astonished, not bitter. He brought the news to the family in Passaic before the "product" appeared in the retail markets. It was his theme for months. The grownups listening to him, as they sat around the table with their after-dinner shots of Scotch, had a look of helplessness and aboriginal curiosity. "It comes in bags like flour; you mix it up," he would say. "It feels like soap flakes." He grieved. "The restaurants, they want it."

I imagined him standing in the shadow of a hairy-chested cook, the pink fingers of each lilliputian hand stretched to their limit to hold a huge roughly oval potato while his head and shoulders drooped in disappointment. The men around the table would toss back their drinks and nod, as if they really understood, but they never made the leap to the abstracted potato—even when they finally saw the product. I'm not sure this actually happened, but I remember Louie at that same table, opening a box of instant mashed potatoes and pouring it into his hand. His hand overflowed, the white stuff was all over the table, but none of the men touched it. My mother swept it up and threw it in the trash. For them it was never "potato."

Their parents and great-grandparents had eaten potatoes in Europe. In America, Louie had grown up eating potatoes served with praise and unspoken thanksgiving—potato pancakes, potato kugel, potato blintzes, baked potatoes, roasted potato, potato soup. He had even made his money in potatoes. During a short-age when restaurants were desperate for potatoes, real whole potatoes to mash, to roast, to boil, to fry, to grate, Louie de-livered. The family story was that he had scoured Long Island, ferreted out the farmers who had potatoes, and persuaded them to sell to him. He needed; they needed; the restaurants needed. New York could not live without the potato; without the potato Louie could not "make a buck." Who could have predicted the fall of the potato? The horse maybe, but the potato?

Louie was a practical man. In a short while, he was whole-saling processed potatoes, which he refused to eat, refused to have in his house, and he was still in business when New York restaurants returned to fresh potatoes.

After he had made his money, bought a house on Long Island and remarried, he would come back to Paterson once a week to eat deli and play cards with his friends, the former boys he had gone to grammar school with. After the game, they'd go to the steambath, the *schvitz*. When he told me that he loved to sit in the steam—I was a grown woman by then—I could hear the Jacobs intimacy in his voice. How does he do it? I wondered. Con-vince me in a few words, that he's giving me his life? I was taller than he, but he managed to eyeball me and hook me in. Perhaps he sensed that I wouldn't criticize him for his card playing the way Bessie did. He couldn't know that I was off on my own riff: Louie in the steam—his Polack-white hair, which he was wear-ing longer, limply curling yet seeming about to unpeel from his compact, beautifully made head; his small feet were pink from the thick clouds of steam, which filled the room and enveloped his slightly plump body, the oddly broad chest for a person that small; he seemed so relaxed, but as his face emerged from the steam, moisture dripping from the almost invisible blond-white eyebrows, I could see that the wet heat had softened only a little that ironic I-told-you-so look in his eyes. Maybe he had been born with that look. The irony was foreign—like Sam's inflected speech. It went back to Lodz; maybe it went back to Egypt.

A few months after Gert came back from that awful vacation in Boca Raton, Louie died. He had gotten up just before dawn, perhaps believing that it was later in the morning. He packed up his small bag with his shaving things and towel, as he did every morning, and headed for the pool, where he would usually shower quickly and then swim. He'd then do his complete toilette before returning home for breakfast. Perhaps the dim light confused him. He thought he was heading for the pool, but he kept walking and walking across the low flat land that surrounded the condominiums until the houses were out of sight, and the grass became sparser and sparser.

Bessie discovered that he was missing around seven o'clock. The police found him later in the day, floating face down in a shallow canal. Louie had taken off his watch and carefully tucked it into his bag.

I had to wait to tell my mother about Louie's death. She was in the hospital in Boston. When I finally told her, Gert stared past me, silently contemplating Louie in his bathing suit, dropping away from her into the warm Florida waters.

Postscript

A few years after Louie died, and after I had written this memoir, my cousin Audrey told me that she was sure that her father had killed himself, "He was a strong swimmer," she emphasized. "He never made a mistake in the water." Audrey did not believe that he had had Alzheimer's disease. Louie's memory problems, she said, had begun years before when he was knocked down by a truck in New York. (Gert is still certain that he had been diagnosed for Alzheimer's.) Before he died he had made a special trip to New York to see Audrey. "He told me that he was not going to die in an institution," Audrey said. "He gave me family pictures." Bessie, his second wife, hadn't come with him. Louie talked. With an echo of her father's passion, Audrey told me that he had handed her Lily's picture and said, " 'She is the only one I ever loved.' "

Passaic

Junction

One day, when I was visiting my mother in Passaic, I offered to take her to visit my father's grave. He was buried in Passaic Junction cemetery. She had been wanting to go for some time, and my brother, whose job it was to take her, had been too busy. I hadn't been to the cemetery since the unveiling of the tombstone ten years before, and I wondered what kind of trip it would be. I didn't much like cemeteries.

Gert gathered up her gardening tools and gloves, which she stuck in a shallow basket, and put on a wide-brimmed straw hat. She wore a full-skirted dress with softly puffed sleeves, made less girlish by its dark brown and beige flowers. She looked like a cross between a flower girl and a garden-club matron. I couldn't imagine how she assembled these costumes. One Christmas she had appeared in an enormous white tam, a white turtleneck sweater, which came down over her skirt, and a five-foot-long white knitted scarf, the winter costume of her youth: skater.

The ride to the cemetery took about half an hour. We were very comfortable in the air-conditioned rental car. When we got out, the heat almost knocked us over. There was no shade in the section of the cemetery where my father was buried.

The sun's glare off the white tombstones and high enclosing

white wall was Mediterranean. The ground was sandy and dry and rose in a gentle, oddly welcoming slope, unlike the new flat bulldozed prairie cemeteries designed for the mowing machine. Those had flat plaques laid in the ground—also for the convenience of the mowing machine. At Passaic Junction there were stand-up tombstones, and most of the graves were bordered by stone curbing.

I couldn't get over the foreign look of the place. It might have been Israel or Greece. America occasionally furnished these unusual scenes, not reproduction English Tudor houses in Westchester or Spanish villas in Beverly Hills but these odd pockets of true foreignness.

My mother and father had belonged to a burial society, which they called "The Lodge." The members were buried in the same neighborhood, their gravestones baking in the same unvarying August heat. It must have been a hundred degrees.

The cemetery was small, and the section that enclosed my father's grave even smaller. Where had all the Jews in New Jersey gone? Florida? Most of my family had chosen to "go" either to Riverside Cemetery or to Passaic Junction. There were also a few in King Solomon. They would say, "I'm going to Riverside," the way some people would say, "I'm going to Miami."

Some relatives, like Uncle Louie, had actually gone to Florida. My father's sister Bella was also there. A few years before, I had spent an afternoon with Bella and her husband at their cabana at the Breakers in Palm Beach. We were all in bathing suits; my aunt's perfectly manicured nails clicked against her icy glass, a vodka gimlet. Her face was calm; she was happy. Earlier she had shown me around the grand hotel, pointing out the coffered ceilings in the reception rooms, as if it were her home. In a way, it was. She and her husband lived in a Palm Beach condominium but had rented a cabana at the Breakers for twenty years. They came here every day and relaxed. My uncle's blood pressure had gone down.

Their friend, a retired owner of a wildly successful car dealership in New York, joined us for drinks. When he found out Gert was from Passaic, he tried to sell both of us two lots in King Solomon Cemetery on Passaic Avenue, a few blocks from Gert's apartment. "What do I need them for?" he asked. What indeed? His tan was the color of mocha frosting. His nails had a mother-of-pearl gleam. His capped teeth were white and even as a movie actor's. He looked as though he would live forever. And what was *I* going to do with cemetery lots? Maybe I'd end up in Florida like my aunt. Maybe I'd be burned.

As I read my father's name and dates, 1902–1976, I felt the loss. I looked into Gert's eyes and saw the loss registered there, in the darkened pupil. That's how it is, her eyes said. Quick sadness, then goodbye. It never occurred to us to say a prayer. Besides, I don't think my mother knew any prayers. The only ritual I had ever seen her perform that could in any way be connected with religion was her placing a small pebble on top of a tombstone as a sign of her visit, a custom that must date back to ancient times. Like my grandmother she never went to shul, but unlike my grandmother she seemed to have completely erased from habit all religious practice, even the lighting of Sabbath candles. Although she never discussed it with me, I could sense that she was recklessly pleased to be free, especially of the labor of keeping a kosher house, which she had done for a while.

I had never heard her utter a pious word—ever. She had no ready-made phrases of consolation. She never even ventured, "Time heals all wounds." She'd say, "I dreamed of Joe last night." In these dreams they were always going somewhere. And that's how I remember the two of them together. She packing food in the kitchen, always fresh fruit, a couple of cold roasted chickens, and rye bread prickly with strong-tasting caraway seeds, and then they would be carrying these packages out to the car, their faces serious, absorbed. They would be going to visit relatives in hospitals, but more often to Bear Mountain, or just out for a ride.

We got down on our hands and knees and began weeding my

father's grave. Before he died, cancer had so wasted him that his head had become skull. When he looked at me the last time I saw him, he smiled; the smile was still his. What was left of him was now deep under our hands: his unhinged bones, his black hair uprooted from his fleshless skull. The weeds came out easily from the loose sandy seasidelike soil, far from the ocean. The grave was planted with foot-high silvery green sedums, which were just beginning to bud, and which would soon put out flat stiff pink flowers. Most of the graves were covered with these desert plants. Gert and I worked well together. We did the job as if we were making a bed. At first Gert moved too quickly, then she found a less taxing rhythm. We got it right. We shaped the grave; we cleaned, but not too furiously. We did the job. The grave had taken on domestic proportions, had lost—especially in this heat, which would kill any mold—its Poe-like horror.

"I want to see Sam's grave," Gert said, as she collected her gardening tools. I took the basket as she wiped her face, and we walked to the other side of the sloping gravel path, which separated this part of the cemetery into two even sections. My uncle Sam's grave was bare except for a few straggly weeds. A section of the stone curbing had sunk at the corner. The bare plot disturbed me. I told Gert that I would come back the next day and plant the grave. I knew sedums would do well here, but I wanted to try a different variety from the watery pink ones on every grave. I wanted dragon's blood sedum. Dark rose. "I'll make it beautiful," I said, already seeing Sam's grave covered with flowers. (Now in July, as I write, the sedum is in flower, drawing bees.) She hesitated. "Don't you like the idea?" I asked. She smiled, "Of course, of course. I don't know why we never did anything before."

I was ready to go, but Gert had more business. "I haven't seen my sister Esther's grave for years," she said. "Who knows when I'll be back?" All I knew about Esther was that she had died young. In a family photograph of the Jacobs and their five children—Louie hadn't been born yet—she is the youngest, a plump alert one-year-old with dark bangs and big dark serious eyes. Esther, having been born between Gert and Louie, had, like them, not been infected with syphilis.

Gert was sure Esther's grave was on the other side of the cemetery. We got in the car and drove down a dirt road that quickly narrowed and became swampy. Water came up to our hubcaps. I had to back out. There was a young blonde woman on the road. As we got closer, Gert immediately recognized her. She was the daughter of the man who for years had been the cemetery's caretaker. Now he was sick, and she was doing his job. If you wanted "perpetual care" given to a grave, these were the people who did it, generation to generation. She cheerfully pointed out a path that would take us to the other side of the cemetery. "If you can't find it," she called out, "we'll look up the site in the office."

I followed my mother, who would go down one path, correct herself, turn onto another path, and correct herself again. She seemed to be finding her way. She was so absorbed, I hadn't the heart to interrupt her, even though I was getting hot and tired. She was following a memory. Her wide straw hat bobbed in front of me. "It has to be against the wall," she said. We crossed another path, this one lined with stone walls broken by rusting gates. Each gate had a different design and bore the name of a different burial society. Gert was getting confused, but finally she recognized "Zion Camp No. 6." What could they have meant by "camp?" I wondered. Were they Zionists who had intended to immigrate to Israel but made it only as far as New Jersey? This was an old section of the cemetery. No one after the concentration camps would use the word "camp" in a cemetery.

Most of the stones in this section were carved with Hebrew letters that I could not understand. There were dark gray granite stones in the shapes of trees, that is, trunks of trees, five or six feet high, carved with knotholes, bark, and cut off at an angle to symbolize lives cut off prematurely. One tombstone was completely covered by a rambling rosebush that had gripped the stone and was sending huge arching canes into the air like antennae. Set in some of these stones were photographs of the dead, glossy cameos with melting sepia brown hair. It seemed as if the photographs had passed through a fire that clarified and yet softened the images. Most of these graves—the ones with the pictures—were overgrown. And the rest I imagine had "perpetual care." The graves dated from the twenties and thirties; they might have been as old as Pompeii. Photographs dropped into a jungle or onto the moon.

We came to the far wall, the last wall, the boundary. It was cool and shady here. Gert took a few more false turns, corrected herself, turned right again, and walked right to her sister's grave. Gert told me that Esther had died of "double pneumonia." She was eight. The tombstone was a small white tablet about three and a half feet high and carved with a small weeping willow tree. The surface of the stone was rough with age and looked porous.

In the same small square plot was a large stone, really a monument. The speckled granite was polished; the tip of the triangular pediment, which was mounted on a square base, reached over our heads. A rich person's tombstone. Charles Jacobs, my mother's uncle, her father's brother. "The one who hanged himself," my mother said. "They used to bury suicides against the wall." The first time he tried it, my grandfather had found him in time; he was still breathing when my grandfather cut him down. Eventually Charles succeeded; he did what he wanted.

"They had money," my mother added. "They had a chandelier." Charles had owned a silk mill in Paterson. His brother, my grandfather Abraham, had also owned a mill, Jacobs and Shein, but it hadn't prospered, and eventually he went out of business. I wondered whether my great-uncle Charles had hung himself from the chandelier.

Gert went on talking. "He killed himself just before Esther died." I looked at the gravestones: Charles and Esther had died in 1918. "My parents didn't have a plot," Gert said. They didn't have the money, I thought, and also they may not have wanted to put her in the cemetery all by herself. The suicide and the little girl: their graveyard coziness came from a family intimacy that had long ago disappeared. My grandfather blamed the wife for his brother's suicide. The family split. The wife made more money, and that was that. My mother was still blaming the wife. "She was hard; they called her 'The Cossack.' She drove him to it."

I didn't hear about Charles until long after I had left Passaic. As I stood between the two graves, I remembered having been here with my parents, playing as they weeded Esther's grave— happy. I didn't remember the tombstones. They hadn't been important, so when I had learned about Charles, I had never connected him to this monument. Suddenly he and his wealth became real. Even though I had known about the mill, I was amazed that anyone in my family would have such a stone.

I got interested in Charles. First of all his name: it was unusual in a family that called its sons Abraham, Samuel, Isaac—heavy, dutiful, biblical names. The name "Charles" seemed so French, so dandyish. He'd probably given himself the name, changed it from the Hebrew, from Chaim, perhaps. Maybe he was gay, I thought. Maybe that's why he killed himself.

I asked my mother what he looked like. "Reddish hair, fair," she answered. I gave him a moustache and put him in a stiff white shirt, an immaculate white shirt. I had heard that my grandfather was fastidious, nasty neat. So I made Charles even cleaner; his skin was intact except for the rope mark burned into his neck. I gave him elegant hands like my grandfather's. I made him "imperially slim" like Robinson's Richard Cory (Perhaps, "imperially" could not fit a Jew, but Charles did own a big mill):

And he was rich—yes, richer than a king—
And admirably schooled in every grace:
In fine, we thought that he was everything
To make us wish that we were in his place.

So on we worked, and waited for the light,
And went without the meat, and cursed the bread;
And Richard Cory, one calm summer night,
Went home and put a bullet through his head.

"How could you do it?" I asked despite what I knew about suicides. "You had so much. You got the biggest stone here. You
got what we all wanted."

I saw Esther. She was eight; she was dressed in white, her dark
hair damp, frizzled at the temples from fever sweat. She could
read. She could think. I imagined her speaking one minute, then
dead. I put them together, she and her uncle: the rich uncle and
the poor niece. They were poor, my mother's family. My mother
had written to an aunt, begging for a white sweater. Her father
was furious with her for having shamed him.

Esther's small white stone seemed to be tethered to Charles's
big dark monument, like a delicate cart to a heavy carriage. The
style of the tombstones was closer to the nineteenth century than
to the twentieth. Charles was Empire; Esther was Civil War.
How odd it was, how historical. I had found style in the cemetery. There wasn't much else from the past, a battered box, and a
cracked vase that had belonged to my grandfather, a small ivory
pick from the silk mills, which had been around when I was a
kid, now lost. There had also been a wonderful photograph of
the Paterson strike. I had seen it. That too had disappeared.

My grandfather had been in the strike, but I wanted, more
than politics, more than history: I wanted style; even if it was in
the graveyard, I'd take it. I wanted markers. I couldn't say with
Whitman that I wanted to be the dust under your feet. Besides

there had been enough Jews turned into dust—well, to ashes. I wanted something hard. I wanted stones.

I didn't want to look for my family's history in Europe. In Europe, I was a tourist. I had not gone to Auschwitz. I could not define my Jewish identity by the Holocaust alone. I'd rather look at the grave of a suicide who had chosen to die. "What's better about it?" I can hear uncle Louie ask. "You're still in a cemetery." And I read in his eyes that cemeteries are for Jews. "O.K.," I finally answer him, again accepting an irony that had as its truth that whatever is Jewish can't be completely funny. It was no comedy, but it wasn't Auschwitz. If they had left a beautiful house, I'd go look at that, but they didn't. The family had chosen the stones, and they had lasted. For almost a century. I wasn't looking for eternity. I needed stones and stories. I was sick of shame, and since Charles was not my father or my brother, I felt no shame. I was fascinated. Style was a kind of redemption. I loved a gorgeous suit, a stylish tombstone. Besides, why not a pantheon of spirits? The Angel of Death and Eros— and whatever else . . .

"She was so young," Gert said. "She was dead in a day." I was ready to go. "O.K., Ma? Are you ready?" She wasn't. It seemed a little cooler now that it was close to suppertime. We'd been in the cemetery all afternoon. "Wait a minute," she said. "I think it's over here." She disappeared. Now what? Another grave? Then I spotted her wide-brimmed sun hat sailing above the gravestones about a dozen rows away. She was moving quickly. I heard her strong cry, "Here it is. Right here."

I caught up with her at a grave about fifty feet from the Jacobses' plot. This one I recognized. I had paid attention when my parents stopped here on their yearly visit. This was the grave of a girl who had been murdered by her stepmother, drowned in her bath. It had been a famous case of the forties, reported in all the local papers, and since I was born in '39, I must have seen this grave when it was quite new. On the stone was a poem with the line, "struck down by a vengeful hand." I remember my mother reading it out loud. The poem was a curse. "How unusual," Gert said, "to have such things written on a tombstone."

"Yes, Ma, no 'Rest in Peace.' "

She hardly heard me. She stood there even more rapt than she had been at her uncle's grave, at her sister's grave. She had taken off her sun hat, and her brown hair—now with just a few strands of gray—curled against her high forehead as it had in her baby pictures, but her face was adult with intelligence. "I knew the family," she said, "they were from Paterson." "What happened to the stepmother?" I asked. "I'm not sure. An asylum or prison. They put her away."

I looked at the dates. The girl was eight when she was murdered. I imagined the stepmother coming up behind her as she sat in the tub, her back to the door. Eight. You're big at eight. She must have put up a struggle.

A memory came of my mother cornering me in the bathroom, where I crouched terrified, jammed in between the toilet and the tub; she was shrieking, "I'll take a piece out of you." Many times I felt that she could have put my head down on a stone block and slit my throat.

I gave as good as I got. Early I had learned about power and cruelty. My cousin Leo, who was just three years younger than I, used to follow me around everywhere. We ate together; we played together. Leo adored me, and usually I was kind to him, but sometimes when I felt evil, I would sit Leo down in his rocking chair and gaze into his big trusting eyes. Taking hold of his hands, I would say, "I love you." His small rosy mouth would curve; his eyes would light up; delighted, he would let out a burbling laugh. Then, still staring into his eyes, I would let go of his hands but bring my face closer to his. Making my voice as deep as I could, I would slowly say, "Leo, I don't love you." I'd watch with cruel fascination as his eyes widened and slowly filled with tears. It seemed to take forever before the large tears would roll down his cheeks. His mouth would quiver. After he had sobbed for a while, I would tell him that I really did love him. And I did. Dear Leo. His face would immediately brighten. Horrified and thrilled, I would kiss him, and sometimes begin the game again. After a few weeks of this, I grew sick of myself and stopped.

Gert and I stood at the grave. "How could anyone do such a thing?" she asked, as much of me as of herself. She knew the answer. It was as if she were saying, You want style, I'll give you style. With wonder, my mother and I contemplated the passion and violence in our own hearts, both of us now tellers of tales, and finally we went home.

Father

and Daughter

In the first memory I have of my father he is fully in the flesh—sleeping. Joe was a genius of sleep. I stood at the side of his bed, holding onto the sheets with both hands. I was very small, my head barely level with the mattress. The bed in that front bedroom filled the space; the mattress tilted toward me with my father's weight. The bed was pushed sideways against the two windows, which were open partway, the ivory-colored shades pulled down to the sash. The screens were black even in the bright afternoon light piling up behind the shades, which softly flapped, revealing the lines of the mullions like bones through transparent skin. My father was naked. He lay face down. I saw first his strong, wide feet, looked up his muscled legs, across his flat buttocks. One leg was bent in sleep as if he were swimming, one hand stretched over his head, the other next to his thigh, his head turned to the side, his mouth open as if for air before he put his face back down into the water. He seemed to move, but was still. Because his leg was bent in a sleep crawl, I could see the dark curve of his sex, the whorl of hair in the crack, and his balls but not his penis. His muscles were long and relaxed in sleep. His shoulders flared with all his strength. A pulse throbbed in his neck. His hair was black and thick—no gray yet. He was white, pink, and black. His skin was rosy in the heat, a fine mist of sweat across his almost hairless back.

I breathed his smell, the faint musk his hair gave off. The room smelled of fruit—apricots, I would say now, but it couldn't have been. We didn't buy apricots. Always apples. He had eaten one, before falling to sleep. The ravaged, browning core lay on the floor next to my cool feet.

No wonder I would later feel a shock of recognition in Rome. The shapes of the baroque were the shapes of that front room on Lucille Place. As a grown woman, I stood at the great crossroads of the Quattro Fontane, where the corners of the four buildings are canted. Carved out of each slanting plane is a berth for a sculpted river and its male water god. I stood there in wonder again, a small worshiping figure. Each way I turned I saw water-oiled flanks, eye level. Water when it coats stone or flesh thickens to the eye. My father was anointed.

He was a swimmer. "Bathing," Joe called it. He liked to take us to tree-bordered Lake Sebago in the Bear Mountains of New York State. He preferred the lake to the seashore: he couldn't stand to bake in the sun and never tried to tan.

Shining white, he stepped out from the dark green shade. There was no splash when he dived, no break between the water and his body. "Plashless," Emily Dickinson calls it. He usually swam freestyle for a while, then treaded water to see where he was—he seemed to do this endlessly. He finished with his favorite, the breaststroke. His large head almost out of the water, the greenish water lapping his chin, his violet black eyes just over the water's surface, he looked like a seal.

Joe swam toward me where I stood in the shallows with my pail and little watering can. He stood over me, water dripping in rivulets from his hair, then lowered himself so I could climb on his back. He took me out into deep water, my hands loose around his neck. The currents that rocked him rocked me; my small legs curled against his sides. How light we both were.

"How do you swim?" I asked him. "You just do it," he said, the Natural, smiling with what seemed to me secret, unattainable knowledge. He couldn't instruct me. Ever. He would carry me or leave me alone. I didn't have his talent for the water or for sport, which he excelled at. He was a gifted prizewinning amateur athlete. I eventually learned to swim—not very well, though I can manage a backstroke with ease. In my father's view, a person either had it or didn't. There was no idea of just learning to be competent.

After we swam, Joe cooked a second breakfast—we had eaten lightly at home before we left. He heated a grill a friend had made for him out of a short length of wide pipe with handles welded to the sides and smaller pipes welded across the foot-and-a-half diameter to hold the food. Joe was the only one who could lift it. When he had a deep bed of coals, he fried potatoes until they were brown as nuts, their centers white and sweet. We ate them with eggs scrambled soft in unsalted butter.

He rested, reading the paper in the shade, and entered the water again. All the late morning and early afternoon it seemed he never left the water, but he must have. I saw him swim beyond the ropes until I couldn't see him anymore. He had become water. I forgot him as I played on the shore, in the shallows. I looked up and saw his white arms break water. He was stroking back.

Joe parked the car, and I followed him up the long hill. Fireflies came on in the tangled grass under the trees. We passed weedy lots and reached the steep, rocky front grounds of an apartment house overlooking the stadium. It was July 4, Joe's birthday. He was taking me to see the fireworks. Although he could afford the small fee to get into the stadium, he returned to the place he had always watched from, since he was a boy. We were trespassers. We stood together in a mob of young men who had come up to Passaic Park from Dundee, Joe's old neighborhood. I heard the laughter of the few children with their young fathers. When someone lit a cigarette, his face would flare out of the dark and then be extinguished. I reached out for Joe's hand and for a moment couldn't find it. I smelled sweat. Sharp, stinging. The corn and watermelon smell of cut grass. I let go of Joe's hand when the first rocket went off. Orange at first, dissolving, then the second-stage surprise of whirling pinwheels—like gorgeous insects. I loved best the white, the red spangles that held their shape, then melted in streamers, dissolving in smoke like quenched candles, *lumi spenti*. "Oooooo," the crowd sang as the rockets exploded from their siren spin; "Ahhhhh," they burst out at the second detonation. I was quiet, breathing with them, the air filled with yearning and release. I stood in the dark with my father, on his birthday, outside the pale. All the light there was was far above us.

His fair skin was subject to prickly heat. Every spring when the weather turned warm, he slathered his trunk and arms with a sea-ooze-gray salve, rotten smelling as clam-flat mud. He pulled a white, long-sleeved jersey over his salve-smeared body and didn't take it off for a week. When he came to the supper table in his soaked jersey and rough work pants held up by a wide, black leather belt with a large metal buckle, he looked as if he had just come off a whaler's rig where he had stirred boiling vats of blubber. When he bent to his soup bowl, my mother and I exchanged bemused glances over his head. After a week of the salve treatment, he stripped off the jersey, scrubbed himself down in his bath with a brush whose bristles were as sharp as barnacle-encrusted rock—and emerged reborn in his smooth white skin. I thought that Joe would never die.

His body rarely let him down—a cold, a little arthritis. Joe never went to doctors. For his only-minor complaints, he dosed himself like a peasant, like his mother Molly. His cure for almost every vague malaise was "to take a good physic." When he offered this advice with a tremendous sense of his wisdom, I howled with laughter, which he didn't seem to hear. "I'm going to give my stomach a rest," he relished saying, "and clean myself out." Once, when he hurt his back, he went to a chiropractor and had Gert lay on burning mustard plasters. He packed an aching tooth with a wad of cotton soaked in oil of cloves. He lost most of his teeth. For an earache he filled a clean white sock with coarse kosher salt, heated the sock in the oven and held it to his ear. He refused the hot water bottle Gert held out for him. "Salt holds the heat longer," he insisted. (My Italian friend's mother twisted a double sheet of newspaper into a cone, put the small end into her aching ear and set fire to the broad lip of the funnel so the smoke and heat would enter her ear—a torch! I wonder whether they called it a Vesuvio.)

Joe didn't chauffeur me around to children's events as parents do now. Between the ages of seven and eleven I spent long weekend hours in his world. I was glad to be with him but felt out of place, the only girl among men. A virgin in the underworld.

In the humid, smoky Jersey summers I went with him to Memorial Park to watch the softball games on Sunday mornings. I usually wore my pink sundress with a short-sleeved jacket edged with narrow lace. The pocketbook my grandmother Molly had made for me swung on my arm. Joe watched with total calm absorption, as the players moved around the scruffy field. The long slow turns at home plate, the fouls, and the short pop flies bored me. Red dust rose from the field. I could taste it. The sweating players scratched their crotches; they jiggled and spread their legs, cupping their balls. They hawked and spit. At Giants football games in New York I sat, bundled in a heavy blanket over the good, gray, woolen coat Joe had bought me. I liked this game— the huddle, the snap, the players breaking from tight lines, sometimes covering the field. The game contracted and expanded. Even the plays that went nowhere were exciting—the pileup, the unpeeling of men from men. The quarterback's getting clear to pass seemed a miracle. Joe and my uncles washed down their brisket sandwiches with Scotch; I was uneasy surrounded by the rank smell of their boozy breath. Joe forgot me and told risqué stories. They didn't bother me; I only half understood them, and Joe was always so happy when he drank. But one of my uncles coarsely bragged about his sexual powers, "I really fucked her," he told Joe in a loud whisper. I was revolted and shamed. Joe took me to the bowling alley, the old lanes dark and smelling of must and linseed oil. On the smoke-stained walls were pinups, red-lipped Kewpie dolls with breasts. Their pink pastel nipples showed through air-brushed sheers. My cheeks burned. There was a bar near the entrance. The liquor and wine shone in the gloom—amber and red. The men laughed together as I watched them from the raised benches. The large, heavy black balls sped down the boards with a low, deceitful hum. When the ball connected—and it always did—the loud crash exploded; I felt it in my bones. I shuddered. The pin boy—that had been Joe's first job—leaped from his hidden perch like a monkey sprung from a cage, his arms swinging close to the floor. Crouching, he set up the pins. When a man hit a strike, he jerked his bent arm as if he were pulling a train whistle, his elbow banging against his side. The gesture reminded me of the fuck-you sign the boys used in the playground, the same motion except without the fingers of the opposite hand jammed in the crook of the bent arm.

Joe turned into a maniac when I was twelve. Maybe he smelled my new menstrual blood. He never touched me and he didn't want any one else to. I was friends with Ed Bitterman, a "roughneck, a loudmouth," according to Joe. He believed that Ed, who was in high school, was trying to seduce me. If he were, it would have been seduction by cynicism. I loved Ed's irreverent mocking take on his teachers. When Joe went to the park to watch the softball games, he heard Ed's loud voice over all the other voices coming from the gang of boys hanging out on the corner across from the park. He would see me talking with Ed. He would see us laughing together.

"I don't want you talking to him," Joe told me one night. I protested, "We're friends." When Joe saw me talking to Ed again, he came back from the park after I had come home, his face black and red with rage. "If he doesn't leave you alone," Joe said, "I'm going to kill him." He went to the kitchen drawer and took out a long thin boning knife. "I'll stick this knife into his heart." He made a jabbing and twisting gesture with the knife. I saw the bones move in his strong wrist. "Remember," he said after a silence. Again I protested. Before I could finish my sentence, Joe began yelling. I went into my room. He banged the door open. I had never seen him so angry. He roared, "I don't want you to talk to him." On and on, he raged. Joe had an enormous voice. It filled the small front bedroom, which was now mine. The knife was no longer in his hand, but I kept quiet. I was sitting on the edge of the bed, which was pushed against the two windows. Joe came dangerously close. I couldn't stand up to face him. Joe had hit me only once—a heavy blow to the back of my head after I had stung him with a sharp retort. He had calculated the force: enough to stun me but not to knock me out. I knew better than to answer him now. I felt his hot breath against the top of my head. My ears hurt as if he were pounding them with his fists. He clutched his huge hands next to my face. I didn't cry. My viscera hardened. I felt a stubborn resolve grow in me. In silence I triumphed. I hated him.

I waited for my chance.

He had the idea that academically brilliant boys were "gentlemen," not like Ed Bitterman. What did he think his gentlemen did? Only talk? When he heard that my best friend Vickie Tansky and I were friends with Barry Eiseman and Ivan Hammer, he was happy. Barry was wiry, intense; his dirty brown hair, thick as a wig, had no part. He wanted to be a physicist. Ivan was also headed for Massachusetts Institute of Technology but wasn't yet sure what he would study. The four of us would play spin the bottle after school, exchanging hard, close-mouthed kisses. We copied the movies. I liked Barry to bend me over his arm until my long black hair dragged on the floor before he lifted me for a kiss. Brainy Barry brought a camera to our spin-the-bottle sessions. He approached sex the way Leopold and Loeb approached murder: he had to have proof that he had done it. We were all thrilled to take pictures; we ordered four sets. Stiff in our stylized poses, we stared at the camera. The boys' faces were either dazed or sly. Maybe their penises were hard. I never felt them. Vickie thought that she looked like a Spanish dancer. I could have been a mermaid in the north Atlantic. I was cold.

"They're good boys," Joe said for what seemed like the hundredth time. "The type to marry." Marry? I had just turned thirteen. I reached into my skirt pocket and pulled out the stack of pictures. "Here," I said, handing them to Joe. "We play spin the bottle." He turned white, a safe sign: he wouldn't yell. His mouth hardened. "What are they doing with you?" he spit. "We were only kissing," I answered. I saw something in his eyes: a thought. I had faked him out and nailed the shot. He shoved the pictures into his pocket.

I attacked Joe at the supper table—with ideas. I was reading Thomas Paine's *Age of Reason*. His iconoclastic statements electrified me. I quoted them to Joe while he ate his pot roast. "I do not believe in the creed professed by the Jewish church, by the Roman church, by the Greek church, by the Turkish church, by the Protestant church, nor by any church that I know of. My own mind is my own church." Joe, always a fast eater, ate even more quickly. His knife grated on the plate. His face grew stormy; he looked as if he were choking, but he wouldn't answer me.

"It's all human reason," I went on. "Reason, thinking, logic."
By this time Joe the Roarer's face was red. He wasn't religious;
he just couldn't bear my know-it-all tone. I was thrilled by my
"it's all" statements. I read Freud's *Psychopathology of Everyday Life*. "It's all sex," I would say, holding up the book at the
table. With my newly acquired theory of the Freudian slip, I had
a verbal weapon, "It means." A Jewish doctor had said so. Joe
fumed in silence.

I swam in my own secret life. I found myself walking
toward Sal on the playground before classes just to watch him.
He had come to Memorial School in the ninth grade after being
thrown out of the Catholic parochial school. None of us knew
why. His skin was dark gold, his slanted eyes tawny and speckled
with green. Fine gold hair lit up his forearms. His evenly spaced
teeth were white. He always looked tan, even in winter, as if he
had come from a long summer at the beach. When I followed
him around the playground, we didn't have anything to talk
about. He smiled his dazzling smile and said hello. He seemed
like a person who did not have control over English, but he had
no accent. He always looked as if he had just opened his eyes
on a new bright day and found it good. I remember going with
him to his house after school one day. He wanted to show me
where he lived. I followed him up Paulison Avenue until we
came to a large two-family house. As we stood on the street, his
father—the same dark skin, but deeply lined around the eyes—
came around the side of the house and they spoke to each other
in Italian. The father looked at me sideways and did not speak to
me. He looked angry. I felt safe standing there on the sidewalk,
holding my schoolbooks. Sal said that he had to go in and help
his father.

That spring when the days grew longer and we could go out
again for a while after supper, he and I finally left the park
benches to go home for the night; we crossed Myrtle Avenue

together. I walked with him up the slight hill. The maples were dropping their pale green bunches of keys. The air was mild. Over the tops of the trees, which bordered the fields across the street, the sky was soft and violet. I was walking a few steps behind Sal on the slanting slabs of blue slate that formed the pavement. He turned and reached out his arms and touched my shoulders—his hands were so light. He brought his face close. I raised my mouth to his. Our lips were half-parted, warm. Our bodies touched lightly. A wave of cold-shivering heat rippled from my scalp down to my feet. Desire. Melting. Tender. The first real kiss of my life. Once. Virgin heat. We touched hands and said goodnight. We never touched each other again. I can't say why. I could surmise. Why bother? That kiss was my awakening—quick, at dusk.

Years later a friend told me that Sal was in the rackets, in the Mafia. If so, he must have held a low-level job. Back in Jersey a few years ago, I saw him in an Italian restaurant reportedly owned by the Mafia. He was a waiter. Dressed in black tie, he served me with such professional skill and near silence that his deft gestures seemed an ironic comment. The plates were hot enough to burn my fingers, but his skin had toughened in service: he put the plates in front of me with bare hands.

There is a legacy from Joe that I no longer want. His shame. Perhaps he never gave it to me. As a young child, so attached was I to him that I took his shame as my own. It entered me in shocking epiphanies. My pity bound me to him. Then too, I was beholden. But what really was his shame? And what was mine?

Joe had left school at fifteen. He told me that they had "put him" in the shop class, automotive repair. "I didn't want that," he said. "I wanted to learn printing." He worked in various garages and at one time bought a gas station, which he soon sold. The fumes from the gas made him sick. When I was in grade school, he was driving a large flatbed truck, delivering pipe. He would leave the house before dawn in all weather. His territory was north industrial Jersey—Newark, Bayonne, Hoboken, Paterson. If his route brought him close to Passaic, he stopped for lunch at home. That stop was a miracle to me when I was little. I would be walking home for lunch recess; when I saw his massive truck on narrow Madison Street, I would run. Once Gert said, as she ladled out some soup for him, "Did you see Daddy's great big truck!" "What's so great about it?" Joe answered. I had never heard that ironic tone from him before. There was also anger in his voice. He stared at something I could not see. He ate his lunch and kissed me goodbye. His beard was rough against my face.

Almost as soon as I could write, for Gert's birthday or for Mother's Day, Joe gave me the job of writing the card. For a number of years I did so without finding his request unusual, until I found a card in his drawer that he had bought for Gert himself. (I was, as I've said, a spy, a searcher of drawers.) He had written his own message to his "dear wife." The letters were all different sizes, a child's hand. The words slanted haphazardly down the little page, labored, as if he had been carving rock with a dull chisel. I stared in shock at my father's secret, my head reeling. His writing seemed unborn. His secret was inside me. I slipped the card back into the drawer and never talked about it. Aside from his signature, that was the only time I ever saw my father's writing.

Yet as crazy as it seems, his mispronunciations were never a source of shame. They weren't secrets. Toothpick was "toot-pick"; film was "fi-lem"; ask was "ass." "I'm assing you," he would say. That last so-called mispronunciation is standard usage among many people of Joe's class. After a few attempts, Gert and I stopped trying to correct him. He was unselfconscious about his speech. He made himself understood. I also came to appreciate his exactness and lack of false modesty or smarmy gentility. He always distinguished between "bath" and "toilet." He never used the word "bathroom." When he was looking for a toilet, he asked for the toilet. When he was going to the toilet, he said so. A bath was what you bathed in. "Bad," his mother Molly called it. Joe had an ear for the subspeech, the tone. He could always hear hypocrisy. Joe despised Nixon, especially after the famous television "Checkers" speech. Joe would mimic Nixon's wheedling, calculated sentimentality.

Sometimes during the summer when he was too busy to leave work for lunch—usually when he had a large parts delivery to put away—he called me and asked me to bring him a thermos of coffee and a sandwich. I walked down Monroe Street to Main, to his shop next to the railroad tracks. Joe would come out of the dim back room. The lights were turned off when there were no customers. The help could sit in the dark. Joe would walk lightly between the high wooden bins filled with greased parts—elbows, valves, nipples, half nipples, ball cocks. Oh, the language of plumbing. Once the owner found us at the counter. I was handing Joe his lunch. The owner spoke to Joe. "Yes, Boss," Joe answered. The word "Boss" broke into my head. I wanted to yell, "He's not your boss. Never." Joe's face was shockingly youthful, vulnerable, respectful. I felt a sickening throb deep inside me. I felt betrayed.

I felt ashamed *for* him.

I thought I was my father's redeemer, his validation in the world, his writer.

It turned out that I was not my father's redeemer.

When Joe was close to death, he said to me in his hoarse, cancer-wasted voice, "I don't know if it was all worth it." A cracked sob broke from his lips. I had heard him cry before, but those sobs had been soft. Now his body seemed too wasted to produce tears, but he cried. His angry sorrow seemed to suck moisture from his bones. "You had me," I said stupidly, offering myself in the old way as his validation in the world.

He was silent.

The current changed—as it always had with him, I realize now. Mercurial feeling was still in him. Life. "You know," he said after a while, "when I was a boy I bought a raffle at the candy store on Third Street, in Dundee, and I won. I carried home a big Easter basket. Big." He opened his ravaged arms. "Bigger than I was. I brought it home to my mother." He described the transparent violet cellophane that crackled as he opened it, the dark purple bow, the spill of shining jelly beans, the pounds of chocolate that he shared. "I won it," he kept saying. Blind luck, fate had smiled on him. And he had had to do nothing for it. The current changed again. He noticed the voices coming from the next room. "Let's go see the company," he said. The changing current that flowed in him, in all of us, was his redeemer.

When I told Joe that I wanted to go away to college, he said that he didn't know whether we could afford it. "Didn't you save money for my education?" I naively asked in my British-novel young lady's diction. He looked dumbfounded. He had been lucky to survive the depression. After a few days, he told me that I could go. He had spoken to the owner and arranged to work extra hours cleaning the shop at the end of the week. He would be a janitor. As I reconstruct it now, he must have first asked for a raise. Joe was running the entire wholesale parts department by himself. The owner had hired various assistants but had to let them go because they hadn't been able to remember the complicated inventory or add a column of figures. Joe had a strong memory, and his math was accurate. And like his brother-in-law Louie, he could lug. Over the years I had heard Joe mimic the owner's response to his request for a raise, " 'Business is bad. You know how it is, Joe.' " "He just bought a new Caddie," Joe would say, "but he cried." Joe's ironic use of the word "cry" captured the owner's constant unrelenting complaint. In all their years of work, Joe and Gert had never heard a boss say that business was good. They "cried." If a "boss" threw herself into her child's grave, crying, Joe and Gert might believe the lament. Once again the boss cried to Joe. Instead of a raise he offered him the janitor's job. The owner continued to get twelve-hour days out of Joe at the counter and a sober janitor he could count on. Joe's cleaning didn't have the extraordinary depth of his sister Jennie's, but he cleaned well. I now had a father who was mopping floors and swabbing out toilets so I could go away to college, but Joe was elated by his enterprise. His heart was in it. "The work is easy," he said about his cleaning job. He had no sense of martyrdom or sacrifice. He also liked my daring to ask to go away to school and his daring to agree. Not one of the fathers of my neighborhood girlfriends would send a daughter away to school; they scraped up the money for their sons.

I was exhilarated when I was accepted at Boston University. My college board scores were high, but my grades were uneven. Douglass had not admitted me.

I increased my work hours at Nadler's Department Store, where Gert sold children's clothes. Mrs. Nadler "put me" in the glove and pocketbook department. She showed me how to measure hands. I would loop and snugly pull the tiny tape across the customer's knuckles. I was so bored in the gaps between customers that even when I had a customer I was still bored. I soon began to arrange and rearrange the counter displays, fanning out the gloves, tilting the hard plastic pocketbooks of the late fifties, the kind you see now in "vintage" clothing shops. Mrs. Nadler assessed me, "Selling, no. You're not a seller. Your mother is a seller. You, you're artistic." Her hazel eyes, which I had called shrewd, now looked wise. She wore her usual black tailor-made dress. The lines followed, yet masked, her body. One string of good pearls. She was a millionaire, ruling the business, while her silent stooped husband did her errands. She was notorious for her unfriendliness. When Gert once wished her good morning, she snapped back, "Who asked you?"

Her grandson Harold Fiebach was in my college prep English

class. Mrs. Miller, Passaic High's Radcliffe lady, had pulled my essay out of the pile, held it in the air, and announced to the class that it was the only essay with "distinction and originality." Harold didn't like that. He had disliked me ever since I won a prize at Sunday school for my portrayal of Rebecca at the well. I wore what I thought were real biblical clothes: I dressed like an Arab—a white burnoose that I made from a heavy sheet, a white headdress fastened with a braided band, sandals. I carried a large water pitcher that had belonged to Gert's mother. At the awards presentation Harold Fiebach told as many people as he could that my mother worked for his family. I was the only working-class child in the Temple school. In senior year, I unthinkingly gave him my yearbook to sign when he asked me for it. "See you in a few years, when you're working for me at Nadler's," he wrote under his picture. He thought that he would be my "boss."

I was already a resister of authority. As president of the Current Events Club, I had spoken out against Senator Joe McCarthy, to the anger of my teachers. One of them, when she saw me reading a Howard Fast novel, warned me that he was a Communist. "Be careful," she said.

Mrs. Nadler stood near me as I cleaned out the dusty display cases and arranged the new pocketbooks and gloves. An almost gentle hum came off her, a kind of surrender. She actually raised my salary. She had me dress the windows. I couldn't persuade her to display fewer items. She knew her trade. Nadler's was lower middle class, although she would also buy a "better line." "My customers like to see everything," she would say when I protested about the racks of items her floor manager had given me for the fall window. "It will look like the five and ten." "You'll do it fine," she would answer, flattering me. "Inside you can put less," she added, pointing to my counter. Sometimes, she had me work in the office, totaling receipts. "You have a smart daughter," she told Gert.

I handed Joe half my salary, which he gave back to me in the fall for spending money. With the rest I bought clothes at a

30 percent discount, scanning the "better line." A black leather toggle coat came in. I bought it. A dyed-to-match violet skirt and sweater came in. I bought it. I bought a white trenchcoat at Wechsler's. Black leather jacket, white trenchcoat. No coed polo coat for me. If Joe had had an eye for the meaning of style, he would have worried.

On my way to the high school to take my final exams, I walked up the Paulison Avenue hill, feeling light and strong in my slim body. I always came through on finals. In the cool early morning air my head was clear. I didn't think any more about the course. For the first time in my life, I saw myself whole, felt the still point inside me, even as I moved. I felt my being and knew it. With double consciousness, I could see myself walking, my legs working easily on the hill, the sun glinting off my hair, which I had tied in a long pony tail, the silk blouse I had splurged on slipping across my back, one thin notebook of essential notes in my hand. I was light; I was easy, I was in my medium: the body and the word.

I sat down at the desk, looked at the first question, and began to write.

Joe and I were lit up with excitement. We were driving north to Boston University. Joe drove confidently, his hands light on the wheel. He looked young again; he had shaved twice that day. Not usually a talkative person, he talked. His voice had lost its heaviness. He made plans about money. At one point he said, "A person is lucky if he can count the number of his friends on one hand." Family was what counted. I understood that he was talking about himself. He was taking me to Boston. We were going up a day early, before the dorm opened up.

We drove on the Merritt Parkway, a road he loved. There were no trucks, little traffic. We crossed into Connecticut, past towns with white church steeples, under small bridges, past roadsides deep in old trees. We crossed into New England.

His friend, the office manager at work, had suggested that we stay at the Beacon Street Motel a few miles from Boston University. The room with two double beds was light, large and airy—fifties modern. Joe, finally tired, put on his pajamas—both top and bottom; at home he wore only the bottoms. He fell asleep quickly. I couldn't sleep. From the windows I could see across wide Beacon Street to the row of brownstones that looked so foreign. A streetcar would pass. Finally I slept.

The next day we ate lunch at the Union Oyster House in the North End of Boston. The sawdust-sprinkled floor, the worn oyster bar like an ancient doorstep, the dark old wood shining, the small windows, and the clatter of dishes made me feel that I was at the center of an old-new world. We ate littlenecks, briny and stinging, followed by fried sole. "This Yankee food isn't bad," Joe laughed as he finished his meal with Indian pudding. "It's cornmeal, try some." I ate a few delicious spoonfuls. The yellow meal was dark with black molasses.

Joe leaned forward, reached behind him, and drew out his wallet from his back pocket. He loved to carry money. "Someone's going to hit you over the head," Gert would warn. He was never robbed. Blind luck. By that time he had a steady job—two jobs—and Gert was working. The rent for the two-bedroom apartment on Lucille Place was forty dollars a month. They never took vacations, seldom went to restaurants, almost never bought clothes. Joe was a saver. Sometimes he would carry a thousand dollars in his wallet. He never had a checking account or a credit card. Money was real, no abstraction—the thickness, the smell, the weight in his pocket. He didn't love money; money was good as his green soul. He thumbed through the green bills as if he were thumbing a deck—he was a fine bridge player—and drew out a hundred dollar bill. He paid the check at the Union Oyster House, and we drove through the brick-sidewalked streets of Boston.

We had carried my heavy suitcases to the fourth floor of Charlesgate hall in the Back Bay. Now we stood on the street together in the brisk, reviving September air. Joe lingered. I put out my arms, and he burst into tears, raising his fists to his eyes. His hands seemed too massive for such a gesture. I felt tears come to my eyes, but I did not cry hard, as he did. "O.K., O.K.," he said. I watched him walk away, his broad back straining the material of his suit jacket.

"You look like an immigrant," a tall blonde girl said to me as I climbed the steps of Charlesgate Hall. Startled, I was silent for a moment. "I am," I laughed and walked into my new life.

TRANSPLANT

Angelo Bertocci
at Boston University

In the late fifties and early sixties our great books course met in the large hall on the second floor of Boston University's block-Gothic building on Commonwealth Avenue. The room, which smelled of chalk and old wax, was dark with dull brown woodwork and brown wooden chairs. In wet weather our boots would leave gritty puddles on the brown asphalt tile floor. The old incandescent lights, which you never see in classrooms anymore, were dim and yellowish; unlike fluorescent lights, they left the room shadowy and soft. Here and there a vivid sweater—red, or yellow, or violet—would light up the comfortable gloom.

The windows did not invite dreaming—no sky, a few branches, telephone wires, gray winter light. Occasionally we would hear the muffled sounds of the streetcars scraping along that flat stretch of mall that divides Commonwealth Avenue.

At nine-thirty, Bertocci would burst through the door, slam down his beat-up briefcase, and begin lecturing. He had the face of a commedia dell'arte puppet: a Punch-like sloping nose, close-together eyes, a flat wide mouth, which pushed up duckbill-like against his nose—an unsaintly feral face. His odd dark eyes were angry and intelligent. His hair was thinning, but the old hairline still showed, like a shadow, or a scar, or a painter's cartoon: you could see the younger head inside the old.

He wore heavy tweed suits, the jackets always too long. Bertocci was a short man, but still his boy-sized ties were too small for him, the clip too high, the tail flapping. His rumpled shirt collars would curl up. He'd forgotten his collar stays. His clothes seemed to spring away from his body.

As he talked, he would dance. His arms would jerk back and forth. He would tautly cup his outstretched hand and stare at the palm, as if, in fact, he held the burning heart of Patroclus plucked from the funeral pyre or the ravishing face of Dido. He would gallop to the blackboard. I don't remember his writing many words; instead, by the end of the class there'd be an elaborate tense choreography of arrows, dashes, and wild intersecting curves.

In the two years of great books, which as a comparative literature major I had to take, I remember his pausing to ask a question of the class only once. A former student of his recently told me that at Brandeis, where she went on to graduate school, she was stunned when asked to participate in a dialogue with one of her professors. "Dialogue?" she said, "Who heard of dialogue?" Bertocci's method had its pleasures. Anonymous, alert and free, I would lean back into my heavy coat wadded against the hard slippery chair and think.

He spoke about characters in literature as if they were real. Life became a conflict between the deepest passions, between the hunger for safety and the love of glory, between the desire for salvation and the love of pleasure. We learned by contrast. After Homer's war-crazed Achilles cramming the river Skamandros with so many corpses that the river overflows blood, and Dante's Mahomet in hell—Dante has him sliced from chin to anus, his shit-filled gut spilling between his legs—we, though young and wild, could appreciate Montaigne's calmer soul. The epic and the essay were not just literary forms: they were ways of being.

A few years ago when I read Primo Levi's *Survival in Auschwitz*, I was deeply moved by his account of trying to teach

Italian to Jean, a young Alsatian prisoner, by reciting to him "The Canto of Ulysses" from the *Inferno*. Being able to remember Dante made Levi feel human. Levi is working with five other men, cleaning and scraping the inside of a filthy underground oil tank. It's damp and cold; their only light comes from a manhole. Every day Levi and Jean hurry to the canteen and carry back a heavy vat of soup for the men. When he translates into French for Jean, first straining to remember the lines himself, Levi feels that he is hearing Dante for the first time, that he is hearing God's voice. When he forgets a line, he says that he would actually give up that day's soup to remember. Reciting the lines describing Ulysses's fate, Levi has an epiphany: perhaps there is a "reason for our fate, for our being here today." Levi has only fifty minutes to teach Jean on their walk to the canteen. He feels a tremendous urgency to make him understand: the next day they both might be dead.

Levi's and Bertocci's situations were in no way analogous: we were in a safe classroom in Boston. Yet Levi's passion to explain, his belief in the poet whom he hears "like the voice of God," so that for a moment he forgets that he is in a concentration camp, were something like Bertocci's belief and urgency. Culture was not an ornament.

As a young man, Bertocci had been through a religious crisis, which had split his life in two. He had experienced true despair. He then discovered Charles Du Bos, the French Catholic critic who believed that literature was "the language of souls." The living forms of the imagination rescued Bertocci as orthodoxy could not. In class, we witnessed Bertocci's salvation over and over again. And since he had a brilliantly dialectic mind, tension, contradiction, and yearning were the turbulent communion he offered us.

We learned that one could not live out every possibility in a lifetime. Yet every choice had its sting, and oddly the sting was thrilling. Dante's hell was terrible; Emerson-without-hell terrible in its own way. "Glad to the brink of fear," Emerson wrote.

Bertocci gave us the most lucid explanation of Plato's ideas I've ever heard. But the voices of the *Dialogues* were embodied. Socrates had lain all night next to Alcibiades—his ugly crumpled face next to the gleaming shoulder of the most beautiful man in Athens—and had not touched him. Bertocci dwelt on this episode, no doubt to show us Socrates's virtue, the Christian-before-Christianity line. But as always when he retold stories of passion—acted on or renounced—he lit up. I remember his paraphrasing St. Augustine's explanation for his stealing pears: "For the pleasure of it, the pleasure of doing evil." Bertocci curled his tongue around the words with relish. Whether he knew it or not, in the classroom, he was passionate about excess.

He had a way of asking insinuating questions; in his "Predicament of Man in the Modern Novel" course, he wondered exactly what D. H. Lawrence had meant by "the deepest life-force. . . . at the back and base of the loins." He never answered the question. Anal! thought the more advanced students—also silent—as if they were pronouncing Eureka! Bertocci was also troubled by Joyce's creation of Molly Bloom in *Ulysses*. "How could a man write about a woman that way?" he asked, shaking his head. A few of us exchanged glances. We knew that women farted and talked about penises. But Bertocci wasn't so much disturbed by Molly's vulgarity as by what he believed was the one-sidedness of Joyce's portrayal.

If Bertocci could have found a way to reflect on these matters in print, his writing would have been more interesting, but he was no Leslie Fiedler. In his writing, Bertocci kept the lid on. He published two books of highly condensed, abstract criticism. I couldn't finish them. In his early thirties, he had written a wonderful memoir of his mother for *Harper's*. But mostly he had been educated away from his past, and therefore from what I believe was his authentic voice. My friend, Ivo, one of Bertocci's graduate students, said that Angelo "had turned his back on the Mediterranean sun." Ivo had just cooked a spaghetti dinner for a group of us, and I was helping him serve the dessert. He watched me for a second as I took down some white bowls for the chocolate ice cream. "Use these," he said, handing me bright turquoise blue bowls, "they look better." "What a dandy you are," I said. Ivo looked angry. "No," he said, "an Italian! It makes a difference what kind of dish you put food in."

When I knew Bertocci at Boston University, he was married, a father, a homeowner in Wellesley. He and his wife Aili would give buffet suppers for the comparative literature majors. We would eat bland Swedish meatballs and salad. Bertocci would play us his record of Gounod's *Faust*. The living room was sprightly and a little prim: lots of white woodwork, neutral colors, a firm settee, rugs precisely set on polished floors.

By then, Bertocci was no longer a Catholic. He attended the Unitarian church in Wellesley but never joined. His students speculated. He didn't really believe, we thought; he needed a social structure. It was an intellectual decision, a liberal decision. Though I had seen his New England parlor, I couldn't imagine him in a Unitarian chapel, praying to a disembodied God-That-Wasn't.

His immigrant parents were peasants from Gaeta. Bertocci had been born in Italy and was three when he came to America with his parents. His father worked in a packing plant; his mother by a ferocious economy—she made the children's underwear from flour bags—pulled the family into the middle class. She saved. They were able to buy a small house in Somerville. Four of the six children went to college.

Bertocci had the relentless energy of the son of immigrants. He absorbed his mother's lesson: work, work, work. In his memoir, Bertocci said that she kept him "tense for long years," but he accepted her direction and believed in it.

He was working himself away from the brutal physicality of working-class life. His father labored in thick woolen underwear and thick-soled boots; his mother had fourteen pregnancies; eight premature babies died. Bertocci said that the huge piles of dirty laundry made him ill.

He brought home clean gold stars from school. He would go on to win a scholarship to BU. He was a prizewinner like my own father, four years older than Bertocci, and also the son of immigrants. But my father's gift, unlike Bertocci's, was his body. He was a poor student and left school at sixteen, yet he won almost every prize it was possible to win in the YMHA athletic leagues and in various state leagues. I have a box of his gold and silver medals for basketball, football, and handball. On one of the heavy silver medals bordered with victor's laurel is a small rectangular relief, like a painting within a painting: in the silvery room with a single window, the floorboards marked by raised silver lines, a slim youth, completely alone, swings his graceful arm toward the floating ball.

My father thought my boyfriends should be playing ball instead of hanging around with girls. When he said this, he looked angry and contemptuous. Years later I would see Bertocci's lips curl in the same way when I reached for a second glass of sherry, which a graduate student poured for me. Sherry! Not even the strong French brandy I had begun drinking after reading novels about Paris in the twenties. In Bertocci I had found another high-minded, hardworking, prizewinning father.

Only once did I see Bertocci tired. He was sitting at his desk in his shabby cramped office. (Boston University in the early sixties was shabby.) He smelled of sweat. His face was gray. He would have had to shave twice a day to look clean-shaven. He was eating his lunch from a brown paper bag. He looked bitter. Years before, he had been offered a chair at Harvard, which he refused. There must have been times when he regretted his choice. He once told me that his fault was in hanging onto things too long out of loyalty. Perhaps it was the same fear of change I saw in my own family. No one ever quit or changed a job—

ever! (In his sixties he finally left Boston University to teach at Iowa, where a chair has been named for *him*.)

Bertocci encouraged me. He liked smart women. I don't know whether Bertocci would have fitted in at Harvard. At Harvard, Harry Levin told Susan Sontag that women did not belong in graduate school.

I had fallen in love during my freshman year; after the breakup of that affair, I couldn't study and left school. When I came back, I did well in Bertocci's classes, and eventually he suggested that I apply for a graduate assistantship in comparative literature. He disregarded my atrocious early record. He may have wondered about his choice when I misspelled the name of one of my referees on my application. I was careless.

Bertocci's brother Peter, also a professor at Boston University, announced, as if it were a new idea, that higher education for women was justified because educated mothers could better educate their children. Angelo brought up his brother's ideas in class; some of the students insisted that he too believed them. It didn't seem that way to me. Bertocci said that he had asked his wife, who was trained in classics, whether she regretted leaving her profession. She answered that it gave her something to think about when she was doing the dishes. His tone echoed her irony and sadness.

As for me, I was being educated in the literature of empire, although we didn't have that term then. When Bertocci said that Aeneas had to leave Dido—"After all, he had to found Rome"— I sympathized with Dido, but I did not really consider that a hero who chose love over glory might be more interesting than Aeneas or that the founding of the great Roman Empire might not have been such a glorious thing. There was no room in this world for the women's writing I would come to love: Dorothy Wordsworth's journal, Colette on her mother, Emily Dickinson's hundreds of poems to her sister-in-law, Katherine Mansfield's diary, and so many other lives and works in which I could find myself.

Dante's Beatrice and Goethe's Gretchen were so unreal, so insipid. In the early sixties, I was excited by the stories of heroes
who kept moving on to glory and transcendence. I hadn't yet
found the personal mode, its private heroism.

I went to work as Bertocci's graduate assistant in 1962.
My job was to grade the papers for the great books course, for
which I got free tuition. My father, who was speaking to me
again now that I was back in school, sent me a small but welcome
monthly check. For the rest of my money, I waited on tables at
the old Boston University Faculty Club on Bay State Road. Hays,
the chef, fed the student help on roast beef and roast potatoes,
heaps of greens, and peppermint ice cream. That late lunch, with
half gallons of milk on the table, was our main meal of the day.
I wore a black uniform with a white collar and a white apron.

A well-known professor lunched regularly at the oval table in
the big bay window. He wore three-piece suits, the vest a padded
prop for his Phi Beta Kappa key. He ordered the daily special
with ringing pomposity and discouraged his guests from leaving
tips: "We take care of the help at Christmas." At Christmas we
checked. He had left thirty-five cents. I heard that one of the
students urinated under his office door.

I had an apartment for forty dollars a month on the edge
of the South End, at 31 Harwich Street, across from Back Bay
Station. I'd sit at the kitchen window and watch the gulls take
off from the long steeply pitched roof of the old armory. My
cat, Pepper, a small dark gray and black male, would rub against
my ankles, tense his back, and spring from the floor to the small
counter and then to the wide windowsill. Unlike the dog I have
now, Pepper would never plop himself down on my papers and
books. I remember him as innately tactful and gracefully con-
siderate. Just outside the chain link fence that enclosed the backyard was a messy thicket of ailanthus trees, the "trees of heaven."
They sprawled over the cracked asphalt and rubble, their arch-

ing palmlike fronds giving the city wastelands an oddly tropical look: foreign and soft. I'd watch the cat and the sky, write in my notebook, and dream.

I wasn't happy in graduate school. Although I loved Bertocci's modern European poetry seminar—loved the poems, that is—I felt my brain drying up with theory. I had to force myself to do the work. Reading theory was like listening to oversubtle rabbis fattening on the text. After all, I was going to be a poet. I was forming my intention in private. On one of my papers, Bertocci had written, "Bright but not judicious." A wonderful description of a poet, I thought.

In November 1963, I left class and walked up Commonwealth Avenue to Kenmore Square. People were standing in the street, crying. John Kennedy had just been shot. I ran back to school and burst into Bertocci's tutorial. He and the woman student looked up from their books. I cried brokenheartedly. Dramatically, I announced that the country had lost its honor. Quietly, Bertocci said, "Well, we can't work today." I was glad. I wanted everything to stop, especially Bertocci's usual talk.

In the spring, the air suddenly warm and dusty, and the light, before the trees filled in, bright and hard, I went out to Bertocci's house in Wellesley to take my comprehensive exam. One question asked me to trace the influence of Kant on modern literature. Somehow, I did it. I felt like a great head without a body. Actually just the top of the head, all brain behind the forehead. Lorca says, "Verde que te quiero verde." (Green, I love you.) With friends after the exam, I found myself saying, "He meant *real* green." I loved it too.

A few months later, I dreamt of Bertocci. He and I were on a bleak island in the north Atlantic. Everything was black and white like an old horror film. The trees were theatrically stunted. I was running along a sea wall, and like a huge big-headed spider, Bertocci was running after me. He was Dr. Frankenstein, Dracula, and the Wolfman, and he had the rolling gait of Charles

Laughton in *The Hunchback of Notre Dame*. Obviously, I had to get away. It wasn't anything Bertocci was doing to me. I simply had to find my own way.

A year later, I was married and teaching at Emerson College. After the birth of my son in 1968, I would begin publishing poetry, return to graduate school, and complete a Ph.D. I found I liked memoir, biography, and cultural history.

When my first book came out, I sent it to Bertocci. He warned me against pathos, but he praised me. About a poem that affirms life in the dirty wasteland of northern New Jersey, he wrote: "Brave girl and how modern." I liked that, especially after a painful experience at the unveiling of my father's tombstone a year after his death. The rabbi, whom I had never met before, had read this first book. When we were introduced two steps from Joe's grave, he began railing against "these authors of modern and immoral books." I felt my legs go weak; it was the first time I had been at my father's grave since the funeral. I turned my back on the rabbi and walked away.

After Bertocci had retired from teaching, I visited him and his wife in their Vermont farmhouse. It was like going home to family during school vacation. They fed me well. Bertocci pushed roast chicken at me. After dinner he asked his wife Aili to show me their pictures from India. In doing so, she called one of the Indian gods by the wrong name. Bertocci corrected her in a particularly cruel way. She turned red and mute. I felt like the favored bright girl I had been at home, my father's girl. This was my family scene.

The next morning at breakfast, offering me pancakes, sausage, butter, and great pours of Vermont maple syrup, Bertocci tried to explain. "Sometimes, I can be very impatient." I wondered if he had apologized to Aili for humiliating her in front of me.

He put on his gray woolen plaid jacket and a red cap. It was hunting season. We walked out through a foot of snow to the edge of his property. I was a little nervous about the hunters.

We were high up. The mountains seemed to make their own weather. The sky was gray as flint, and the wind was blowing from the north. Bertocci's face was pink with cold. He walked easily; his back was straight. He seemed fuller. His shoulders weren't the least bit hunched against the wind. He was talking books a mile a minute. I half-listened; my thoughts were elsewhere—on the sky, the blue in the snow, and the blackness of the pines on the upland slope, on Bertocci heated up, the gray gone from his face. He was comfortable in these clothes, the thick boots, the rough jacket. They fit him. Years later, at Aili's memorial service, I touched his arm in a gesture of comfort and jumped in shock. His arm was as hard as wood.

The Man with
a Satyr's Face

In Bernini's great sculpture *The Ecstasy of Saint Theresa*, in the Church of Santa Maria della Vittoria in Rome, Cupid is smiling with unbearable sweetness; his hair is curled into insouciant locks. His light touch has knocked the saint into an openmouthed swoon—you can see her teeth. She's been surprised. The thick fingers of her right hand are drawn upward like sea plants toward Cupid's crotch. Her big foot—only it and her face and hands are uncovered—dangles like the limp head of a dead duck from beneath the hem of her immense habit. The stiff habit seems barely freed from the original stone block, as if the blows from the sculptor's chisel melted the stone only slightly before it froze again into deeper stoniness. This suavely plump Cupid is free; his off-the-shoulder robe flutters yet clings in places, as if it were wet. We might believe that he had just stepped off a silky wave and waded in from shallow water. He seems to be enveloped in a moist wind. Cupid has not prepared the saint for divine love: Cupid *is* the lover, beautiful and conventional. In my life, he's sometimes taken an ugly shape.

I had stopped at the Eliot Lounge on Commonwealth Avenue, after a late afternoon class during my sophomore year at Boston University. A friend told me that she had done this, ordered herself an aperitif, and I thought I would copy her; it sounded so sophisticated.

Mike was sitting at the bar, his camel-hair coat slung over one shoulder. He was drinking stingers, brandy and crème de menthe. The dark green liquid shining in the cone of the cocktail glass looked devilish, invented. His face was blurry in the dim light. I don't remember what I was drinking, but I was keeping up with him, and he was drinking fast.

Mike offered to take me back to the dorm. There was a Thermo-Fax copying machine—the technology between Ditto and xerography—in the passenger seat of his new light blue Pontiac. Mike sold office equipment. He moved the machine into the trunk. I could see him more clearly under the streetlight; I thought he might be in his late thirties; in the few months I knew him, I never found out exactly how old he was.

He drove down Commonwealth Avenue, but instead of turning onto Marlborough Street, where I lived, he crossed town and went south. In fifteen minutes we were in an empty parking lot whose center was brightly lit by a double row of lights—like a stage. The far edge of the lot was dark and deserted. That's where I found myself. I was drunk; he was leaning against me. I backed across the front seat until I was wedged against the door. The window handle pressed through my coat into my back. I was trying to get away from him, but I also did not want to get away. In a second—I don't know how—he was into me. He was quite gentle. He had got his pants down with one hand, and my panties down with the other. He still had his coat and jacket on; his tie was tied. He couldn't get into me all the way, and he didn't force it. I could feel the fine tip of his penis; it was as sensitive and probing as a tongue, but hotter. I came—for the first time. I had had a year-long affair—the first—in my freshman year at school with a man who kept telling me what a good lover he was, with a man I loved, and yet with him I had never felt this kind of pleasure.

I saw Mike for the next few months; he would reach me on

the dormitory phone, which was in the downstairs hall at the foot of the wide staircase. The small dorm, which housed about twenty students, had once been a private home. Voices carried. My friends heard me call him "Darling." I played it up for them, my role as a sophisticated woman who called her lover "Darling."

Sex with Mike was never again as good as it had been that first night. The trouble was, I really didn't like him; in fact, he repulsed me. Mike lost value in bright light. His face looked terrible. It was a satyr's face: pushed-up nose, squinty eyes— his drinking turned them bloodshot. It seemed as if his features were being pulled into the center of his face, where a hole was about to appear.

Once when we were out together during the afternoon, he suddenly stopped the car in front of a Catholic church with grim pointed twin steeples. I didn't realize where we were going until he took my hand and led me to the door. He knelt in front of the altar and crossed himself. The altar was as hard and clean as a hospital sink. His satyr's face looked strangely pious and completely goyish. I could not stand his display of piety. He asked me if I believed in God. He was shocked and angry when I said no and afterward kept bringing up my "lack of faith." When we disagreed about something, especially when we were out driving, he would keep his eyes grimly fixed on the road and mutter under his breath, "Sure, sure, and she doesn't believe in God."

Mike loved to drive. He was good at it. Hands lightly curled, shoulders loose, he drove as if he had been born and had then come to manhood behind the wheel. The road seemed to turn into calm water: we glided, he looked younger. The exact destination didn't matter, but he usually needed to head north. Following his instinct for that direction, he was happy. A fish in channel. Except on our one visit to Sacco.

We drove through deserted weekend streets, past blind-windowed brick factories. His former wife was from Maine, and they had lived in Sacco together. Now it seems to me that he had been looking for her on that ride. He had a son whom he never saw. His face crumpling, his mouth quivering, he told me that one day he had come home and walked into an empty house; his wife and son were gone, the furniture along with them, not a picture on the walls. In certain moods, which now, knowing more about addicts, I recognize as orgies of self-pity, he would repeat the story of his suffering; he would blame his ex-wife. Then he would turn spiteful; his mouth would twist and harden; he would describe her thighs, how they became puffy after her pregnancy. "Her mother had thighs like that," he would say, "I could see the bulge above her knees when she sat down and her dress hiked up. I should have known the daughter would inherit those thighs." Then he would look at me triumphantly, feeling vindicated. I watched him with distaste.

When he wasn't in a sentimental or self-pitying mood, he liked to show me the unusual side of Boston. We went to a lesbian bar on Tremont Street. He was playing guide to the underworld, except that he had chosen a Saturday afternoon. We stepped into a quiet room with a long bar. Two women were sitting together, quietly talking, their dark heads close together. They looked up calmly. Mike strutted down the center of the room with his shoulders thrown back, as if he were the male star. His camel-hair coat swung behind him like a cape. Actually I liked his walk. Toes slightly turned out, back straight and lifted, he would prance and glide—weightless. He seemed propelled by the glossy shine of his expensive leather shoes. The women ignored him. We had a beer and left.

I realized that Mike was running out of money when he couldn't pay a hotel bill at the Ritz in Boston. This was before credit cards. The clerk had given us a room on the strength of Mike's Mark Cross suitcase and his persuasive charm. He did have charm. He had been a successful salesman. We were to pay when we checked out. Mike encouraged me to order breakfast from room service. He was off food. That morning he had gone through two bottles of iced champagne. My scrambled eggs and ham, muffins and toast, orange juice, and pot of coffee were silently wheeled in on a large round linen-draped table. Mike watched me lift the heavy metal domes from the plates and asked with polite curiosity if the eggs were still hot. He would have liked to buy me completely, and something in me wanted to be bought. In her memoir, *Smile Please*, the novelist Jean Rhys has written, "The whole business of money and sex is mixed up with something very primitive and deep. . . . It is at once humiliating and exciting." I could have gone that route with Mike, but he was on the skids. When it was time to leave, he told me that he was out of money. I had about ten dollars. We snuck down flights and flights of back stairs and raced out through the basement to the street.

During the next two months, he was drinking more and more; the sweet, perfumed, cloying scent of stingers came out of his pores like sweat. He was going under. His car got shabby; there were frantic trips to the pawn shop; he was pawning office equipment that did not belong to him, and he eventually lost his job.

Mike hung onto me, as if I were proof that things were still all right, that he wasn't in fact drowning—for all I know he could have been dying. He needed to show me off. In Boston we went to a piano bar at the edge of what used to be called the Combat Zone, before gentrification cleaned up the strip joints and displaced the hookers. It was a hangout for statehouse politicians, salesmen, ambulance chasers, petty crooks, gamblers. I liked the scene. The smallish upstairs room was dark and smoky, but here and there the face of a customer was lit from below by a round circle of light from the small red-shaded lamps on the tables, like a cutout in a black curtain.

We sat with a friend of Mike's, a member of the House. His metal crutches were propped up next to him. He couldn't walk without them. He took one side of the booth; his powerful square trunk and heavy arms matched the span of the table length; his shrunken legs and hips were tucked under the table. His straight hair was combed from its side part into a stiff slab.

Local politics often harbors the wounded and transforms their wounds into eccentricities and trademarks. (The former Speaker of the Massachusetts House weighs more than three hundred pounds; his pale luminous head is small above his huge bulk; his hair, pushed to the edge of his blown-up face, looks like a disturbed wig. His face has become too big for his hair; the scalp will not blow up the way the face will.)

Mike's friend looked at me skeptically when, with Mike's urging, I told him I was a student. He asked me how I earned my living. He didn't use the word "whore," but he made his meaning clear. I showed him my red-and-white college identification card. There were limits to my willingness to try out roles. I liked the shady scene, but I didn't like being shamed. He apologized; Mike relaxed. His jumpiness—he seemed to always be bouncing in his seat—stopped for a while. I had validated him.

His large chapped hands folded on the table, the crippled man talked about his daughters; he was careful and courtly but was hiding his confusion, as he continued to size me up. I was going along for the ride; I knew it was temporary; I was curious.

Mike took me to meet his mother, a widow who lived in the family's large, wood frame house in Milton. We went in through the back door into a large kitchen. Mike hadn't called her, but she was ready for guests: her stockings were pulled up tight; her ruffled clean apron tied smartly around her plump, corseted midsection; her pink-flowered housedress clean and freshly ironed. I stared at the gleaming, polished toaster carefully positioned on a clean white doily. She was polite and noncommittal. She wasn't buying. Her son walked around me as if I were a pet pony he had to sell to buy his first meal in a week. She gave us tea. Her hands on the brown teapot were plump and hard; her thick blonde graying hair was wound up in a grandmotherly bun, but its shine and weight signaled a sexual possibility. Mike went into the parlor and came back with pictures of himself in sailor uniform. In the pictures, the thin light smile on his face seemed about to slide off.

When I met his old girlfriend Sheila, I decided to break things off. I didn't know we were going to see her. I thought Mike was showing me his new apartment. Up until then, I didn't know where he lived. It turned out to be Sheila's apartment; she was expecting us; she greeted me with a civility that was belied by her hard, angry eyes. At one point, Mike pulled me up from my seat, turned me sideways to Sheila, and, pointing to my breasts, said, "Look at that." I pulled away; she cringed.

Days later, Mike gave me a present of an expensive green leather belt. I knew somehow it was Sheila's and questioned him; he seemed to be lying. The next day I took the streetcar to her apartment; she was home. The heat was turned on full blast. The apartment walls seemed about to crack. Sheila dressed like an early fifties deb—ballerina shoes, a full skirt with a trim belt, a double row of pearls with a well-tailored blouse. She was getting ready to go out: there were a boxy handbag and a pair of white kid gloves on the hall table. Against her burning face, her dyed blonde page boy looked like hot metal. I returned the belt, which she said was hers. I told her I wouldn't see Mike again. Her sad, stony expression brightened for a second, and then, almost immediately, she looked angry and hopeless; it wasn't the first time he had given her things away or had pawned them.

The next time Mike called, I told him I didn't want to see him anymore. My voice was firm. I listened to its firmness and liked the tone.

My friends were happy that I had gotten rid of "Darling." Roberta, whom I'd known since freshman year, seemed to feel that I shouldn't be seeing men at all. She and I had first met when we were both living in Charlesgate Hall. Roberta had been having trouble with calculus and had been trying to make contact with Eva Lindauer to get some help. Hearing that I was Eva's friend, she came to my dorm room and found me wrapped in a bathrobe, sitting crosslegged on my bed, reading *On the Road*. She stared with judgment at the book by the notorious Kerouac. "Oh, you like the Beats." "Not really," I answered, meaning it. Yet, from the time of that first meeting in Charlesgate Hall, Roberta and I were cast as opposites.

For months before I broke up with Mike, Roberta had been cautioning me about him. One night, she and I were together while I was waiting for him to pick me up. Roberta's slim long bare arms were gleaming white against the tight bodice of her sleeveless black dress. Her narrow shoulders were hunched. She had taken to wearing a hair net, so that, although she moved her head when she talked, her heavy black glossy hair was still. "Even Stephen Dedalus couldn't do both at the same time." She was talking about *Portrait of the Artist as a Young Man*. "You can't have art *and* experience; you have to choose," she said emphatically. I believed her. When Joyce has Stephen say that he will "forge in the smithy of [his] soul the uncreated conscience of [his] race," we couldn't imagine that Joyce's portrayal of Stephen was ironic. We completely missed Stephen's joking comment on his vocation: he calls it "the spiritual-heroic refrigerating apparatus, invented and patented in all countries by Dante Alighieri." Like Roberta I believed that art was superior to life but thought that I wasn't as brave and steadfast as she. We agreed that I seemed to have more talent for experience than Roberta. I knew that I would "renounce"—we used words like that—life for art but not yet.

Roberta and I would remain friends for years. Many times I would try to write about her, without much success, but only now, as I think about Mike and those early years, do scenes of our friendship rise to the surface with some kind of coherence. When we were all in graduate school together, Roberta and Ivo married. Once at a party I saw Roberta get drunk; she was loud and exuberant. Ivo couldn't stand it. He took her arm and pulled her upstairs away from all of us. When they came back, Roberta was subdued. She stared at the floor. "He doesn't like me to drink," she said. "You can say things, you can be as loud and bawdy as you want, and it looks O.K. I can't. It doesn't fit."

In the late seventies, after she and Ivo had divorced, Ivo cautioned me, "Don't ever try to put anyone in prison. Even if they seem to want it, they'll hate you for it." When I saw Roberta after the divorce, she told me that her marriage to Ivo had been the greatest mistake of her life. She had just come back from California and was spending the day with me in Passaic, where I was visiting. At a seafood lunch in a Cuban restaurant done up in every shade of sea blue and blue green, we talked about the past and then went on to films. I told Roberta how much I had liked Nick Nolte in *North Dallas Forty*. Nolte plays a wide receiver with a marvelous pair of hands. He's getting old and has to be shot up with painkillers before games. He refuses to give up the game. It's the only place, he says, where he can use the gift he has. "I want to find a place in the world that will use me," I said with my old undergraduate self-importance. Falling into our past language, Roberta answered, "And I want to use myself." She put her small cool hand lightly over my hand. "It's risky," she said, "but it's the only world we have." I nodded, but I shivered. We were back in Either/Or Land. Suffer and Die for Art Land. Suddenly, I didn't want to take myself so seriously.

Roberta and I walked together to the train station in Passaic Park. It was just before Thanksgiving and still mild. Roses were still blooming, floribundas softening what seemed to be miles of chain link fencing. We talked again about Boston. "Those affairs you had, did they ever give you any pleasure?" Roberta asked.

"Some," I answered, not knowing that her question would stay with me.

Infrequently over the years, I would remember Mike. As soon as his face would appear, I would try to shake it away—literally. I would toss my head as if I had water in my ear. I didn't know what to do with Mike's devilish face, his thieving, with what people were now calling "date rape." It was the one affair I was ashamed of; although I didn't call it shame; instead, I used the word "regret."

Last summer, I saw him in a different way. It must have been early July, because the rambling roses were in bloom. I was driving down Cambridge Street toward Inman Square in Somerville. On every block there were three-deckers being converted into condos—the same awnings, the same two-tone paint jobs, the same black iron fences, the same predictable plantings of rhododendrons and azaleas. There were still many unconverted houses. Jammed into their tiny square front yards were bland-faced statues of the Virgin surrounded by thickets of rambling roses—red, white, pink, and paler pink. They seemed to have just opened at once. Stopped at an intersection, waiting for the light to change, I drifted into reverie, eyes at rest, unfocused but taking in. Just across the street to my right, behind rusting chain link, were shell pink roses surrounding a shrine. In the complicated shadow cast by the roses, Mary's face seemed worked on by a private storm. All facing south at attention, the blossoms stood out like appliqué from the dark wild thorny tangle of arching rose canes. They were in full sun, lit up, translucent, dewy, not a black spot or gnawed leaf. It was too early for Japanese beetles. The roses looked cool. Perfect. And yet, like all roses, their very fullness reminded you that they would soon drop like apples.

As I watched the roses and then shifted into first, I remembered Mike's face; the habitual smirk was now a genuine devilish leer, unselfconscious; his head was tossed back; he was about to speak, or rather, make a sound, one of his buzzing sounds of pleasure. I let myself see the rest of him. There he was—naked, his high broad chest, the glint of fair hair, the flat belly, and narrow hips, and strong, well-shaped legs. His penis was erect, pointing up. His skin was delicate and pink. I found myself grinning into his awful satyr's face. He was ruined and potent. I laughed out loud and let myself remember.

Two Houses

Eva Lindauer, my best friend during my freshman year at Boston University, first told me about Harwich Street. She was having an affair with Paul, a painter who rented one of the apartments in the small brick town house, but it was really the solitary house she loved, and its life of purpose.

Eva was the most brilliant of all of us. She cracked a term's calculus in one night, read the text from cover to cover, and got her A. A Phi Bet, she was offered graduate fellowships at Harvard and Brandeis.

Boston photographers would ask her to pose. Portraits of Eva hung in their Newbury Street windows. On the back of one photograph she had given to me—Eva leaning forward, her face split into light and shadow, hair loose, cigarette (she loved Pall Malls) in outstretched hand—she had written, "To my dearest Mim, *De qui je pense, à qui je viendrai en joie et misère pendant les jours et les nuits de l'an.*"

What did she look like then at nineteen? We first met standing naked in the Boston University clinic after the compulsory physical for freshmen women. We spoke a few words, shared a joke, loved each other immediately. Eva was almost six feet, long-legged, long-waisted, high-breasted, large-hipped. "A Modigliani woman," our friends would say. We all loved comparing ourselves and each other to figures in paintings and characters in novels. Eva's grandmother was Hungarian and insisted that

Eva had Gypsy blood. Her hair seemed Indian: blue-black, thick
at the roots, glossy. Her narrow, definite lips were carmine—
no lipstick. She had a loping walk, though her joints were vulnerable. Her knees would give way, and she'd sometimes fall
without warning. "When I take Eva's hand," a local musician
who played at the old Turk's Head coffeehouse said to me, "I feel
I'm holding the hand of God." He was very short.

The Family of Man photographs had just been published. Eva
came to me with the book, pointed to a photograph of a young
woman in a mental hospital—despair, her head to her updrawn
knee. "Sometimes I feel like this," Eva said. Her father was an
alcoholic, an accountant, an unpublished poet. The drawers of
his shabby Brooklyn office were filled with reams of poetry that
no one read except him. Eva found him on the floor one day. "I
don't want you," he drunkenly mumbled, "I want your mother."

Before she met Paul and began spending time at Harwich
Street, Eva had been in love with Ford Hunter, a student at
Boston University's School of Public Relations and Communica-
tions. We serious types made fun of that program, but Ford, we
had to admit, was striking. His shocking blond hair—so child-
bright that it seemed dyed—didn't go with his manly face. His
complexion was flawless, but against that angel hair even *his*
skin seemed mortal. Ford came from money. When his parents
were away, Eva would stay with him in his family house in
Newton. She wanted to marry him. At Christmas she bought
him expensive presents that she could not afford.

She was starstruck. When a northeaster dumped three feet of
snow on Boston and the streetcars stopped running, Ford, Eva
told us with rapt pride, had skied into town from Newton. He
was kind; he was graceful. "A real gentleman," I can still hear
Eva's grandmother say. "I don't think she lie down with anybody
yet," the old woman said to me when I was staying with the Lin-
dauers in Flatbush, and Eva went off with an old boyfriend. Ford
broke off their affair so smoothly that Eva never got angry.

A few years ago I saw him on TV; he had sailed around the

world alone. It turned out that Eva had been right about Ford: he was a hero. There he is, I thought, in his own movie. His blond hair was streaked with gray. He had been through a deep, lonely experience but had trouble finding the words to describe it. A while ago I listened to a man who had gone around the Horn in a kayak try to talk about his experience. Like Ford, in moments of remembered intensity, he used words like "wild," "great," "neat." Oh, how Eva loved him, her man of action.

As freshmen, Eva and I lived crowded with hundreds of students in Charlesgate Hall, an ugly late-Victorian-Romanesque hodgepodge between the Fens and the Charles River. Most of our classmates clung together with the same hunger to be part of a group, which had once driven me in high school.

Eva and I hated the dorm. We longed for solitude and heroic vocation. After her breakup with Ford, Eva found these things in Paul. She loved his painting of a white hot sun swirling out of a cold black sky. "With all the energy of Van Gogh's stars and planets," Eva said, "except it's cold, it's the coldest thing I've ever seen." At the end of our freshman year she moved in with Paul.

When I first visited Harwich Street, there were two easels set up in the studio: on one, his white sun painting; and on the other, her abstract November forest in browns and black. She had just finished it; the oil was still wet, and the studio smelled of oil paint and linseed oil; it smelled of work.

Eva decided not to go to graduate school. She and Paul moved to California in 1960, when so many people were going west, and I took the floor-through apartment. It was just after my sophomore year; I stayed for just part of the summer. When another apartment became available in the same building a few years later, I was happy to move back. The rent was still forty dollars a month. I would stay until 1966.

There were only three buildings left on Harwich Street. The tight row houses, which formerly lined the block, had been knocked down and the rubble cleared for a parking lot. I'm sure the demolition had undermined the remaining houses. The angles at Number 31 were so out of plumb that my friend Ivo told me that he could never live there: it would make him nervous. The stairs, which led to my second-floor apartment, leaned like a ship's stairs in bad weather, so although you were walking up, you were also leaning left, away from the wall. There was a geological feel to it, as if an earthquake had hit the street, but I never felt that things would spring apart. The shift had occurred, and the house seemed to be holding. In fact, it held until the wrecker's ball crashed through the walls in 1986. (A condo development built around a grassy park has now replaced Harwich Street and the parking lot. The new building, with its bays outlined in green, is a postmodern echo of the old town house. The architects obviously had studied the style of Number 31.)

The original Harwich Street house, plainer and simpler than the large neighboring mansions being constructed at the same time, had been built around 1850. With the quick slump of Boston's South End before the end of the century, Number 31 was converted into three flats.

The shallow black soapstone kitchen sink, its beveled edges cleanly cut like glass, dated from that first renovation. Water turned the stone a darker, more slippery black. The brass faucets and copper pipes were stapled to a wide splashboard nailed above the sink. I painted the one flimsy kitchen cabinet a terra-cotta brown and repainted the walls in the same startling, uncompromising flat white that Paul had used. I invited my friends to help me paint. For the floor, I splurged on a vivid "Daffodil Yellow," put out by Benjamin Moore, an expensive brand then. The dry boards soaked up paint, and even though we had laid on coat after coat—it took gallons—the pattern of the grain still showed through. There were wide gaps between the wide pine boards. The dark cracks, which would quickly fill with wooly matted dust, leapt out against the freshly painted floor. The kitchen was just large enough, so that, if you looked down its length, the glowing floorboards seemed to narrow like railroad tracks in a perspective lesson.

The bathroom door, which was next to the soapstone sink, was usually open, making the view into the bathroom part of the kitchen scene. The massive claw-footed tub, big as a bed, bulked against the toilet. Because the floor tilted so wildly, the tub looked as if it would break loose from its moorings, shoot across the floor, and smash the toilet like a teacup.

I was already spending a lot of time with John; we would marry in 1964. When he stayed over, he would sometimes soak in the big tub while I made breakfast. The door would usually be open. As I worked, I could see him in the steam, his damp head and bare wet shoulders resting against the sloping end of the tub. There was plenty of hot water, scalding water, in fact. We would eat mushroom omelets—canned mushrooms were the most exotic item on my grocery shelf. I'd make coffee in a cheap aluminum drip pot, which I kept warm on a trivet placed over the gas burner.

Except for an old solid-chrome Sunbeam toaster bought secondhand, I had no electric appliances and no TV. They wouldn't have worked: the house ran on DC. Electricity had been brought in around the time of the First World War, and the original wiring had never been changed. I was literally on a different current from most of Boston.

The light at 31 Harwich Street was a miracle. There was nothing to block it. The two big deep-silled kitchen windows, which rattled in any kind of wind, looked out over the tiny trashy backyard and across the tracks of Back Bay station to the sloping roof of the armory. In bad weather, gulls would wheel in from the harbor and down the Charles River to hunch on the armory's long copper-flashed ridge. In early afternoon, a clear cool light washed in across the low nineteenth-century houses of the Back Bay. At those times, the kitchen was bright and shadowless. (Paul had used this room for his studio.) Later, as the sun dropped, a rosy, then a wild red-and-gold light would shoot through the windows. The room lit up and seemed to float in an element between air and water. The woodwork seemed even heavier and the walls porous. I knew that the light was coming through the windows, but it seemed as if the brightness were actually penetrating the walls' secret invisible mesh.

For brief moments, inner and outer life came together. It was enough to sit at the small benchlike table and watch the room fill and then gradually darken. I would feel the cool white coffee mug—I bought it for its thick heavy bottom—and I would experience a brief sensation of clarity and peace.

The New England transcendentalists might have said that I was experiencing heaven's light. According to Emerson, "The sky was the daily bread of the eye." Thoreau preferred reflected blue, which gathered in the hollows of the deep snow around Walden Pond, not these wild sunset reds and yellows.

The commuter trains would roar into Back Bay Station at dusk. Watching strangers get off and on—I could barely see their faces—I would feel that I was sending them off like a friendly spy. In those brief moments, I wasn't lonely. Time stretched out, and there was plenty of time.

The landlord, Aaron Smith, who was black, lived just under me in the first-floor apartment. "You can do whatever you want," he said, "as long as there's no police." He was deaf as a post, and we communicated mostly through notes. His were formal, "Your note of even date enclosing check in payment of Sept. rent rec'd. I thank you and herewith enclose receipt for same." Before I left on a trip to Maine, he wrote, "I trust you will enjoy with much luck the fishing expedition to Northern Maine." (His epistolary style reminded me of my mother's, whose letters to me often began, "Received your lovely missive.")

Mr. Smith and I never used first names with each other. When we passed in the hall, I would shout, "Hello, Mr. Smith." Murmuring, "Miss Levine," he would touch his hat, a beautiful pale gray fedora, carefully blocked, the fine nap smoothly brushed.

Over the black marble mantel in what had formerly been the back parlor and was now his kitchen hung a large, gilt-framed lithograph portrait of Abraham Lincoln. Mr. Smith voted Republican. The dusty heaped-up room, the clean pearly lithograph, each line like a dark gray hair, seemed encased in the must of another age.

Mr. Smith worked as a messenger for a Yankee business downtown. A friend said that Mr. Smith was a "house nigger." He had worked for white people too long. I didn't see him that way. He wasn't servile. He had style, Boston style. What else could it have been? He wasn't from down home.

When I knew him, Mr. Smith was already in his seventies, and there was something antique about his dress. He wore dark three-piece suits, which looked sculpted, and which seemed to gather their own atmosphere like the microclimate around a plant. His stiff white shirts were immaculate though a little worn. His ties were discreet, flecked with tiny nubs of gold or dark red. A gold watch chain looped across the midriff.

Mr. Smith stood very straight. He had the carriage of a much younger man, though sometimes, when I saw him coming down Harwich Street after work, I noticed that he was moving slowly. At those times he looked his age, bony instead of thin and wiry, and his magnificiently constructed suit hung too loosely on the straight pole of his spine.

Mr. Smith was remote. That he was black and I was white must have been partly responsible for our shyness, yet I am sure that he was solitary by nature. His deafness locked him in, but it had been his choice not to marry. He lived with his German shepherd, Blackie. Mr. Smith was correct but not outwardly affectionate with the dog. They were like army friends of different ranks.

He had a nephew who would visit, usually on a Sunday afternoon or evening, and he had a girlfriend, who came occasionally to have dinner with him, a youngish woman with red hair,
light yellow skin, and bright makeup. I could hear her shouted
conversation through the floorboards, and beneath her shouts—
mostly about the food—his low speech, the words just out of
my hearing. There was a habitual though loose formality to all
of these meetings. Always they discussed the same things, as if
to reassure each other. Or rather, she did. She had to work hard
to make Mr. Smith hear her. Sometimes, she sounded as if she
were speaking to a dumb child.

Daily at Boston University I entered the "spiritual-heroic refrigerating apparatus." Sometimes it was thrilling. At home
on Harwich Street, I would listen to the comforting minutiae
of daily life. In one of his novels, Philip Roth has a young
English instructor, who would become a writer, heroically cor-
recting papers, his pencils sharpened, his mind clear. Control and
order: he loves them. There's a different way to tell my story.
The woman I once was sat in her kitchen. The faucet dripped.
Mr. Smith's girlfriend asked again about the doneness of the
roast beef; then it was, "He said. . . . she said. . . . Do you
know what?" I lifted my book, usually a great book, and took
my notes. I stopped and listened to the voices rising through
the floorboards. I was held in the matrix. I filled the kettle and
boiled water for coffee. Water splashed on the stove. Sometimes
I would hear a voice in my book, not exactly the language of
souls, but a human voice, which seemed to come through time
still in its flesh case; the words were flesh: I repeated them.

In our brief encounters in the dimly lit hall, Mr. Smith
was imposing. His reserve was monumental, almost taciturn. He
was so like the immigrant men I had seen in photographs—my
own grandfather dressed in the same correct way, staring at the
camera, his body stiff and slim, yet worn, a body that had been
worked too hard.

Mr. Smith's eyes advanced and retreated; there was a lot of pupil, a lot of burned-out darkness, and also a smoldering light. They were both full and vacant, both alert and exhausted—the eyes of Poles at Ellis Island, the eyes of conquered Indians posed in ceremonial dress, the eyes of Chinese railroad workers in the American West, staring at the camera. I never saw him smile.

Every night he would turn on the Jerry Williams show. (Williams is still on Boston radio. His campaign against the seat-belt law, which he said was fascistic, was responsible for its repeal. The other day I heard him questioning a caller, "So you want mandatory testing for AIDS? Let's just run right out and test every person who wears an earring. Is that what you want? How about every black baby? Is that what you want?") Mr. Smith's radio boomed. The bombastic hectoring voice of the popular talk-show host would fill my apartment: Boston parking, civil rights. For an hour, Mr. Smith and I would get some news of the world.

. . . . .

The two second-floor bedrooms of the house at 207 State Street in Framingham were in the low wing, which had been added to the older main house around 1830. The owners lived in the older part of the house, and my husband, John, and I rented the apartment in the 1830 addition. The larger of the two bedrooms, where John and I slept, was tucked under a low ceiling, which slanted to meet two pairs of square eight-over-eight windows. The windows faced each other like mirrors or pictures in a gallery. The sills were barely a foot above the floor. The back windows, which faced southwest, were hot and bright, the front-facing windows cool and pale. We put our bed between the front windows and faced the hot south light.

The huge headboard of the brass bed, which we bought from our Yankee landlady, curved between two high bedposts like a fabulous harp. The posts were square, rather than the usual round columns, and gave the bed a neoclassical air. Once assembled, the bed was so heavy it could not be moved. The side pieces reminded me of thick-gauge railroad tracks. Yet with the harplike or loomlike headboard and footboard, the bed seemed about to float, to be just held down by the sloping eaves.

We had rented in Framingham because I had just taken a teaching job at the state college, a block up the street. The house had belonged to the landlady's father. "We don't want any wild drinking parties," she said as we signed the lease. "They're teachers," her husband responded reassuringly. We were silent.

We had just come home from a year traveling across Europe. After living out of suitcases, suddenly we were owners, not only of the stupendous marriage bed, but also of a large white refrigerator and a washing machine. We understood that if you rented an apartment without these things, you had to buy them—Framingham was not a laundromat town—but we were dazed by the rapidity with which these heavy objects arrived. My husband's aunt gave us a rose-colored hooked rug for our pale blue bedroom, my parents gave us a blue velvet chair.

We did like the house, six rooms—more space than we'd ever had, paneled doors, and rustically delicate proportions measured out by a carpenter whose intelligent eye you could still feel.

The house had been done over before we moved in: the woodwork gleamed with good white oil paint, the floors shone. The owners had even had the windows washed. All that cleanliness could not obscure the oddness of the rooms, the way our bedroom lofted up against the ceiling but was rescued from any sense of cramping by the four surprisingly generous windows—Yankees pouring out four glasses of delicious sherry, just one for each guest, our tight-lipped landlady lacing her baked beans with strong black molasses.

In a year I was pregnant. A month before I had bought a pantsuit, dark green corduroy. The cut was slim, boyish, like a riding suit. How quickly the waist became too tight to button. Life was just happening. Although I wanted this child, the daily nausea of morning sickness made me feel unmoored and afraid. Even so I was stoical. I would eat a few dry crackers in bed before getting up. They would dull the nausea and I would go to work.

Eva came to see me. She and Paul were living in a cinder block ranch house in Brockton, an even more provincial place than Framingham. Things hadn't worked out for them in California. They had come back east broke, Eva pregnant. She gave birth to her daughter in the ward at Boston City Hospital. Now there were two daughters, Hope and Haven. Are names a fate? I wondered. Paul was working in a plastics factory. John and I had stopped going to Brockton. Paul's gambits drove us crazy. He'd preach about the right way to drive a shift car. "Shifting down . . . , shifting down," he'd intone as if "shifting down" were an esoteric feat. How else could one drive a shift car? Then he'd go on to hardware stores, "I go in and ask for a left-handed rachet with a two-quarter thing-a-ma-bob on the end and a half-cut washer with a friz-em-a-bob on the top and this guy says, 'Sure, how many do you want?' It blows my mind." Sometimes he'd sulk. John and I were a threat. Eva was unhappy, but she wouldn't talk about it to us. When she came to see me in Framingham during my pregnancy, she talked about—what?—I can't remember. She seemed to be hiding. We all had retreated into marriage, discovering like every wife that marriage did not complete us, but we could not admit it even to ourselves. In a few years, with the women's movement, all that would change. Until then we hid our discontent.

Eva's clothes seemed a further concealment: hillbilly wife—wash pants, a long-sleeved man's shirt, big shoes on her big feet. Her hair was wound into a mean bun, and she was smoking a pipe. No hash, just straight tobacco.

In a few years her life and Paul's would change. They began designing and making jewelry—polished bones linked with silver. What could be cheaper than bones? I was skeptical when Eva showed me the bones. Not an idea for the East, not then, but

I had forgotten about the rest of the country. The business took off. The bones sold in California, in New Mexico. She and Paul went south, bought acres, built a house, prospered. Bonesmiths.

Our son David was born on May 1. He slept in the small second bedroom, which opened off our room. From my bed, I could see him in his crib a step away. He'd cry and I'd gather him up while John slept. First I'd change David's wet diaper; his legs were so thin, they looked like loose keys in gigantic white keyholes; then I'd nurse him. He'd suck and fall asleep, and I'd tuck him back in. The first night that I accomplished this, I was elated. Sometimes I would bring him into bed with me and nurse him, propped against that incredible headboard.

John, after hearing stories of babies being smothered in their parents' beds, dreamed that David had fallen asleep between us and that he had carried him back to his crib. John woke up from the dream, bending over the crib holding a pillow, which he believed was the baby. He then became more frightened, "Suppose I didn't wake up, suppose I put the pillow down over him and went back to bed?" "But that didn't happen," I answered.

David thrived. One, two, three months passed. He woke less often. Two in the morning, then three, then four. Just before the first dawn light it is absolutely black. I'd wake to his signaling cry and stumble into blackness. I'd turn on the small light in his room. The light slipped like a heavy drawer through the door into the big bedroom, a sharp-angled slant across our bed. Just over the line, my husband slept in half darkness.

Our nights were peaceful, but once, during the day, I had been downstairs working when David woke crying from his nap. I had left him too long. He had thrashed so that he had rubbed sore spots on his soft-boned fingers. I was horrified.

The cool nights of May and June when David had needed a light blanket were soon gone. Now when I picked him up, his new close dark hair, which grew through the gold down he had been born with, would often be damp, pressed against his head like wet fern. By then we were used to each other. He knew the sound of my rasping off-key songs.

By September he was regularly sleeping through the night, waking by six, sometimes by five. Our night scene changed. I would usually put him to bed by nine and get into bed myself. I'd leave the door to his room open, turn on the lamp next to my bed and read. David would fall asleep with his delightful round face turned toward the light. He saw me there composed, my then long dark hair spread on the pillow, my absorbed downward glance, my now familiar face. The light from the small blue-and-white Chinese lamp shone in a yellow circle; the headboard gleamed dully. The phone next to the bed was still. My friends reached me in the morning. Very little disturbed that votive half hour, when gazing toward the light he fell asleep. "The Reading Madonna" was a title that could have described the scene.

There was a stack of books next to the lamp, a notebook. I relaxed against the pillows and felt that I was gently putting myself on view—like a living icon. It was a little like acting, mastering a technique, but at the same time my heart was loving. David fell asleep so quickly this way, in an instant. I didn't worry about his becoming too attached—Robert Frost was the only person I had ever heard of, besides peasants, who at sixteen was still sleeping in his mother's room.

So we had a moment of balance, my son and I. The rope that bound us became weightless, invisible as an eye beam. Seeing his face turned toward me in trust as he drifted off so easily into darkness made me understand myself: I was restless for adult words. There was the sound of turning pages. In those moments I was there for him and not there.

Outside the wall of that low-ceilinged room, the night was thick and immense. There seemed to be nothing but that room. The windows were black. We could have been inside a cave. The bed might have been part of a theatrical dream set. A bed and an altar both. The mystery of images: how potent they were. You could be a carrier, even a creator of images, and yet not be the thing you created, not completely.

And what about the rapt believer falling asleep, with his face turned toward the light and my face? Perhaps, after years, he would learn that you could be more than one thing.

Courage

I've begun to work small. The vegetable garden of our
Arlington house where we moved in 1978 is only a three-by-
twenty-foot strip between the house and a chain link fence
covered with honeysuckle. There are chives, now past flower,
their stems tipped with purple seed pods, parsley seeding itself,
lemon-tasting sorrel—my grandmother Molly used it for a cold
summer soup—rocket, and whatever dandelion blows my way.
Compared to these biting greens lettuce tastes insipid; so far I
haven't planted any. This summer I'll put in a late planting of
spinach. There's mint. "Invasive, a weed," a segregationist gar-
dener told me with contempt. "You'll be sorry you ever let it in."
I'm not. How could I sneer at anything so fragrant. "Common,"
is another of her derisive adjectives. She likes to name-call, spac-
ing out the words. "Weeds. Common. Common. Weeds." Every
now and then I pull a clump of mint to clear space. It comes up
easily, releasing its sharp clean smell. No pest touches it. There's
basil, with its more complicated heady licorice scent. I've been
trying out different kinds of tomatoes. Because of the limited
sun—half day—early ripening cherry tomatoes do best. I like
them unchilled, plucked like grapes, full of juice, sweet sour.

Last summer a pumpkin vine sprouted out of the compost—
we had dumped the seeds from a jack-o'-lantern—and worked
its way around the house under the laurel and rhododendron

along the front foundation. We let it flower and run but gave up hoping for fruit. In October John found one huge pumpkin under the bushes. It ripened. We carved it and saved the seeds. There are now three vines sprawling around the southwest corner. Yesterday I looked into the soft star of the pumpkin flower lying over a leaf. The blossom was at least eight inches across, open to the point of collapse, faintly ribbed, faintly furred, a pale dome at its heart: a preview of pumpkin or the vine imagining the substance of pumpkin. It seemed the butterfly story in reverse. The winged pointed blossom first. The lighter, freer flower before the heavy fruit. Staring into the flower's dazzle, I asked myself, Who needs the pumpkin? I wonder how long that mood will last.

There are strawberries. Alpine, but they like it here in Arlington, ten miles from the ocean. You can still smell the salt blow in from Boston Harbor. "Have you ever tasted these?" I'll ask, handing over the smallest handful of berries. Have *you* tasted them—small, distilled, winy essence, the taste of red, the taste of roses. "Oh, you have fraises des bois," my art history professor friend says, "I always drink champagne with strawberries."

I'd like to take him by his clean well-manicured hand and pull him down here under the honeysuckle where I keep my compost. I can't manage a large pile anymore because of a back injury, so I have three plastic milk cartons where I layer dirt with green weeds, spent violas, some kitchen garbage—coffee grounds, vegetable and fruit peels, peanut shells, egg shells with their film of slime, clam shells, moldy bread, bones. (I ignore the compost experts who warn against stinking animal remains: bones sprinkled with dirt don't smell. I've heard of someone who scrapes up road kills for his compost pile.) Microbes, worms— café crème with a chill of blue—amber-colored centipedes, and gray insects, which look like ancient trilobites, come up through the plastic grid into the rich waste and do the work for me. I shake the crate every few weeks. Black compost sifts down for the garden. I pull the hornworms off the tomatoes and pinch out the suckers. I didn't pinch enough. This morning I had to get down on my hands and knees and peer into the tomato vines as if I were peeping through a keyhole, then thread my hand in to get at the ripe fruit.

On Sunday—it's August—I had breakfast with a friend from California; Brice was staying in an inn in Newburyport. "See, Mim, even I can be a tourist. It's a stage set. I've got the room with the bay." He motioned to the building behind him— sand-blasted shutters, black paint glossy as tar, sand-blasted clap- boards iced white, red geraniums in neat window boxes. "Why not?" I answered. "The world is now touring America." It used to be the other way around. We all went there, and what were we looking at? Restoration. But the restoration is aging, so it doesn't look so new. So depilated. Brice went on making ob- servations, "Everyone says hello. Hello, hello, hello. They don't stop there. They want to talk. And talk. And talk. And talk. I thought Yankees were tight-lipped." "It's the long winter," I an- swered. "They're let out. Like the vegetation. There's not much time, in a few weeks it'll be cold again. Seasonal affective dis- order." "Oh, yeah, I heard about that. They're selling special full-spectrum lights. Supposed to cheer people up. No winter blues. A scam. You should come to California."

Brice looks like a retired running back. He's massive but now slack. His broad face accommodates a flattened nose. Brice has never had anything to do with sports, but people took him for a football star, or a narc. He stood out; people wanted to talk to him, but he had good reason to be afraid of talkers: he didn't want to be recognized. After his graduation from Princeton, he'd gotten into alcohol and pills, then hijacking. A disgruntled cohort had turned him and the rest of the gang in to the police. That's how most criminals get caught. Brice skipped bail, changed his name, settled in California, where he ran a small business out of a truck, selling frozen meat and fish to retirees who lived modestly in trailers or small ranch houses and ate well: Brice's baby racks of lamb, prime rib, jumbo shrimp. "They like to sit in their garages," Brice said. "Some of my customers, I've never seen them out of pajamas. They don't bother to get dressed." Every year he was making less. "But I like what I do," he would tell me. He had first gone to California on vacation with his parents. "I loved it," Brice said. "Now I'm here. I keep telling you and John to come out." He loved to call us in the winter, "Upstairs I keep the windows open all year round. Drive home at night from some small town—they're still there—flat all around, truck empty, no more stops, turn off the AC, roll down the window, orchards, white everywhere, flowers, you'd like it." Brice was always trying to get his friends to the coast. He has taken the name of a classmate of his who died in his twenties, and he wanted to be with the few of us who knew his real name and his story.

"Have you seen these death penalty types screaming outside the prisons?" Brice asked me in Newburyport. "They don't understand that people can change. They want blood."

Brice's father had been a chief of state police. There was a photograph: the Chief in full uniform, Sam Brown belt, smart cap with visor, gun; he was kneeling. Between his high boots stood the three-year-old Brice, his blond hair in ringlets, his small face alert and helpless. Years ago when Brice had left his first wife for Mrs. Schwartzkopf, as he always called her, his father, his mother, and his wife had followed the couple to Provincetown. Crazed to see his model son breaking out, he had pulled them off the road, using his old police tactics. "What does she do?" the Chief had screamed running toward Brice, "Blow you? Is that what she does?" Brice smiled in wonder when he told me the story. "Samson and Delilah. That's what they think. They were all screaming, my mother wringing her hands. What has she done all these years? Polish her antiques? They want me in a straitjacket."

Brice kept a gun in the house. When I asked him about this a few years ago, he told me that he felt he needed protection. His neighborhood had gone down. There was a lot of action, a lot of drugs. Now he had a different angle on guns. One night, he told me, he had heard louder noises than usual. A man was beating up a woman on the street outside of Brice's house. "He was a big guy," Brice said, "and he was beating the shit out of her." Brice ran out, pointed a gun at the attacker, and told him to stop. "Go ahead, asshole," the guy said, "kill me." Brice went in and called the police. "So much for guns," he said to me. "I never carried that mace you sent me," I responded. (When I hurt my back, I had asked Brice to send me some mace. "I'm so slow," I told him on the phone, "I don't feel safe when I creep around Fresh Pond.") "Did you ever read the cautions? Don't use if your assailant is carrying a gun or a knife, never use if your assailant is extremely violent. You have to position the mace just so. If you don't use it correctly, you can turn a rapist or a thief into a murderer. And I can't run. An automatic assault weapon would do the trick, but they're too heavy to carry, besides, I'll walk with a friend." "You have friends?" Brice teased.

There's still a warrant out for his arrest on the hijacking charge.

The garden is let out, beyond itself. The morning glories along the front fence have done so well that they look for a few hours a day like a solid blue hedge. Parents bring their children to see them. In the neighborhood I've reached an apotheosis: Morning Glory Lady. Deceptively benign.

My neighbor Marge likes to call to me over the back fence, especially when she's heard a juicy item come over the scanner that she listens to as she prepares her husband's lunch. He's retired now, and Marge complains that she's running out of ideas for meals. A few weeks ago, I heard her call, put down my garden shears, and slipped through the yews along the back fence. Marge had on one of her pink flowered aprons. A scrubbed dishcloth hung on the tiny line strung between her back stairs railing and the fence. Every morning the cloth went up like a flag. Marge's voice was breathless and confidential as if talk had to be stolen and our proper place was silently bending over the washtub. "There's a flasher in Menotomy Rocks Park," she said. "They're harmless," I answered in my calm, know-it-all voice. Marge followed her usual gambit. "I wouldn't want to be bringing up kids now a days, what with all the drugs." I knew what was coming next. "And abortion." Marge had had ten children; she took hormones to get pregnant with three of them and blamed her health problems on those early crude drugs. How could she be sympathetic to abortion? "Don't you think, Mim . . ." She would have gone on, tracing all modern evil to abortion. For a second I saw myself as she saw me: sympathetic face, Morning Glory Lady. I couldn't stand it. "As long as there are women," I said, there will be abortion. Better to have safe abortions." I wanted to repeat the word "abortion" again and again but stopped myself. Marge's eyes went blank. Her hand flew from her heart to her throat. "Well, I'll call Sue, and tell her not to send the kids to the park today. You never can tell, don't want them to see a man with . . ." His thing hanging out, I thought. Marge smiled. She had erased my words.

In the early sixties just after my sophomore year in college, I had had an illegal abortion and lied to a grand jury. Sid, my friend and lover at the time, knew a medical student who had done an abortion for a friend. All had gone well. The medical student agreed to help me. We boiled the instruments in Sid's dusty East Village apartment. Sid was a composer, and his place was piled high with yellowed manuscript scores. The medical student—I still won't use his name—did what turned out to be a partial D and C. Using anesthesia was risky. I didn't even take an aspirin.

The medical student told me that if I felt sick or developed a fever I should go right to a doctor. I went home to my parents' apartment where I was staying that summer. I took my temperature. It was a little over a hundred. I was in bed resting. Out of the blue, five minutes after I had put down the thermometer, my mother asked me if I had had an abortion. I said yes and told her about the fever and what the medical student had said. She called a doctor immediately; in an hour I was in the hospital.

I was to have a D and C in the morning. That night I became delirious. I felt myself floating above the bed. The nurse came in, took my temperature, and ran from the room. I remember the wild alarm on her face, which looked huge above me, and the blurry streak as she ran. My temperature was a hundred and eight. They put me on a gurney. I was surrounded by people as the orderlies and nurses frantically pushed me down the long hospital corridor. The IV bottle bobbed and shone whitely, like a ship's light. My father and mother ran beside me, their beautiful tender heads close and large, their bodies wispy and ghostlike.

Also running beside me were detectives in dark suits, holding their hats in their hands, like G-men in the movies. The hospital had reported the abortion that night when I became so ill. We stopped before the double doors of the operating room. The detectives would have followed me through the doors if the nurses had let them. They asked me who did it. I didn't tell them.

I knew by the wild haste of the people around me that I might die. But I wasn't afraid. The high fever had stunned me out of fear, calmed me. Then the drugs took over and I went out.

When I came to the next morning in the recovery room, I felt I was coming back from the dead. A young nurse had her hand on my forehead as I opened my eyes. I believe I had a cloth still wrapped around my head, at least, that's how I saw myself, still shrouded. "You're all right," she said. Her hand was cool.

The police were back by lunchtime. One of them talked about his son Paul, who had been in high school with me. I had last seen Paul at a party on graduation night. It had been warm, finally without any spring chill. We were all standing outside under the newly leafed trees. The air was sweet and musty. We could see each other's faces in the light from the streetlamp. Paul had on a white jacket; he was blond and tanned, his hair was cut like the actor Tab Hunter's, high on the sides, with a high slanting bang. There were a lot of very fair Poles in our class. He looked completely glamorous, so untouchable. We stared at each other. He was more serious than usual, less arrogant, less shy. "Yes, I know him," I answered.

I measured the distance between myself and his beautiful son, the difference between my old life and my new one. I felt a flicker of shame. I could have made myself comfortable by joining with the detective to prosecute the "abortionist." I could become good again, Paul's father was saying in effect. Then I got angry. They were working on me. If they had known my dead grandmother, they would have mentioned her too. They wanted the "abortionist's" name. I told them I didn't know.

Before anything had gone wrong, Sid and I had agreed to keep the student's name secret. He would have been thrown out of medical school; he would most likely have gone to prison. I did not believe in this law that had caused us all so much trouble.

One of the brainy boys I had gone to high school with, who was now at Massachusetts Institute of Technology, came to see me. He told me what a brave thing I had done. He stared at me through his thick glasses, and his eyes, which were usually clear and hard, were dewy with awe, "You didn't put it on the guy," he said. "You took care of things yourself." He had got it all wrong, but I was too tired to explain.

When my mother came to see me, she would tell my story in the third person; she would look into the air over my head, and address an audience: "She didn't tell them, not even when they followed her to the operating room." Her face was thoughtful.

In the hospital, the detective, the father of the golden boy, had assured me that the story would not be in the paper. I had asked him; I was worried. I wasn't that cool. I questioned my mother, and when she told me that the *Paterson Call* had covered the story, I made her bring me the paper. The *Call* reported that I was in the hospital as a result of an illegal abortion; they gave my name and address, my parents' address, in case anyone might have any doubt which Levine I was. I was furious with the detective. The public shame did bother me but not for long. I told myself that I would not hide, that I would not explain, and I didn't. Whatever cover I had was blown. I went home; I looked the neighbors straight in the eye and said hello. With my mother's help—without judgment she had told me about a married woman we knew who had had an abortion—I decided that most people either had their own secrets or that they hadn't really lived. At nineteen, I couldn't imagine any other possibilities. I was glad to be alive. I went to the park for sun; I got stronger.

A girl I had known slightly in high school kindly came to see me and told me her own abortion story. Now in memory she seems such a tender child, her voice was so quiet and firm, her long black shining hair parted on the side, one lock held off her smooth forehead by a large barrette, which seemed to have just replaced a wide child's ribbon tied in a bow.

A week after I got out of the hospital, Sid and I were summoned to appear before a grand jury.

We rehearsed our story over and over, drilling each other in an intense single-minded way. We planned to say that we never knew the abortionist's name or address. Our main problem was to make our contact with him seem plausible. How can you find someone in Manhattan if you don't know his name? We decided that we would tell the jury that the "abortionist" contacted us. We would say that word got around that I was pregnant, and that someone, a well-wishing friend, no doubt, sent the "abortionist" to us. We would say that he approached Sid in a student cafeteria. Sid and I had seen a lot of Cold War spy films. The "abortionist" became a kind of Communist, a nameless, sneaking figure always waiting in the shadows, a man who somehow got the necessary information about our situation and our characters and found his way to us. He infiltrated us.

We had also learned about wiretapping from the movies. In the weeks before our appearance before the grand jury, we were in touch with the medical student only by pay phone. This was an unnecessary precaution, but we were taking no chances. When we were not feeling dramatic, we became grim. We conspired. We knew that we had to construct a story and stick to it, and although our obsessive rehearsals were beginning to bore us, we found that the possibility of our going to jail for perjury sharpened our concentration.

Sid bought me a watch, silver inlaid with gold. I don't know how he managed the gift. His music brought him little money. It was an old watch that had been engraved with initials. An engraver had cut a new design over them. Sid was careful to explain that the watch had a flaw; he wanted me to understand exactly what I was getting. "Nothing had gone wrong, when he did it before," he said about the abortion.

On the day of our appearance, a young tough-talking assistant district attorney spoke to us separately before we went in to testify. After talking to Sid first, he told me that Sid was ready to cooperate. I knew that that was impossible. Sid was fanatically courageous though he looked frail. I imagine that he was the kind of bespectacled kid who, crying, would take on the class bully but never get any credit for it because he looked like a coward, a coward in the movies, small, dark, weasely, stoop-shouldered. Sid had ulcers. His meals were austere. He'd peel the skin off the chicken breasts before he broiled them, insisting that fat was bad for his ulcer. I wondered. He was weird about food. He would marry a woman about whom he said with delight, "She's the only woman who can cook broccoli without making me sick." He could never stand the smell. He had allergies. He wasn't a guy-guy type, but I knew he wouldn't crack. He was too inflexible. His gut would burn, but his head would stay clear. I repeated myself to the assistant district attorney: I didn't know the man's name. He said that I was risking a perjury charge and insisted that he already knew the name of the "abortionist." How he loved to spit out that word. "Then what do you need me for?" I asked calmly but with spite in my heart. He got angry. "We'll get you," he said. "We'll send you away. Lying to a grand jury." He also had seen a lot of films.

I knew I was taking a very small risk. The odds were in my favor. If Sid and I said exactly the same thing, how could they prove we were lying? Then I began to worry. Was there something we hadn't thought of, some small detail that would cook us both? We had had no legal advice; neither of us had any money for a lawyer.

Sid went in first without my having a chance to speak to him. He was wearing an ancient suit and tie, and his new short haircut looked raw. His face was yellow. They'll know he's lying; with that haircut and suit, he looks as if he just got out of jail, I thought as I sat on the bench outside the courtroom, silently rehearsing my lines.

When my turn came, I was nervous but clear. I was pleased with my prim appearance. I had my hair parted in the middle and pulled back in a bun. I was wearing a plain skirt and a short-sleeved round-necked flowered blouse, a student's uniform. The jury sat in front of me like an audience in a theater. I answered some questions, corroborating Sid's story. Then I was asked about the abortion. They wanted a description. Apparently they had to have evidence that the abortion had happened. I was surprised by these questions. I said that I had put my legs back and that he, this person whose name I did not know, inserted an instrument. I burst into tears. Public shaming. At the spectacle of a crying woman, the jury looked stricken. The assistant DA had become the bad guy.

In an hour it was all over. The jury decided there was insufficient evidence to bring a case to trial. We were the only witnesses. They had no way to prove we were lying, but I suspected that most of the jurors knew we were not telling the truth; although there might have been a few fans of Senator McCarthy who bought our story of the nameless infiltrating "abortionist."

Sid and I walked out of the courthouse into the warm early summer day. From a phone booth far from the courthouse we called the medical student to tell him the good news. I was elated that we had stuck to the story and won.

The abortion had hurt me, and I felt grief. I was sorry that I had allowed myself to be injured. I was sorry that I hadn't found a safer way to get it done. If I had any shame, it was about that. I had no guilt about killing the fetus, though I do believe that I did kill what would have become a person. I was clear about not wanting Sid's baby. We were friends, not mates. There was also a slight chance that it might have been not his but the result of a brief single encounter with an artist who had a misshapen face and body. I was afraid I would hate his baby.

Now, years later, my bravery seems to have left me. My son David's girlfriend, Sandy, keeps her pet rabbits in our backyard. Her landlady insisted that she get rid of them. After a few seconds' thought, I told Sandy that she could move them here. She calls them her bunnies. Jagger, a brown Dutch dwarf male, and Bunny Chicken, a white-and-gray female, live in separate cages in front of the hemlocks ten feet from the back door. I can see them from the porch. They've never mated. Sandy and I feel sorry for them, particularly for Jagger, who has chewed through the cords of his outdoor run trying to get to Bunny. Jagger is four; he won't live much longer.

We've been reading a book about rabbits, which advises restricting a litter to seven. Rabbits can have as many as twelve at a time. "Foster the rest out," says the writer, or "dispose" of them. In any case, "dispose" of "runts." I'm sure the writer is British. Only the British have this calmly sadistic tone when talking about animal training or animal husbandry. A famous British dog trainer on TV savagely yanked a spaniel's choke chain as she sweetly intoned "Walkies," her favorite command. "Dispose?" Wring their necks? Throw them in the furnace? Drown them in a sack? Perhaps, if I did it with rites, prayers, and bloodletting, then buried the tiny bodies in the compost heap to rot and be scattered on the early blooming scarlet tulips near the rabbit cages. No, I can't do that. Every time I think about "priestesses," I see Martha Graham, the priestess of modern dance, with her stage face. She plays vatic. One needs long training to be a witch, one needs a tradition not to look phony like Graham.

Sandy and I are still talking about mating Jagger. We'd have to do it this spring. Jagger may not make it through the winter.

Some years ago I went regularly to visit a friend in prison, one of Brice's group who had faced the trial and been sentenced to two years. Not a bad bit, as the cons say. Friends had told me that the prison was not prisonlike, so the first time I went, I took David, then two years old, with me. I had strapped him into the car seat, and, on the advice of a neighbor, took the quiet back roads instead of the bleak superhighway. We rode through old farm country, past stone walls, apple orchards, and star magnolia blooming early in the cool New England spring.

The grounds of the low-security prison, which was nicknamed "The Farm," were sterile as a military base. A big flag flapped in the wind, making a stupid sound. Unthinking, resolute, I carried my son into the visitors' building. I had to leave my bag and pass through a double set of iron-barred doors, which slid and clanged. My son nestled against me, not frightened. He was a compact, strong boy, rounded, but not soft. His weight sank into me in a delicious way. A cloven fresh weight. His round head against my neck, just fitting in between head and shoul-

der. He didn't squirm, but he wasn't passive. He didn't hang.
He participated.

Just as the first door slid open, one of the guards offered to
carry the baby so that we could more easily pass through the
cramped space. I clutched David to me and said, "You're not
going to take my baby." The guard looked at me, surprised and
offended, "No, lady, we don't take babies." I didn't believe him;
my legs were weak, my arms felt too strong, too heavy. My heart
lurched with fear. I felt done in.

At later visits, I would experience the same kind of fear but in
a milder form. I began to wonder whether my fear had become
stronger than my courage. Would I ever have the strength to
fight, to lie, to pick up a knife? I didn't know. I wanted to be able
to kill a runt and stand up to the cops. But ever since I'd had a
child, I felt as though I'd lost those powers.

Yet this morning when I thought again about courage,
I came to the conclusion that my definition of heroism was too
narrow. Just having a baby was an act of courage, for all women,
for those who go into it without thinking and for those who
think and decide. Pregnancy and childbirth have been sealed in a
kind of silence, like a taboo. And the films, which were so popular now, of mother and father training for the event in special
classes, laboring together, even the films of the actual birth, did
not really convey the mystery of the journey.

Don't you remember what that was like? I asked myself. In
those last months you were helpless before the life that would
with its own power break out of you and leave you who knew
how. You were afraid, you went into the dark, you suffered, and
it changed you.

Devotion

*S*andy's rabbits have been here for a year, and I find
myself more and more drawn to them, especially to Jagger, the
Dutch dwarf. Jagger is five, old for a Dutch dwarf, yet he looks
new. His dark brown fur shines as if he's just been washed; his
brown eyes are clear, outlined in darker brown, shaped like a
watermelon seed. I never get tired of watching him.

Now that it's the end of March, the sun has come around to
the front of his cage. Yesterday I let him out into his run and,
slipping a carrot between the wire, crouched down to watch him.
The sun shown through his short stiff ears. Lit up by the sun,
they were pink; along the back of each ear, from tip to root: a
thick, dark rose vein from which branched paler veins. His ears
looked newly sprouted, vegetable, sensitive. They seem to have
just broken through the skin and fur; seem to have sprung from
deep inside his small skull. Between his ears a faint I shaped
mark, a pale brown stitching, makes the top of his head look like
miniature carefully tended plowed fields, side by side.

Dutch dwarfs have rounded snouts. In fact "snout" is the
wrong word. Jagger's soft nose is black as a truffle against the
dark brown fur of his head and shoulders. Along his lower back
and flanks, the fur becomes faintly streaked with butterscotch,
and here and there are sparse odd quill-like tufts of white hair
of a more downy texture than the minklike fur. Only when you

look closely do you notice that Jagger is not completely dark glossy brown. The white fur is hidden, an undercoat of down, the fine white tufts breaking through like the tip of a feather sticking through a pillow.

He'll stand up on his hind legs. Only when he presses his front legs against the wire mesh of the cage can I see the white bottoms of his paws. Two clean white flakes otherwise hidden. There's always rabbit shit in the cage, but somehow his paws are clean. The white is so unexpected, a kind of ravishing signal, unintentional—a woman lifting her heavy hair with both hands and revealing the nape of her neck, the short damp tendrils at the pale hidden hairline.

Jagger is a neat eater. I've watched him deconstruct an apple half. He chisels the edges; round and round goes the apple. The flat half, with its red border of skin still intact, diminishes. His tooth marks are like the cuts from a small chisel, the kind you use for cutting woodblocks. In the same way, he chews the stiff brown oak leaves that drop into his pen. He turns the leaf round and round, scalloping again the deep-cut edges of the leaf, until a little leaf beard sticks out of his small precise mouth and then is gone. His lapping is daintier than a cat's. His tongue is so small; he makes no noise as he drinks. His whiskers spread out on the water like a long-legged bug.

When Jagger is resting, his paws hidden under him, he looks like a duck on water. His small spine makes a faintly bumpy line, which emphasizes his suave haunches. The sleek, close-lying fur does not obscure his shape; the fur is like a glove, a poured glove; it flows over the sleek muscles.

If I try to touch him, he'll hop away. He's not like Whitman's ideal animals. In "Song of Myself," Whitman writes that he "could turn and live with animals, they are so placid and self-contained." The stallion responds to his caresses. "His nostrils dilate as the [poet's] heels embrace him, / His well-built limbs tremble with pleasure." Jagger is also self-contained, but he is truly wild. He doesn't want my caresses. He doesn't respond with pleasure. He's not grateful or loyal. He doesn't care for me. I'm just the servant. He's completely himself. He never nudges me for food; he never rolls on his back so I can pet his stomach. The most he will do is come close for food.

Jagger is not cute. Anyone who has read D. H. Lawrence's *Women in Love* knows that rabbits are not cute. Lawrence describes Bismarck, a big buck, "The long, demon-like beast lashed out again, spread on the air as if it were flying, looking something like a dragon, then closing up again inconceivably powerful and explosive." Lawrence's character Gerald has picked up the rabbit by its ears. Bismarck scratches, he draws blood. Lawrence makes the clawing deliberate, devilish, and sexually male. But every rabbit, male and female, will do this if you leave its rear end dangling. It will flail and rake with its hind legs—a reflex action. If you get your hand under the rump, the rabbit will not scratch. Bismarck would not have scratched if Gerald had held him correctly. Now that I know a little about rabbits, Lawrence's rabbit scene doesn't quite come off for me. But he's right about the wildness of rabbits. He understands that rabbits are not Beatrix Potter creations.

Sometimes when I open Jagger's cage, he bolts out and does a furious pivoting run from one end of the fence to the other. As he runs, he jumps sideways like a quarterback faking out a tackle. He runs for joy. His eyes are fixed on something I cannot see or even imagine. He doesn't relate to the audience—me— the way a dog would. He's like Nijinsky leaping and dashing. He's the airiest mammal I've ever come close to.

He looks, but he doesn't seem to take things in. He's "autistic." You can't find out anything about yourself by looking into a rabbit's eyes. Nothing looks back. Jagger's innocence is shocking.

Rabbits can scream—when they're frightened to death and when they are being killed. Otherwise they might as well be mute. I've never heard Jagger scream. When he's startled he stamps, setting off a tremendous racket, but mostly he's silent.

The crows that patrol Jason Heights are quarreling over carrion, probably a dead squirrel. They're in the tops of the seventy-foot Norway pines. The treetops are swaying with their weight. The crows are screeching and cackling. Rough and angry, they keep it up. They sound hysterical. The dog pants. She needs to have her thick curly winter coat clipped away. She farts; she moans as she stretches; she barks. The gunmetal gray cat, who likes to visit my garden, gives off an electrical purr.

Jagger's silence makes him more mysterious than a cat; he's a genius of self-possession.

Last winter, when it was ten below zero, I worried about Jagger. Snow piled up roof high around his cage. I'd go out to make sure he was alive. I'd have to get very close before I heard the thrumming rushing sound of his paws against the wire cage. He'd burrow into the hay we put out for him. His coat thickened; he got fatter. A mammal heat pulsed in the hutch and reassured me, but still, despite myself, I felt pity. It was misplaced.

Jagger emerged in the spring, sleek and glossy. "I told you that he'd be all right," Sandy said. She was good with animals and she knew them. She and her sister kept a horse at Pony Boy Stable in Medford. They were both skilled riders and had that straight-backed carriage of riders; they seemed to sit straight on their hips, even when they were walking. I had once driven Sandy to the stable and followed her in. Pony Boy had been added onto over the years, and the stalls backed up to each other at odd angles, the dirt-floored aisles zigzagging in the gloom. I jumped at the snorting, stamping, pawing horses. Confidently, Sandy moved ahead of me, stopping here and there to pet a horse. "This one bites," she said and firmly batted a black two-year-old between the eyes as he went for her coat buttons. "He likes to pull them off," she said. Sandy was the one who groomed Jagger. She held him, washed him, and cut his claws. I was timid about holding him.

Sandy and I watched Jagger rake the newly thawed ground with rapture. He digs and digs. He's made himself a rabbit hole. It's large enough for him to turn around in. He's camouflaged the entrance. I've tried to look into it, but Jagger has placed his den in a corner of the run I cannot get to unless I take apart the wire fence. It's his.

A neighbor came by the other day with her grandchild. I was planting some roses near the front fence, "Brownells Rambler." The *Roses of Yesterday and Today* catalog promised that they would produce a shower of gold and survive subzero temperature. "Planting roses?" my neighbor asked. "We ripped all of ours out—mildew, black spot, aphids, leaf miners, Japanese beetles. Maybe you'll have better luck," she added with malicious innocence. "Show her the rabbits," I said, pointing to her grandchild. I must have looked gaga. "I'm Italian," she said. I wouldn't have known by her name: Charity Marks. She's solicited me for various liberal causes. I give to everything without much enthusiasm and little hope: MASS PIRG, CPPAX, ACC, SANE, MCCADD. "We raised them for food. My mother butchered them. She'd slit their throats, nail them up by the ears, and strip the skin off in one piece." "Oh, so you're not thrilled by rabbits." "No," she answered and continued on her walk, pushing the stroller in front of her. Well, I'm thrilled, I said to myself. I like to watch rabbits. Maybe I'd eat Jagger if I had to. But I don't have to.

In Julien's, in Paris, I saw a Frenchwoman—pale green eye shadow, red lips—feed shreds of smoked salmon to her little black terrier. He sat next to her on the banquette against the wall. He was well behaved, not like Jagger. But when I feed Jagger fresh clover and carrots, I think of that Parisienne. I too like to have animals take food from my hands.

Is Jagger a substitute for the second child I never had? I don't think so. Actually, Jagger is my idol. I do not go to church or temple. Instead I contemplate the mystery of the rabbit. A mystery is a religious truth that we can know only by revelation and cannot fully understand. Whether or not Jagger is worthy of my devotion is not important. Contrary to the faith of my forefathers, I have become an idol worshiper.

I adore Jagger.

Mute, oblivious of me, he affords me the gift of his beauty, his shocking innocence, his brown eyes with their purplish blue haze, which do not know me. Jagger ravishes me.

Postscript

One day when Sandy was cleaning the cages, I plunked Jagger down next to Bunny Chicken. In about a month Bunny had a litter of five. Two died, the runt soon after its birth and the other after an unusually cold spring night. We gave away the two we called the gray sisters and kept the fawn-colored one, which looked most like Jagger. At first we called "her" Fawn Hall— the Iran-gate hearings were on—but discovering our mistake renamed him Ollie. The three rabbits are still here in the backyard. When I went out to look at Jagger this morning, I noticed that mushrooms had sprouted in his run. Jagger was sitting in the corner of the cage that the sun reaches first, washing his face and paws.

· · · · ·

It's the beginning of May, and we're all out of our houses. We and our immediate neighbors all live on subdivisions of the Hornblower estate, which was built before the Civil War. Tim and Marge have the old servants' house, an upper-middle-class home by today's standards. The first thing I heard this morning was Tim's cranky voice tense with years of unexpressed resentment. Only lately has he begun to gripe to us out loud. Our property borders his on the south side. He was complaining to my husband about our oak trees: the branches arch over his house; twigs drop into his chimney; the oaks are a nuisance. Tim was aggrieved. Nature, he seems to believe, was created to make work for him. We've already pruned five cords of wood off the trees. He wants us to have them trimmed up to his property line. He wants us to butcher these old plantings from the Hornblower estate, so he won't have to sweep up twigs. Of course, Tim knows that we can't control the oak trees. We've done all we can. I believe that he'd like them down. He hates trees. He has only a few pines, which drop their needles discreetly. Messy deciduous trees, dropping leaves, acorns, seed—the oaks send down long chains of tiny flowers by the bale—don't fit his idea of order, and neither do we and our garden.

Tim's privet is a masterpiece of tight pruning. He uses a hand shears, not an electric trimmer. June, July, and August the clipping goes on. Tim's face gets tighter and tighter. Each glossy leaf looks cleanly washed. If allowed a few inches of freedom, even well-trimmed privet will flower—small white sprays, yellow-centered blossoms with a troubling, sophisticated scent of chocolate and smoke, sugar and faint rot. Tim's privet has never flowered. His front lawn is cleanly edged. There are no weeds in the beds. Even the forsythia, a difficult shrub to prune, is gracefully thinned. Flowers are where they belong: in window boxes and hanging baskets, every year the same salmon-colored impatiens, a splurge of color. In the middle of the immaculate lawn is a flagpole flying the American flag and, in front of the flagpole, two wooden pinwheels, one white, one yellow, a chaste debauch.

He winces and sneers when he passes our front garden. We took out the lawn and planted flowers: lamb's ear; pink, white, and yellow yarrow; old-strain pink moss roses; yellow ramblers; purple globe thistle; bee balm; iris; tickseed. He thinks it's a mess, and to him it is. His taste is French, like Edith Wharton's: cool green, suavely clipped and smoothed, set off with one color. She liked to edge with nasturtiums. When we planted day lilies in the tree strip, Tim incited a town-meeting member to call the police. He said that they were an obstruction, a danger to children who couldn't see over them. The amused policeman who came to investigate decided that we hadn't broken the law. "Them's not flowers," the affronted Tim wept to me, "them's weeds." Old-strain day lilies, escaped from early Puritan gardens. Edith Wharton would have agreed with him.

Before he retired, Tim worked as a house painter, going off early each good morning, dressed in white. "That's what they taught us when I was an apprentice," he told me. "Always white, not like these kids, College Pro. They don't know nothing." When I painted my front threshold cranberry red, he shook his head, "If your front door is black, your threshold should be black." "I like the color," I answered. Tim looked at me with incomprehension.

He's been friendlier since he misunderstood something I said about Hildegard Betancourt, the Massachusetts Institute of Technology professor, who lives across the street in a "twelve-room Italianate Victorian mansion"—the real estate ad description; the house just went on the market. Tim and I were standing— he on his side of the south fence, I on my side—looking at the pile of junk in Hildegard's yard. "Well, that's one way to do it," I said with a surprised awe, which Tim took for disapproval. The house was a falling down wreck when Hildegard bought it. The men she'd given board to in exchange for their doing repairs would just throw the debris out the windows. "Get off," Hildegard would shout at the kids who liked to climb on the pile, which grew larger and larger during her ten-year stay. "It's not a *public* dump, it's a *private* dump," she laughed. Before the house went on the market she hired four trailer-sized dumpsters. I was out front on my hands and knees, carefully coaxing my "natural" garden, when the first dumpster rolled up.

Yesterday I saw Tim sweeping his driveway. The heavy rain of the night before had knocked down green leaves. "And I haven't got a tree on my property," Tim lamented as he swept. During a snowstorm Tim will be out with his snowblower on the hour, blowing the snow off his driveway as it falls. He can't wait until the end of a storm.

I've seen Tim almost every day for the fifteen years I've lived here. His hands are always full—ladders, paintbrushes, buckets, lattice, gutter lengths, lime, fertilizer, grass seed, broom, rake, patching compound, linseed oil. The list has no end. Every few years he paints his "piazza," an Arlington word for porch. During the spring and summer, the period of his most intense activity, his conversation will go like this: "I've got my nails, and I was just over to my friend in Lexington. He give me some nice boards. So I got my boards. I got my paint. I'll finish up that job." "I got my" is Tim's universal. Over the years I've heard that phrase applied to just about everything in his world. Everything in his world is in parts, which he will bring together, but he will seldom, if ever, appreciate the whole. No completed job ever looks quite right to him.

When he was operated on for a hernia, he had to slow down. His recuperation took longer than usual. The surgeon apologized. "We cut the wrong side," he said at the first post-op visit. "We'll have to do the other side." "I told him not to go to the VA hospital," Tim's wife said, "but he wouldn't listen. Now he's got *two* scars." Tim took the mistake meekly. A doctor was a doctor. A priest was also a priest. Tim took a job as a part-time handy man at Sacred Heart; it was Father this and Father that. "What a brownnoser," I said to John. "No, Mim, it's feudal," he answered. John was right. Tim served the priest. Since his two operations, Tim's been walking bent over. He's been told to stay off ladders, which he does, but he's back at work at home and at church.

I was told that Tim once kept pigeons. I wonder whether he kept them in the long-gone cupola. "One thing less to paint," he told me, "got rid of it." In the same spirit he covered his nineteenth-century house with aluminum siding. "Can't paint it anymore," he said. The house wouldn't need painting for at least twenty years. The clapboards were in magnificent shape. The one square foot that peeled, high up on the north side, bothered Tim. He couldn't live with it. His wife is blamed for the pigeons' removal: she made him get rid of them, the talk goes. At first he must have loved to see them fly out over Jason Heights, and return, swooping down through the pink afterglow, but all Tim's pleasure turned to work, and the work became too much for him. Sometimes he reminds me of myself—after I've revised a poem to death.

He's begun to hate his house. "I'd like to get out of here," he says, his face turning mean and sour, "get a little ranch on a slab, but Marge doesn't want to move." "They'll have to carry me out of here in a box," Marge says, in her confidential whisper.

"I love all weather," said Ridley Good, my neighbor to the east. He was wearing faded vintage polyester, the yellow shirt paler than the inside of a summer squash, the pants gray as wash water. His long, ascetic face tilted toward me. How old is he? I asked myself again. Sixty? Eighty? When Ridley looks at me, his sapphire eyes seem to send out blue beams like flash-lights. If I step closer, I feel as if I am falling into his head. Our Augusts were usually dry, but this August it had been raining for two weeks. When the sun came out, the trunks of the oak trees steamed. "How do you like the rain forest?" I had asked, cutting through his back garden on my way to Robbins Library.

Ridley was an art restorer; he also bought old houses. He'd

never married and lived on Maple Street in the house he'd been born in. All the houses on Maple Street, which backed up to Academy, where I lived, were built on Hornblower land. One by one, Ridley bought the four properties that abutted his land, a collection of nineteenth- and early twentieth-century houses: Gothic cottage; stick style; Greek revival; 1890—what is it?— hip roof, steep center tower, long narrow front porch, a Charles Addams house. There's also an enormous barn with a deep stone cellar. The Tower House, the Greek revival, and my 1941 colonial share one driveway, which seems more like a private street. Ridley let our house go by. It wasn't old enough to interest him.

Before I got to know Ridley, I had sized him up as another bleached-out Yankee who needed his "things." The poet Robert Lowell describes his mother as having "a window-seat, / an electric blanket, / a silver hot water bottle / monogrammed like a hip-flask, / Italian china fruity / with bunches and berries / and proper *putti*." That's all they have left, I would think, their class goods. Who buys these things? I would ask myself as I thumbed through the Winterthur catalog: gold-leafed cachepots, tiny Limoges porcelain boxes, needlepoint pillows with the patterns of tulips and hibiscus, another porcelain box, this one in the shape of a cat, modeled after one that supposedly belonged to Madame de Pompadour. Her name was a selling point. Yankees with nothing better to do, I would say. Or people who wanted to be Yankees. Ridley just needed bigger things.

His full-time man, Jim McCullife, took charge of the houses. Jim was a master carpenter; he'd hire people to do such jobs as pointing chimneys, repairing roof slates, replacing copper flashing. They'd get the outsides into shape—roofs, clapboards, shingles, slates, gutters, chimney. Those houses were tight. No rotting sills.

The exterior trim was complicated: gingerbread on the Gothic cottage, fluted pillars on the Greek revival, a maze of sticks on the porch of the 1890: Jim could cut wood any way. The rhythm of his work was unhurried but not slack. He was as old as Ridley and had learned not to exhaust himself. He liked what he did. From my windows, I'd watch the pieces come together. Jim would stand back and appreciate his carpentry. A friend of mine who had once worked as a laborer on a construction job told me that appreciating was not allowed. If any man stood back to look at his work, he was screamed at. The men were not allowed to sit down when they drank their coffee.

After years of work on the exteriors, Ridley would finally send Jim inside. Jim would put in new ceilings. He'd take down the plaster on the interior walls and lay in insulation. He'd rip out the awful accretions of half-measure kitchens and bathrooms, rickety cabinets, and partitions. Then the energy would go out of the job, and he and Ridley would find some more exterior work to do. Two of the houses were filled with Jim's equipment. He was a haunter of yard sales. He seemed to have two of everything: lathes, jigsaws, band saws, routers, drill presses, table saws, reciprocating saws. Another house held Ridley's picture frames. Only the Gothic cottage was rented. "He likes things, not people," I used to say.

Actually Ridley loves what he loves with ardent devotion. "Look at the columbines," he'll call to me. "They're just about my favorite flower. They look as if they've just alighted, those spurs of color, airy." I gaze with him into the flowers' intricate kaleidoscope geometry: cream, maroon, yellow. "Come here," Ridley orders, drawing me into the garage. "I asked for some annuals, and they sent me these." On the table: flats of globe marigolds the color of cooked carrots. "They looked dyed, I'm sending them back." Ridley shuddered.

The breeze lifted; the columbines danced against the lattice of the back porch. A trumpet vine covered a trellis. Ridley planted it to draw hummingbirds. He's waiting for them, "They used to come. None yet this year," he says patiently. Columbines. Hummingbirds. Exquisite. Dazzling. Sexed jewels. In Massachusetts, it would be the ruby-throated hummingbird: a din of wings, a flash of red and iridescent green. Have you heard one? It made my hackles rise. I thought a bee had gotten into my ear.

Ridley restores paintings out of doors to avoid the build-up of Xylol and acetone fumes. His worktable is a length of plywood set on sawhorses. He's outside in all seasons. In good weather there are always two lawn chairs set out for guests. His customers come to him with grayed-over portraits of their ancestors. Ridley will bring out the color. He'll find the charming detail, a bit of lace, a birthstone freed from fog and murk, a half smile. "I like her," he'll say, as he swabs, cleaning, cleaning. Cotton batting permeated with acetone blows across the grass under the trumpet vine. "The mediocre can have charm," he'll say. He cleans whatever he's brought without complaint, but he never confuses quality with mediocrity. He worked in Venice after the floods of 1967. A Gauguin sailed into his back garden for cleaning. John and I, hoes and rakes on our shoulders, were heading for the vegetable garden—Ridley had let us use some of his land. He looked up from his worktable, his long head rising over the trumpet vine. "Oh, look, peasants," he laughed. "Come and see this."

The rain's stopped. When I cut through Ridley's garden early this morning I saw that he had already been out working and gone in. There were still drops of water wobbling on the full sheet of gray-green painted plywood that made his table. His magnifying goggles sat among the drops. Ridley never wiped rain off his table. Cotton swabs were stuck in the thickets of the yew. I caught him on my way back, or rather he caught me. A large black Mercedes sedan pulled out of the driveway. Someone had just dropped off a painting. The world came to Ridley's back garden. "I love the provinces," he once said to me in his teasing way. Ridley did not drive. He had a regular driver at the local cab company. I was told that he once took a taxi to New York. He had his groceries—I wondered what they were—delivered from the two unctuous brothers who owned Stevens Market. They sold beautiful meat, but I couldn't imagine Ridley biting into a loin lamb chop or a rib steak. I had never seen a morsel of food or a glass or cup on Ridley's worktable. I had once offered him a basket of zucchini. He chose a small one, held it uneasily. "This will make my supper," he said.

"Look," he called, "I've got something good." I hadn't seen him for at least a month, and he seemed thinner than usual. His shirt and pants clung to his long narrow body. I moved closer. The clean light shone on a marine painting. The rigging was as fine as spider silk. Above the faint line of the horizon, the sky opened to pink. I looked into the air of the painting. The ship was called "The Mount Hope." Ridley turned on his blue eye beams. His long face tilted upward. His skin was lined, but tawny, gold. "This painter puts in people," he said. "See." On the pier, on the deck, I began to make out tiny dark figures. Ridley handed me his magnifying goggles. There was man with a flattened stove-pipe hat and a sly look. "I'll bring it out," said Ridley. "Marine painting, landscape painting—not quite the right terms. I think these painters got the proportions right. We're not that impor-tant. We are so small. Some marine painters leave out people completely. Eerie. We *are* here. I like the ones with people." He stepped back, I took off the goggles and stepped back with him. I could see the tiny human figures now that I knew where to look.

Ridley picked up a long thin stick and twirled it in a wad of cotton batting. It was time for me to go. Before I stepped onto the path between the garages, I looked back. Ridley was leaning forward over his table, his head tilted down, his cheeks drawn in. With the stick tipped in cotton soaked in acetone, he was carefully, with his light fine touch, stroking the surface of the painting. He took a few steps back, looked at the whole picture, then gently leaned again into his devotion.

Journey

Breaking Up
the Still Life

Every afternoon around five o'clock, the enormous cocktail lounge of the Hotel Nikko in Mexico City would begin to fill up. Sometimes after a day of sightseeing, I would stop for a drink before going up to my room to read and wait for dinner. There were mostly groups of dark-suited Mexican men drinking and talking business with a stylized lightheartedness. The Nikko was Japanese built and owned, but most of the Japanese tourists and businessmen avoided the lounge.

At about seven, more Mexicans would arrive—families, dating couples, groups of friends—and the music would start. The week I was there, an Israeli quartet sang digested international songs accompanied by a synthesizer. There were no deep notes. Their high, bright, nasal voices produced a musical patter of unrelenting cheer, suitable for a "soft" exercise class in Beverly Hills. After each song they would vigorously raise their hands high over their heads as if they had received tumultuous applause.

The lounge on the lower level of the main lobby spread out at the bottom of a deep travertine-faced, steel-buttressed space that just managed to soar despite the improbably jutting angles. We sank into deeply upholstered pale blue chairs and sofas, which were lined up like seats in a train station. The dark heads and shoulders of the customers just showed above the oversized, overstuffed chair and sofa backs, and we looked—small figures at the bottom of this huge space—as if we had just been dropped by an amusement park parachute jump and were adjusting to the effects of a neck-compressing G-force. Perhaps it was the women's long hair that produced this illusion: seen from the back, their necks completely disappeared under their dark hair. Short cuts were not popular with Mexican women.

I'd order the delicious Mexican beer, usually Dos Equis, and read the *Mexico City News*. Every day there would be an air-quality report, which seemed pointless, because the air was either "poor" or "dangerously poor." There had been an article reporting a government proposal to plant thousands of trees as a barrier against the "unhealthy winds" blowing into the city. "Unhealthy winds" was a euphemism for the "fecal dust" that came from open sewage. Shit was blowing through the air, but no one would say so. It was bad for morale, bad for the tourist business. Along with the Mexicans who had money to spend, I was glad to be inside the Nikko lounge, a sort of indoor café.

When traveling in foreign cities, I had to find a place where I could have a slow drink—coffee, mineral water, a beer—and, if I wanted, sit for hours, watching people, reading, writing in my notebook, or simply looking into space. I did a lot of that. Listening to the voices around me made me intensely happy. I'd experience a small triumph of arrival. Coming from a family that had reached America and never moved, I would be thrilled that I had reached a new destination. My mother's mother had always wanted to go to Coney Island. "Joe," she would tell my father, "as soon as you get your car, we'll go." She died before he had his first car. When I took my mother to the Au Bon Pain café in Harvard Square, she would, as she watched the passing parade of students, punks, leftover hippies, say wistfully, "Here you can do what you want. No wonder they don't want to come home. Here you're free."

The places I reached did not have to be beautiful. It was enough that I had arrived. My back would straighten, my shoulders relax. Living *in* culture, I would completely inhabit my body and feel its perimeters as a subtle line of energy, as if indeed I had stood against a sheet of paper and been traced. Shortly after this trip to Mexico I hurt my back; the pain kept me at home for almost two years. I remember saying to my doctor at Spaulding Rehabilitation Hospital in Boston, "I just want to be able to lift a cup of tea to my mouth, to move from the sink to the stove in my kitchen, to sip a beer in a café and watch people." My dream of moving again, rising, walking, pausing, stopping for an hour to watch and write in my notebook drew me back to the world, to civilization.

Chekhov wrote home to Russia from Nice, "Culture juts out of every shop window, every wicker basket, every dog smells of civilization." I hadn't had to go as far as Nice. Culture had thrilled me ever since I was a child stepping into my grand-mother Molly's kitchen. There I had felt culture, both hers and ours, European and American. The things in Molly's kitchen jutted out at me: her coffee grinder, the little white enamel pot with its black handle, the strawberries simmering in that pot, reducing to thick jam, the yellow batter of her sponge cake, her jars of spices, her knife worn to a flake, the Jewish newspaper open on the table, the black "carving" of the Hebrew letters, the radio with its glowing yellow-green dial, Bing Crosby singing "I'm Dreaming of a White Christmas." Vigorous life, refined but not eviscerated. Call it civilization. Travel is longing. I sought the soul of home. And always with me was the first home, the source.

I grew adept at identifying culture, even the hotel universality of the "hospitality bar" in our room. Every inch of its white in-terior was filled with icy goodies: little vials of Scotch, bourbon, rum, vodka, gin, vermouth, half bottles of beer, bars of Swiss chocolates, chocolate-covered cherries, packets of mints, caskets of nuts, four kinds of sugared fruit juice. The makings of a quick fix gleamed in red, black, and gold wrappers. Everything was in miniature and cost an unbelievable sum, even the mineral water.

• • • • •

The next day, I decided to take the subway downtown. Passing the lined-up taxis outside the hotel, I cut through a small park that faced the Reforma. Because construction had blocked off the pedestrian crossway, a temporary bridge built of planks and staging had been constructed over the busy road. I followed the fast-walking Mexicans up the stairs and across the rickety-looking bridge, trying not to look down between the planks to the roaring traffic below.

Although there were streams of people crossing the Reforma, I was not prepared for the crowds in the subway. Hundreds of thousands of people—there are more than twenty million people in Mexico City—moved patiently through the giant underground. Almost everyone was carrying something: shopping bags, notebooks, books, shabby suitcases, frayed briefcases, flowers. There were carpenters carrying levels, hammers, saws, packets of nails; there were painters carrying brushes and buckets of paint; there were masons with trowels, electricians with toolboxes, plumbers with snakes and wrenches. There were young boys selling ballpoint pens, old women selling candy, young men selling lottery tickets. And in the midst of all this selling and carrying, a blind beggar would somehow move through the crowded car, singing as he went.

Every other person was carrying a baby. In Mexico you are a baby until you are three or four years old, and babies are carried. All the time I was there, I saw only one baby carriage. Mothers, fathers, sisters, brothers, and grandmothers all carry babies. On the subway, mothers would often hold the babies while the fathers offered them a drink from a clear plastic bag wrapped tightly around a straw. (At home, you sometimes see children carrying goldfish from the pet store in such bags.) When they weren't eating or drinking, the babies would be sound asleep, their sweating heads pressed against someone's chest. They rarely cried. A young Indian mother with long braided hair had her two-year-old daughter bound to her hip by a dark blue rebozo. The lower part of the child's body, from the waist down, was hidden by the shawl; she didn't seem to have any legs. She sat up straight so that her large head was parallel to her mother's. They looked as if they had both sprung out of the same pelvis and were sharing one pair of legs.

The stops in the Mexico City subway were marked by pictures as well as names—for the illiterate. We passed Patriotismo, Chapúltepec, Sevilla, Insurgentes, Cuauhtémoc, Balderas, Salto del Agua, Isabel la Católica—there was also Barranca del Muerto, the Ravine of the Dead—names that I liked to believe were more evocative to Mexicans than the Boston subway's Park, Boylston, Arlington, Copley, Auditorium, and Kenmore were to us back home in New England.

Outside the Pino Suarez station, were posters supporting Cuauhtémoc Cardenas, who was running as the leftist opposition candidate against the revolutionary party, the PRI, in power since the twenties. His father, Lázaro Cárdenas, a former president of Mexico, had named him after the last Aztec emperor, a hero to many Mexicans. Both the right and the left were insisting that the PRI rigged elections by stuffing the ballots; "made them pregnant with tacos" was the idiom.

From the station, I walked north along a narrow treeless street of crumbling buildings with store windows filled with the same faded gray shirts, pants, and aprons. Ahead of me was the Zócalo. The immense space, next to Red Square, the largest square in the world, was filled with gray fumes, as if a canister of gas had just been exploded. Dizzy from the smog and the heat, I made my way toward the cathedral by walking under the colonnade that framed the east side of the square. No one ventured out into the steaming open space. In contrast, the buildings bordering the Zócalo looked like tiny blocks slipping off the edge of the plaza.

. . . . .

The marble floor of the Catedral Metropolitana sloped and rippled. Built over a lake, like most of Mexico City, the church was shifting as it sank. I didn't know whether the recent earthquake had additionally undermined the foundation. Avoiding the gilded giant credenza of the main altar, I found myself at a shrine dedicated to Our Lady of Zapopán. In a painting above the small altar, the saint rose out of a black horn-shaped moon tipped with stars. Her tiny doll-like face was concentrated under a minute crown of stars, and her flat robe stuck out in a triangular shape from her shoulders as if the robe hung from precise poles. In the middle of her chest was a gold medallion, thin as a wafer. The small saint seemed to be drawing energy up from the black moon into her wicklike dowager empress slipper-shod feet, up through her chest, into the galvanized knob of her face. An Indian couple gave me a curious look. I was staring like an idiot. I was transported. It must be the heat, I thought. Or the altitude. I just need something to look at.

Strolling counterclockwise around the perimeter of the church, I came to a chapel near the door that was getting a lot of action. There were mostly young men in the chapel. Just at the head of a broad short flight of stairs was a large crucifix. The entire body was dull matte black and looked as if it had been burned. I expected to smell ashes. Christ's overlong arms were spread like the wings of some giant seabird, and his tense angular torso, with its fragile-looking ribs, strained out from the cross. The face of the *Cristo Negro* was hidden by a mess of wild dark dusty hair that had a burned reddish tinge. I got down on my knees along with everyone else, looking up into the hidden face, trying to see something. The larger-than-life Christ filled the chapel. I felt as though I were trapped in a cage with a wild animal that had been subdued but was still alive: malevolent and crazed by pain. The men on their knees looked alert, excited, and afraid. The hackles rose on my neck as if a cold wind had passed. My heart raced in wonder. The voices hummed in prayer. This was the apotheosis. They were deifying Him now. Working Him over. Their words seemed to mold spirit. We spun on the wheel.

There was an Indian woman with white hair and a deeply lined face, begging just outside the church door. I didn't have any small money, so I gave her a handful of subway tickets. *Mamacita*, little mother, she called me, touching me lightly with her rough bent hand. I thought of her all day between my bouts of dizziness.

• • • • •

On Saturday morning, a middle-aged shoeshine man dressed in dark blue pants and light blue shirt like a bus driver's uniform unfolded his portable stand in a plaza near the Mercado de la Merced. The entire outfit—the customer's chair with its padded seat, the attached sunshade, the work stool—were all bright red. The chair had a built-in drawer under the seat; the stool, which was also a supply chest, was decorated with pasted-on diamond-shaped mirrors. On the sidewalk next to the stool were a half a dozen dented pots, a round bushy paintbrush, a smaller brush with a pointed tip, two oblong polishing brushes, a bunch of rags, and a shallow tin can, which served as an ashtray.

The first customer of the day arrived, an elderly man wearing worn, neatly pressed clothes and a crisp panama hat. He declined the newspaper that the shoeshine man offered him and with an approving encouraging expression watched the man begin work. First the shoeshine man slipped in a pair of shields to protect the customer's socks. They stuck up on either side of his ankles like orthopedic devices. Then with elaborate serious motions he dusted and soaped the ancient shoe as if he were going to shave it. At least five minutes had gone by. After the shoe was washed and rinsed to his satisfaction, he applied the oily polish; the shoe darkened and dried in the warm air. Moving smoothly from the waist without any strain, the shoeshine man brushed the shoe over and over again. That will last a week, I thought. But he wasn't finished yet. Dipping into a different can, he coated the shoe with a second polish and brushed and brushed until the shoe gleamed. Then a third layer of polish. This time he looped a rag around the back of the shoe and pulled it back and forth until it squeaked. The customer noted each stage of the job with approving chatter. The shoeshine man smoked as he worked, placing the cigarette in the shallow tin can with its lighted tip facing out. Dipping the small pointed brush into the smallest of his pots, he deftly painted the edge of the sole and the outside of the heel. After the dye had dried, he gave the shoe its final brushing and began on the second shoe. When he was finally finished, he took the customer's money with a matter-of-fact, I've-seen-it-all expression on his heavy face. The old man walked away with a light step. His shoes looked new.

In between jobs, the shoeshine man would sit in the customer's seat, reading the newspaper, but the breaks were short because it was Saturday morning, and many men wanted their shoes shined. A surly-looking man in his thirties arrived with his wife and daughter, who silently withdrew to wait on the low stone wall that edged the small grassy square under the trees. The customer grabbed the newspaper and held it in front of his face. Every once in a while he'd glance suspiciously over the paper and grunt. Step by step the shoeshine man massaged his shoes. After about ten minutes, the surly customer put down the paper and began to speak quite pleasantly. He wasn't smiling, but his face had softened.

Again with that same taciturn I-know-what-I-know look, the shoeshine man took his money. *He* had not been changed. Seeing his skill predictably work its transformation on the shoes and on the customers, he had grown bored. Did he look for surprises: the customer who could not be made happier, the shoe that would not yield to its rebirth? He was a superb technician, a masterful shrink who had become cynical. He needs a vision of himself, I thought, a story of transformation and redemption. Maybe he needs to polish women's shoes. (Only gringuitas had their shoes polished.) American to the core, I ended with: he should be making thousands.

• • • • •

Guillermo was the leader of the tour to the Pyramids of Teotihuacán just north of Mexico City. A friend, who was back in Mexico for the first time since 1960, decided to join me for the trip, and as we made the rounds of hotels, picking up passengers, Nancy happened to mention to Guillermo that there were no longer any pulquerías in Mexico City. Guillermo seemed startled by the mention of pulque, an alcoholic drink made from the maguey plant. On our way out to the Pyramids, he kept interrupting his rambling tour speech with uneasy references to the maguey.

The microphone sent out hair-raising high-pitched squeaks, and finally Guillermo decided to do without it. "Can you hear me?" he kept asking. As soon as he began to speak, he would twitch. Then I noticed that his twitching had a complicated pattern. His left arm would shoot out, his left hand would quickly move from the wrist as if he were maniacally screwing in a light bulb and then somehow end up behind his back. At this point, he would usually pivot, and we could see that the wild hand was lodged between his shoulder blades in a yogilike twist. The elaborate tic had a rhythm; you could dance to it. Guillermo must have had Tourette's syndrome and had somehow harnessed the tics to animate his speech. He spoke with a volatile rushing speed that did not match his age. Guillermo looked past seventy; he said that he had been in the tour business for more than fifty years.

We passed through squatters' villages made up of low one-story hovels set on white unhealthy-looking dust. "This makes me feel very bad," said Guillermo. His arm shot out, and the hand twirled—this time with a magicianlike flourish. I expected to see a theatrical tear roll down his aged Pierrot's face.

His obsession with the maguey plant was explained as we pulled into the parking lot of El Maguey. With the pinnacles of the pyramids tantalizingly in view, Guillermo explained that we would be treated to a lecture on the virtues of the maguey plant and then would be free to browse in the shop. He assured us that we were under no obligation to buy. He seemed embarrassed. The owner, from whom Guillermo would collect a kickback, poured out tequila for the tourists. My touch of turista had put me off alcohol, and I went to find a shady place where I could munch on my rice cakes in peace. Nancy, who had listened to the maguey lecture given by the shop's owner, told me that she had learned something. She held up the sharp point of a leaf that was attached to a long thread. "You draw the needle and the fiber all in one piece from the plant. Nifty." "Great," I answered. "I bet a lot of Mexicans sew that way. If I'm ever in the desert and I need to sew a button on my Girl Scout uniform . . ." Carefully wrapping up her "needle and thread," she urged me to come and see the donkey.

The maguey expert was leading the group toward a donkey tied to a tree. He asked if everyone had their cameras ready. Then he stuck an open bottle of beer in the donkey's mouth. The animal lifted its head and sucked down the beer. "Doesn't he get drunk?" asked a California woman who was dressed in bright pink; around her puff of bleached hair she wore a white bandana-sunshade with a tiny lace border like a baby's hat. The Mexican shrugged. The ground was littered with bottles. The donkey had bloodshot eyes.

Inside the shop were dusty looms that hadn't been used in years. There were piles of luridly colored factory-made blankets and tables and tables of crudely made trays, machine-carved "figurines" of lifeless-looking animals and birds. Everything looked like everything else. There were thousands and thousands of things. I bought a bottle of mineral water. Nancy bought two of the ugly blankets for her boss in the States. "They're hideous," she said, "but they're exactly what he asked for, and for once I'm going to give him what he asks for. Who am I to judge? He'll love them." I smiled, and we both laughed at our temporary magnanimity.

Finally we got to the pyramids and the first blue sky I had seen in a week.

· · · · ·

The Mexican artist Frida Kahlo wore her long thick black hair Tehuana style: pulled up straight above the ears, up off her forehead, and wound with wide ribbons into a large braided crown. Sometimes the crown would be stuck with sprays of tinsel flowers, or stiff bows. Emily Dickinson was always crowning herself—the word "diadem" appears in so many of her poems. Her coronation was a kind of spiritual affirmation. Kahlo liked the actual weight on her head.

There was no such thing as too much. She would wear a large ring—silver and onyx, gold and amethyst, silver and jade, silver and obsidian—on each of her fingers except the thumbs. On those she wore thin gold wires. Her long Tehuana skirt had bands of gold and orange, and satin-stitched flowers in yellow, white, pink, burned red, blue-purple, and more gold. When she had still been able to go out to parties, she would remove the everyday gold caps on her upper incisors and replace them with "dress" caps set with rose diamonds! Her smile must have had a barbaric glitter.

In one of her self-portraits she stares out at the viewer with a wary, sober, unsmiling expression stripped of conventional charm. She is not tranquil. The thin red ribbons, which encircle but do not quite touch her long neck, have an ironic curl. She has painted in her heavy black untweezed eyebrows; they meet above her nose. She has also painted in her distinct moustache. A pet monkey looks over her shoulder; his eyes have the same wariness; his long-fingered hairy hands curl around her shoulders. She has posed herself as a tense madonna, the monkey her holy baby. Kahlo had longed to have a child, had become pregnant, and had experienced a gruesome miscarriage.

Kahlo had been crippled by childhood polio and then by a terrible bus accident when she was eighteen. Her right leg, pelvis, collarbone, ribs, and spine had been crushed and broken, and she had been impaled by the steel guardrail of the bus. The impact of the crash had somehow ripped away all her clothes, and a sack of dry gold paint carried by a workman had broken open, spilling gold powder over her naked body. She recovered from the accident. Although Kahlo walked with difficulty, for a number of years she still managed to lead a full life. She gave herself to her many friends and lovers with a passion that sometimes overwhelmed them. Kahlo married the painter Diego Rivera in 1929, traveled widely, and became a painter in her own right. But in her last few years—she died in 1954 at the age of forty-seven—the effects of her injuries more and more crippled and confined her. The year before she died, her right leg was amputated. Some doctors are now saying that it was spina bifida, undiagnosed, that ultimately crippled Frida. Whatever the cause, the pain tormented her. She became addicted to morphine. Worn out by the struggle, she took a suicidal overdose of drugs. On the night she died, Kahlo wrote in her journal "Viva la vida" (long live life).

In Kahlo's house at Londres 127 in the Coyoacán section of Mexico City, which her Jewish immigrant father built in 1904, the single bed where she painted looks out from the cool narrow hall to the garden below. A door-sized wooden canopy spans the four posters and would look like a lid except for the large mirror over the pillow.

Next to Kahlo's daybed is a small worktable that holds pencils, bottles of ink, bottles of nail polish, pastels, and a round makeup mirror with a white plastic rim like the kind you can still buy in the CVS store. Often plastered into an orthopedic corset, which kept her flat on her back, Kahlo needed to have her painting tools within easy reach.

A panel of dreary official portraits of Kahlo's saints, Engels, Marx, Lenin, Stalin, and Mao, deadens the wall above the bed. (There is no picture of Trotsky, who had been her lover and who lived in this house under Kahlo's and Rivera's protection from 1937 until 1939. Kahlo left the Party in the thirties but was later readmitted when she renounced her former anti-Stalinism.)

The daybed is echoed by an almost identical nightbed in the adjoining room, but instead of a mirror attached to the similar lidlike canopy, there's a black-framed window of iridescent blue butterflies. A Christmas tree ornament, dark blue and big as a grapefruit, hangs from the end of the canopy along with a frightening papier-mâché skeleton, only one of the many Day of the Dead figures that Kahlo and Rivera collected. Embroidered on the pillow: "Despierta Corazón Dormido" (wake, sleeping heart).

The names of the six people closest to her in these last years are painted on the pink wall of her bedroom.

Kahlo bought and arranged almost everything in the house in Coyoacán. Her students, who came to the house for classes, said that Kahlo had them arrange and rearrange her dining room and kitchen things as exercises in design. She loved to buy, and had a knack for choosing, objects that are uncannily alive. On a mirrored chest of drawers, a combination altar and miniature theater, a smirking pottery pig plops down next to a pair of white porcelain hands that look as if they've been cut off a bloodless saint. A tiny ship made of gold wire and pink seashells sails toward an open black and gold fan. There are cunning thimble-sized coyotes carved out of obsidian, a white stone frog so cleverly made that you believe it will leap. In the yellow-and-blue-tiled kitchen, which Kahlo designed, are green-glazed pots with covers like curled-back maguey leaves, a pottery tray with a dark shiny glaze and a deeply crimped edge like a pie just out of the oven. The wooden floor of the dining room is painted violet. On green shelves, on yellow shelves, are cheap blue glass vases covered with little white "tits," cat vases, pigeon pitchers, rabbit jars, duck jars. She liked things in twos: pairs of green and blue plates, pairs of brown luster mugs, pairs of chicken-yellow cups.

On those mornings when she had been well enough to paint but found that for some reason the work just would not come, she would go to the local market and return home with her purchases. She would fill the dining room vases with flowers— she wouldn't arrange the flowers but would just stuff them into the vases. Then she'd lay out the things she had bought, a sugar skull, a white straw horse, a frail wagon hitched to a fat ox. Friends would arrive. She'd have her own animals around her: the pack of hairless energetic Aztec dogs; Caimito de Guayabal, the monkey; Bonito, the parrot (Gertrude Caca Blanca, the pet osprey, was kept in the garden). Rivera would leave his studio in the adjoining suburb of San Angel and join her for a lunch of chicken or fish, tortillas, and guacamole. And together they'd break up the still life.

· · · · ·

Just before sunset in San Miguel de Allende, a wild troupe lurid with shabby glitter—shabby because they were poor— broke into the respectable scene of family strollers in the square in front of the pink stone church called the Parroquia. My heart lifted. The masked and costumed dancers who led the procession spread out and began to waltz and then to samba to the music provided by the beat-up band of mariachis. It took me a while to realize that the dancers were all men. The ones dressed as women wore huge, cone-shaped falsies; every once in a while a long skirt would lift to reveal a hairy muscular leg. One man, wearing a devilish Aristotle Onassis mask with painted-on slicked-back gray hair, danced alone, smoking a cigarette in a holder. The green and the yellow masks seemed to have been lifted right out of the jungle. All the faces—monkeys, parrots, whores, devils, skulls, clowns, angels, princes, princesses with hectic rouged cheeks—were unnaturally still above the swaying bodies. One man held a gyrating puppet; he spun one way, the puppet another. No one went unmasked, and no one stopped dancing, sealing the illusion.

A wavering double line of little girls trailed from the edge of the plaza around the corner of the church. They all wore yellow dresses; the white collars were tattered; buttons were missing; bows were undone, but the uniform yellow held everything together, the yellow and the black straw hats with strings hanging from each neck and resting flat across the shoulder blades.

Old men who had lined up against the iron fence in front of the church watched the dancers with suspicious curiosity. Just as the music picked up and the dancers bobbed more wildly, an enormous flock of magpies—they looked like a black funnel—whirled into the square and disappeared into the tightly pruned box-shaped fig trees that bordered the park, forming a dense hedge held up by thin whitewashed trunks. Occasionally bird shit dropped from the trees onto the crowded benches below. No one seemed to mind. The church bells rang nine times, and the dancers, the band, and the little girls walked off into the dark.

Bad Women:

A Visit with Jean Rhys

On the day I arrived in London I walked down Frognal Lane to Church Row and then cut across the High Street of Hampstead. As I came down Flask Walk, I heard the furious voice of a woman and the loud pitiful sobbing of a child. I had left my son, David, at home in Arlington for these two weeks, our longest separation, and I found myself staring at mothers with their children. This mother and child were in back of me; I could feel their voices break against my neck. We came abreast as we stopped for the traffic, and they overtook me when we crossed the road into Hampstead Heath. The woman was thin and tall. She looked about twenty. Her hair was blonde, and she had painted her face black around the eyes—the punk look in 1977. A jack-o'-lantern with the candle blown out. She wore high spiked heels, a flowered skirt that came to her knees, and a short black leather jacket. As she spoke, she swung a small handbag, a pouch with long drawstrings. She was beautiful—something of the model about her—but her bony face was terrible. I couldn't tell if her eyes were blue or black. I had seen blue eyes turn black with rage. And she raged. The child had stopped sobbing and was crying quietly. The mother was walking furiously ahead of the child, and the child was trying to catch up. She carried a doll under one arm; its legs flopped against her delicate hips. She was about seven or eight. I couldn't see her face, only her straight slim back and slim legs under the flowered cotton dress, which buttoned down the back to the waist. The bow had come undone, and the fine cotton was limp in the humidity of that day. Her blonde hair came to her thin shoulder blades. I don't know what I was thinking, but I followed them. The mother kept changing directions, zigzagging. At one point, she stopped short, and the child walked into her. She bent over her daughter and caught hold of her ear. She shook her. Then she charged ahead of her again, and the child followed doggedly, with determination. She had stopped crying. I wanted to put my hand on the girl's thin shoulder and tell her, "Don't worry. When you grow up . . ." I didn't yet have the right words for the mother, and I hadn't been brave enough to stop her. But I saw who she was—a woman.

It was 1977, and I was in England to interview the novelist Jean Rhys, whose work was the subject of my doctoral dissertation.

Born in Dominica in the West Indies, Rhys had left home for England, worked as a chorus girl, married, had a daughter who was raised by her husband's family, lived in Paris in the twenties, published, disappeared, was rediscovered, and became famous with the appearance of her extraordinary novel *Wide Sargasso Sea*. In 1977 Rhys was still an outsider, a woman who had lived a shady life and wrote flawlessly about shamed women.

I would be staying until Saturday with Yvonne and Bob, two writer friends who had rented an apartment in West Hampstead in the house where Evelyn Waugh had been born. It was an ordinary brick house, too narrow for its height, jammed in a row at the top of the hill. The attic apartment was anonymous and modern except for the flowers. There were bunches and bunches of vivid anemones jammed in vases, in glasses, in cups, in bottles:

scarlet, black, and yellow. Yvonne's extravagance was thrilling. If I hesitated about a dress or a blouse when we went shopping together, she would cry out with angry impatience, "Buy it!"

The last time I had seen Yvonne we had spent a weekend together in Boston, walking the brick-lined Back Bay, stopping for endless cups of tea and coffee, talking with a mixture of confidence and anxiety about our writing. We had tried to figure out how we—as writers—fitted into this century. Yvonne, who had been born in '46, believed that her generation was elegiac: "We are near the end of the century, explaining, trying to understand what happened to us. We keep looking back—with loss. We are not like Gertrude Stein, creating the twentieth century."

"That's true," I responded, "we're minor."

Yvonne shuddered. "Oh, don't say *minor*."

I smiled, then grew immodest. "We may not be creating new forms, but we're still trying to live freely, to have experience— like Katherine Mansfield, like Jean Rhys in the twenties. That's brave, isn't it? We seem to have to relive all the old struggles." I told her that I had been thinking about the paper Virginia Woolf had read to the Women's Service League in 1930. Unlike the feminine ideal she had been brought up to emulate, that of the utterly unselfish woman, the "Angel in the House," Woolf realized that she did not have to live on her charm. "How freeing that must have been: to understand that you don't have to be *nice*," I said. "And her image is so violent: she grabs the angel by the throat and strangles her. Woolf was angry, all right; it doesn't show in her pictures—she looks so ethereal."

"I don't think she ate much," Yvonne said. We both looked at our clean plates and laughed.

"She was still hung up, but she knew what the problem was: she said she couldn't write about her 'own experiences as a body.' She couldn't write freely about physical life. Maybe that's what I'll be able to do someday," I said to Yvonne. "Maybe that's where I fit into things."

Soon after I arrived at her London apartment, Yvonne cleared the table for lunch, moving the pile of thick black-and-red-bound notebooks to the bookcase and sweeping up her papers. She had just come back from France, and her description of Paris typed on the yellow legal pad paper began with lilacs. As she bent over the table, laying out the pâté and a plate of sliced tomatoes, her thick brown hair, which was just beginning to gray, hung straight down on either side of her face and seemed to encase rather than frame her head. She was very thin—too thin.

While we were drinking our coffee, a large brown-and-orange Angora cat with a huge fluffy tail appeared at the window. Bob explained that he and Yvonne had found the cat starving on the roof outside the living room window. He was sure that it had belonged to the previous tenants. The cat would climb up and down four stories across roofs and terraces and spent most of his time in the back garden. Bob absentmindedly spooned out a can of cat food and put the plate down on the floor near his feet. The cat ate without stopping. After he was done, he looked huge and lordly. Because I was allergic to cats, he had to be put out. Bob seemed afraid to pick him up, and I hesitated, not knowing the animal. Yvonne forcefully picked up the cat. Glaring at Bob as if to say, "You're a man, this is what you should be doing," she firmly set the cat down on the roof outside the window.

Later that afternoon, she and I had tea at Louie's on the High Street in Hampstead. Yvonne had been reading Willa Cather's *Song of the Lark,* and as I tried out the rich English cream and pale green gooseberry flan, eating very slowly, she began talking about Thea Kronborg, Cather's heroine: "She's an *anima woman.* I find that term useful. Sometimes, I think that they have been sent into my life to cause me pain. They bring you love and adoration; you are glad to be loved and admired, especially since you've reached thirty; then they sleep with your lover and they keep on wanting to be loved. They take everything and they don't understand why anyone should be angry. They get what they want from men, and men either see everything in them, or see right through them. Mostly they see everything."

She asked me if anyone had written about this from the point of view of the betrayed woman. "Colette," I answered. "But that was friendship between women who slept with the same man, not about women who loved each other first. And not about a woman who felt herself charmed and deceived by a beautiful woman." Yvonne was looking down, staring at the gooseberry flan. "This sounds so literary," she said. "I've been talking about Mary Lou and Bob. It was awful." She gave me a significant look, "I couldn't bear to go through that again." She doesn't trust him, I thought, and she is afraid of me.

At the table next to us were a mother and daughter, and a baby in his stroller. His cheeks were ruddy, and his hair pale blond. He was squirming and fussing; his face was flushed and he was ready to scream. Just in time, his grandmother unbuckled the strap, lifted him from his chair onto the leather banquette, and plopped a sugar cube into his bright red mouth. He sucked and coughed—the shock of sugar. Mother and daughter smiled, looking into each other's eyes, indulgent and knowing, having offered the baby—after ignoring him—a surprising comfort. They laughed, connected. The baby smiled.

The day before I was to leave for my visit with Rhys in Devon, I decided to have tea at Harrods. A balding man with a dim face played genteel music on the piano. There were so many tinkling runs I couldn't hear the melody. The large pink room was crowded with middle-aged shoppers and tourists like myself who wanted to "experience" tea but for one reason or another had decided against Claridge's or the Connaught. There was also the occasional child being given a special treat. For less than two pounds you could have all you wanted from the heaped buffet.

Directly across from me, at the table in front of the French windows was a group of women. I am trying to remember each one. Five friends meeting for tea, perhaps to celebrate. I couldn't place them, their class, their lives. They seemed to be in their late twenties, early thirties. Four of them wore pale cotton sundresses with full skirts that came midcalf; all of them were wearing the "new" daring high-heeled shoes. Back home we were still triumphantly celebrating the comfortable shoes that had come in with the women's movement. I was shocked to see in England how quickly things had already turned around. The women looked like actresses or show girls, delicate-faced and bold-faced. Their conversation rose and fell; I didn't catch much. They were gorgeous, and I watched the movements of their bare arms. I decided that they were school friends.

The fairest had a baby. He sat in his highchair and ate cakes, one after the other. When he got restless, his mother lifted him out and let him walk. When he became tired of that, she would reach into her bag and pull out a toy or take him on her lap, and then after a while he would squirm and get down again. He didn't go to the other women, although some of them talked to him. That's how I heard his name, "Ben, Ben, what do you want now?" His mother picked him up and went to find a toilet. She passed near my seat. In fact, I looked into her face, pale gold line of brows, a small pale violet mouth, upturned nose, and thick expertly cut shoulder-length hair. She was so close I could see the shades of color in her hair: silver, gold, and brown. Ben was pressed against her party dress, against the low-cut heart-shaped scallop; her shoulders bent forward with the strain of his weight. He was about three years old and wore sturdy oxfords that swung heavily and clumsily against his mother's slender thighs.

While she and Ben were gone, one of her friends, who wore a white short-sleeved pantsuit, much gold around her neck, began to talk quickly and vehemently: "She gives him everything he wants. Just has to ask and she hands it to him, and he doesn't stop from morning to night. All the way over here in the car, it was Ben, Ben, Ben!" When Ben and his mother came back, the friends composed their faces into a blank placidity. From her thoughtful and sadly wary expression, you could tell that she sensed that they had been talking about her. When she spoke, there was a tremor in her voice.

She had been judged and isolated. Perhaps, they were jealous of Ben; perhaps they missed her attention. It came down to the old truth: unless you had a child, you could not imagine what it was like. She was now separated from her friends as her own mother had once been separated from her; and she could have warned them in the same way her mother had once warned her: "Just wait till you have kids of your own. Then you'll know what it's like."

The next morning, Paddington Station was crowded with people leaving for the weekend. As I stood in the long line waiting to reserve a seat, I began to realize the seriousness of this holiday. It was the Queen's Silver Jubilee. At first I was told that there were no seats. Finally an extra train was put on, and I was able to buy a ticket for Exeter.

A woman entered the compartment with her son, who looked ten or eleven. After hesitating, standing in the middle of all of us for a few minutes, she asked a man to change his seat so she could sit next to her son. She gave the words "my son" a strong, intimate emphasis. This mother and son on the train stood out in their deepest intimacy. The lovers I saw holding hands, kissing, did not seem intimate or tender, nor did the married couples or friends traveling together. Their manners were social. But this mother and son, like the woman and her child at tea in Harrods, were so much together. The way their heads inclined toward each other. Everyone else seemed to be hiding.

When we got to Exeter, I left my baggage at the station and went to call Jean Rhys. The woman who worked for her answered and gave me directions to Cheriton Fitz. She asked me to hold on. I could hear her speaking to Rhys, and Rhys's voice in the background but not her words. I was worried that something had gone wrong, that she wouldn't be able to see me, but no, it was all right for Sunday. I had planned to take a taxi from Exeter, but the woman I spoke to told me to take the bus to Crediton and then a taxi to Cheriton Fitz. The muffled voice in the background stayed with me all day. I was excited to know that Jean Rhys was really there.

That night, I dreamed about Rhys. In one of the dreams, I arrived at a small village, which looked more French than English—Brittany, perhaps. It was a village of women in wartime, the forties. Most of the women were tending shop and wore large shopkeeper's aprons with long ties that wrapped around the waist twice; perhaps the aprons had been left behind by husbands who had gone away to war. I went from woman to woman, trying to find Jean Rhys, asking directions, asking if anyone knew her or had heard of her. Finally, a woman told me that she thought she knew of such a woman; if I wanted, she would take me to her. We walked along a stone pier around the curve of a small harbor, then into a shop. There, my guide introduced me to Jean Rhys, who was sitting in the back of the store among barrels of fish, dried hard as wood, and sacks of grain and dried beans. There was a pungent, salty odor coming from the fish, which stuck out of the barrels in a rough heap. Rhys wore thick brown stockings and stout shoes, but her face was strong-boned and thin, with high cheekbones and blue eyes. Like everything else about her, her hair was in the style of the forties, combed up in front, combed down in back, and held in place by a hair net. Rhys, who had begun publishing in the twenties, literally disappeared during the war. Her novels went out of print. Her professional life stopped.

Just before I woke, I had another dream. I was walking in the country. The grass was brilliant green, like Devon, and the sky a shining, polished blue. I came to a high stone wall with a small round iron door, like the kind you see in illustrations of fairy tales. I was able to look over the high wall. On the green grass was a fierce child dressed in a spotless white dress that reached her thin shins. She clenched her fists and set her jaw, jumping into the wind and dancing defiantly. She had an elfin face like Hawthorne's Pearl or the child Anna in Lawrence's *The Rainbow*. Her elf locks were fine spun gold. She didn't seem quite human. When I questioned her, she told me that her mother and father had sent her away because they could not stand her hunger and rage. She lived in a world without people, in a meadow that was always green, always spring; her dress never got dirty; she lived on spider's silk. She wanted to drink milk. We needed each other, she and I. She wanted to get out so she could grow old and die, so she could love me. Her heart was small and cold, she said. I decided to free her, to teach her to bend and break, if she would teach me to be true, inviolate, straight to the mark. For those things, I would need her will. I already understood how to be human. Since I had been in the world, I knew what she must hide, and I told her not to hiss like a snake or bare her teeth. The bargain was struck. I moved toward the gate, and she quickly warned me, "No, don't touch it, it's dangerous. I can fly out." I asked her why she hadn't flown out before. "Someone had to come to rescue me," she answered. Marveling at her blonde hair and amazing face—strongly sculpted adult bones, tight child's skin—I noticed that she had an English accent.

On Sunday morning, Exeter was shut up tight. In England a holiday was a holiday: no business. I went back to the cathedral close where I had seen flowers for sale. The shop was closed; the tearoom was closed. I tried Exeter's two hotels, hurrying so I wouldn't miss the bus. No flowers. Nothing. All I had for Rhys was a copy of one of my books. I got to the bus just in time. It turned out that I was the only passenger. On the outskirts of Exeter, we passed the first-class Imperial Hotel. I was sure that they would have flowers, but it was too late; the bus went on.

At the stop in Crediton, I looked for a taxi. The High Street showed me its blank face. A woman with short, badly bleached hair and a ragged mouth told me that I wouldn't find a taxi: "There are none today." Her tone was spiteful. At last, I found an open garage; a man came out of the back room and offered to give me a lift. I'd come too long a way to miss this meeting with Jean Rhys, but I didn't trust the man. He was looking me up and down, a calculating expression on his face. "If I don't find a cab, I'll be back in fifteen minutes," I said.

I walked up the High Street again and finally saw another person. He was dressed in a tweed vest and tweed pants, a leather jacket—a cap, a walking stick, a bent back. "Just walk back the way you've come," he said. "There's an alley on your right, next to the pub, walk in and ring the bell." I did. It was just as he said. A small red sign, five inches wide, two inches high: TAXI. The driver came to the door with a full mouth, holding a napkin in his hand. He swallowed, "Of course, I know where that is. Just be a moment." When I came out, I realized that I was just across the street from the garage where the shifty man had offered me a ride. I had come to the taxi office by the back way.

We drove through fields. The roads narrowed. Every space seemed tended. There were flowers in the hedgerows and occasionally on the side of the road the purple-pink spikes of gladiolas. We passed through tiny villages with cottages decorated with flags and banners for the Jubilee celebration. In seconds, we were back in the fields. The cows raised their heads as we passed; we seemed to be driving straight into the glowing green. The roads became even narrower, the hedgerows higher. Now the driver stopped and blew the horn before taking a curve. The trees grew close to the road. The freshly turned-over earth was red and rich. Devon dirt.

We stopped at a small whitewashed cottage. There were no decorations for the Jubilee. Jean Rhys had sent me directions: "With your back to the pub called the Half Moon, go straight ahead." We hadn't come past the pub, but there was, as she had written, a large trailer parked next to the house, which was deep below the level of the road. The cottage was so small that over-night guests had to use the trailer. Jean Rhys's neighbor answered the door, smiling and relieved. "Easy on the booze," he whispered. "Sometimes, after these things, I find her passed out on the floor." We walked down a short narrow hall lined with book-cases; there were two closed doors on my right, which must have led to the kitchen and the bedroom. He opened the door directly ahead of us.

After the dense green of the hedgerows and the darkness of the hall, the pure white of the sitting room was startling. I was half an hour late, and it was obvious that Jean Rhys had been waiting in her chair. She had arranged the room and herself with care. Each color stood out against the white walls like a piece of glass in a blown egg. The details were finely beautiful but not luxurious: a purple landscape over the mantle, a blue vase of smoky glass filled with purple flowers, harebells perhaps. We sat in rose-colored chairs; the rugs were deep and white like the walls. There was a silver rose against the wall to my right. It looked like a perfect rose that once had been alive and then coated with silver, a rose that had been enchanted, stopped in time. I usually didn't like that kind of thing, but it worked here.

In one of her stories, Rhys had written that there were many pretty girls now but fewer great beauties. Rhys was a great beauty. The pictures I had seen of her did not do her justice. She looked straight at me, giving me her charming smile, offering me her face like a gift. (Like Colette, Rhys had been professionally interested in beauty and was briefly in the cosmetics business.) I wondered whether she had read Virginia Woolf on charming women, but then Woolf might not have the final word.

If you had a face like Jean Rhys, you could easily expect that fortune would be on your side. Her blue eyes were enormous and clear and seemed to take up half her face. They looked dark against her ash blonde hair. She had a strong, well-shaped nose and a wide mouth, the kind of face that was supposed to photograph well—no, now that I think of it, to *film* well. I remember reading a description of the ideal model's face, the kind that would photograph well, written by a woman who ran a modeling agency: large but widely spaced eyes; small nose; a well-shaped mouth that must not be too wide; and nicely curved lips that must not be too full—all in all, the look of a one-year-old baby with a big blank space in the middle of the face. Rhys's features did not conform to those insipid specifications: her nose was too big, too strong; her mouth was too wide.

She was wearing a heavy knitted sleeveless dress, crimson with a black pattern worked in at the hem and under this a white blouse with a blue stone brooch at the throat. Over her shoulders, she had a very fine openwork scarf—pale blue. The colors were as bright and clear as wet ink.

She crossed her legs, and I could see her slip. Does anyone you know wear a slip like this? Thick creamy satin, a color you never see anymore, beige pink, like flushed skin, a narrow band of lace at the hem, banks of lace insets up the length of the slip. A gorgeous piece of goods, thick as clotted cream.

Giving me a sharp glance, she said, "No tape recorder." I had arrived in England with the usual equipment: tape recorder, half a dozen cassettes, an instant camera and film, flash cubes, and an x-ray-proof film bag—all the paraphernalia for the modern interview. I used none of them.

Jean Rhys was sixteen when she came to London from Dominica in the West Indies in 1910 and attended the Royal Academy of Dramatic Art. I asked Rhys whether she had wanted "to play a glittering part," like her character Marya in the novel *Quartet.* Rhys answered, "Yes, I meant a big part, an important role, a star role. I wanted to be famous." "What was it like being on the stage?" I asked. "I wasn't *on the stage*," she said scornfully. "I was in the chorus. It was a terrible life. We toured the North and the Midlands. They had to leave me behind in Newcastle. I was sick with pleurisy in a bed-sitting-room in Newcastle, alone with only the doctor coming to see me. I was brought up to get married, to be dependent; the theater was a way of escaping. It worked for a while."

Sarah Bernhardt wasn't as beautiful as Jean Rhys, but she had a thrilling voice; no one who heard her ever forgot it. When Rhys had a chance for a part, she could barely speak and flubbed her lines. Her voice caught in her throat. Her beauty had not brought her what she expected.

As I turned to get matches—we were both smoking—I caught a view of the fields through the casement windows in back of me. Her neighbor returned, carefully carrying a brimming cock-tail glass. Rhys had asked him for gin and vermouth. I wasn't drinking; I felt that I had to keep a clear head. Rhys began telling me about a present, "From Harrods. Wrapped like the crown jewels. I clawed it open. It was good brandy." Then we chatted about what kind of presents we liked to get. She loved liquor, flowers, jewelry. I hadn't expected she would want toasters and vacuum cleaners. She gossiped about the cleaning woman. Then she talked about Gypsies in what seemed to me a perversely delighted way. Her friend had been sleeping in the trailer, she said, and "this long long pole came in through the window. Her bag was stolen. An old Gypsy trick. Now I have locks on all the windows." Next we talked about spiders. She was afraid of spiders. "I am very superstitious," Rhys said, "are you?" Wanting to please, I said, "Yes, I never kill spiders; they bring good luck." She gave me another one of her scornful looks.

As we talked, I felt she was offering me a series of set pieces; she was posing. But then, why should she confront everything in a new way for me? I also felt that she thought I had more power than I actually did. She was trying to impress me, to charm me. Finally, she grew impatient. "Well, when is this thing really going to get started?" she asked. I began shuffling through my questions.

She took a big swallow of gin and vermouth. "I did a satiric piece on interviews," she said. "I called it 'Building Bricks without Straw.' They did a terrible piece about me in *Women's Wear Daily*. Mizener lied about me in his book on Ford [Ford Madox Ford had been her lover]. Some critic sent me this long article comparing me to Anne Radcliffe. You're not going to call me a Gothic novelist, are you? I've never even read *The Mysteries of Udolpho*."

I don't know what I'm going to call you, I thought grimly. I moved closer, pulling my chair across the deep, resisting rug, looking at her head-on. "I'm going to tell them how good you are and what you mean," I said with smooth calculation. She responded to the flattery and smiled her charming smile. For a moment her beauty made her unreachable. "Did you ever think of creating a character who was a writer, a woman like Jean Rhys, who had the kind of will and mastery of form it took you to write your kind of novel?" I asked. She jumped; a little door seemed to crack in her wide clear blue eyes. She hesitated for a long time before answering. "No," she said, "I never thought of that." I had a straw and I was going to build with it.

I wondered why a writer would imagine characters more helpless than herself, as if admitting to will and mastery would be admitting to a disgusting obscenity. The heroines of Rhys's autobiographical novels are first innocents and then victims of men who often buy them. Ruined ingenues who cannot act for themselves, they seem drugged by shame. I asked Rhys about the Spanish singer in *Quartet*. "That's Raquel Mer; it's a tragic song that she sings; there's always something a bit tragic about innocence because it's often defeated."

She pulled her large head back; I put my large head forward. Rhys went on, "They're always saying my work is autobiographical; it's not just that, a lot is imagined. I never saw those rats in the shed. The shed *is* there [she pointed over her shoulder] but I never saw the rats." (She was referring to "Sleep it Off, Lady," the title story of her then latest book of short stories.) "*After Leaving Mr. MacKenzie* is imagined. The room was mine, but not the rest!"

I looked up from my notes and caught her expression as she turned in her seat and reached for her drink. Now her face was tired. As we went on talking, the contrast between her animated face and her tired face became extreme. It cost her something to see people, to keep up the role. When she thought I wasn't looking at her, she appeared weary and bitter.

She sipped her drink as I talked, "One of your characters says that she 'wanted to go away with just the same feeling a boy has when he wants to run away to sea—at least, that I imagine a boy has. Only, in my adventure, men were mixed up, because of course, they had to be.' " I tried to ask Rhys if she thought women paid a heavy price for sexual experience. This seemed to me to be at the heart of her heroine's suffering, but I couldn't get my question out. Rhys jumped at me; her voice was sarcastic, "What? Are you suggesting a life without men?"

Apparently believing that I was criticizing her life, she began to explain, "If you didn't have any money, you couldn't do it alone, and I was brought up to marry, to think men would take care of me." When she did not succeed as an actress, she "ran away" to France with her first husband, over the objections of her family. "I wanted very badly to get out of England. Neither of us had any money, but he helped me free myself."

"I never *wanted* to be a professional writer," Rhys continued. "I just wanted to be happy." "But you did write," I said. Rhys told me that she had always kept a diary. While trying to sell her first husband's journalism in Paris, she met Mrs. Adams, the wife of a *London Times* correspondent. Mrs. Adams asked whether Rhys had written anything herself and persuaded Rhys to let her see the diaries. Mrs. Adams typed up certain parts of the diary, added some connecting narrative, and showed it to Ford Madox Ford, who was then in Paris, editing the *Transatlantic Review*. "Other people encouraged me," Rhys said, "Other people wanted me to write. I had the manuscript for *Quartet*, and someone told me to take it to London." Rhys saw herself as a private person who kept notes for her own life, who used the diary to ease unhappiness and record her impressions. Yet unlike Dorothy Wordsworth or L. M., Katherine Mansfield's friend, truly private writers who do not seem to have had any ambition for a public role, Jean Rhys did become a professional writer. *Quartet* is a novel, not a series of journal entries.

Jean Rhys disavows her will. "Other people encouraged me," she repeats. "Ford encouraged me. I guess I wasn't fair to him in *Quartet*, but I'm not sorry. I must say that he loved writing and writers with a real love." (The character, Heidler, in *Quartet* is a satiric portrait of Ford who became Rhys's lover and supporter when her first husband was imprisoned for illegal financial speculation.)

She said that she believed in fate, that at certain times in her life people appeared to help her. After Rhys's third husband died she couldn't stand being alone in Devon and "ran away"—that same expression again—to London. She became ill, and the doctor told her that she had had a heart attack. After leaving the nursing home, she returned to Devon. "Life was horrible," she said. She couldn't write or think. "A man came and helped me," Rhys said. She told him that she "was afraid of everything." He came everyday and talked to her, calming her, telling her that there was nothing to be afraid of, the way we calm a child. Rhys emphasized his reassuring manner and the way he kept repeating his soothing message. I found myself being lulled by her repetitions.

Finally out of this difficult period, she wrote *Wide Sargasso Sea*, her masterpiece. "It took five years," Rhys said with bitterness. Where another writer might talk about how she had got through, how she plotted and fought, how she decided to survive, Jean Rhys gave credit to a strange man who appeared out of the blue and barely mentioned herself except to say that she was helpless and suffering. She also seemed to resent having had to do the work. The man had helped her, but he had also expected her to produce.

"But you did write it," I said. "You did survive! You are a survivor." The proof was in front of me, the beautiful strong bones, the beautiful room, her design and choice of colors. The body of work on the shelf: five novels, two collections of short stories.

Now she turned her large eyes on me, "I don't want to survive anymore. . . . My life has no meaning; when you don't want anything anymore, life doesn't mean anything."

"Do you ever dream about Dominica?" I asked, trying to change the subject. "No, I used to have vivid dreams and remember them, especially the blue sea and the green mountains, but now I take sleeping pills and don't remember my dreams—if I have them at all." She got out of her chair when I stood up to open the window. There was a walking stick near her, but she did not use it. Instead, she held on to the mantel, stiff and awkward on her feet. I looked away as she sat down and looked again when she was back in her seat facing me. Her eyes had become clear again, clear as a child's.

"Do you still miss Dominica?" I asked. She looked up, "It was so beautiful, but nature doesn't care for us, and people are intent on destroying the beauty. . . . I think it's a kind of revenge." She mentioned groups that were trying to prevent further damage, but admitted that she could never join any kind of group, especially a political group. "I don't think we can do much," she said. "People will believe anything, want to believe anything. I met a woman the other day who told me a great leader was coming. I told her that Hitler had come. But she insisted that this leader would be moral. They all start out that way." Rhys went on, "London must be full of rich Arabs. Money: that's all they care about. Ruined Dominica, cut down the trees, cutting down the trees here."

We talked about her years in Paris—she was there for most of the twenties and had known Hemingway. "He took such pleasure in everything. He was so vital," she said. "Did anyone call herself a feminist?" I asked. "No one I knew. The word wasn't used. To get started, women had to be better than men; men only had to be half as good." She stopped to think and went on. "The best male writers are better than the best female writers." She seemed uncomfortable with that idea. "The writing of men has a greater scope; we write about ourselves and our immediate circle. Men have a different kind of brain, not superior, but different." Perhaps she had wanted a larger field for herself.

She returned to the subject of France. "I loved Paris. Perhaps it's not true now, but I felt that Englishmen disliked women. The actual position of Frenchwomen and Englishwomen, I'm sure, wasn't much different, but in France you felt men were interested in you, what you looked like, what you wore, what you were thinking. It was wonderful after England." In France, she was not made to feel shame for being a woman, for being beautiful. She came to depend on it.

When I asked her about her hatred of respectability, she said that respectability and goodness were two different things. She didn't want to be thought of as an outlaw: "There have to be some laws." "What about what you've called 'the soul-destroying middle?' " I asked. She sat up straight. "I prefer the extreme." So do I, I thought. She had stopped smiling and looked thoughtful. Her position was strong and contrary, and I liked her for it. Her rebelliousness was still alive, and though she drugged herself to sleep, the tensions and conflicts of her life were still present.

She had asked me to turn the heater down, and now the room was cold. I felt chilled. It was late afternoon; the light in the room was dimmer, the sun no longer coming in through the windows in back of me. The fake coals of the electric heater looked hot; the red was painted on. "Just a few more questions," Rhys said. I asked her about her work habits. "Oh, I never have a plan. When I get an idea for a book I work all day and into the early morning." Rhys is a careful reviser; all her books show a form impossible to achieve in a first, or even a second, draft. "I've never worked like a professional writer, turning out a quota," she added. Then she turned in her seat, turned her large head away from me, her jaw lifted on its thin stalk, "I can see the shape of the book; it's like a mathematical figure." She stopped talking and moved her hands out from her body. (All during our talk, she had kept them at her sides except to lift her glass or to smoke.) Now she traced a figure in the air with grace and strength, as if she held a tool, and leaned out of her seat instead of sitting small. I could see the energy move out from her spine, into her shoulders, into her hands; the angle at which she held her head was firm. "I know what to take out, how to make the figure clear." She pressed her fingers together and cut through the air without apology, her arms extended to their full length, nothing held back, the hands decisive and sure. The woman who moved her arms so confidently, without hesitation, is not the woman we find in Rhys's work.

When she looked back at me, her eyes were smaller, darker, "willful." I mean the word in its old sense, "proceeding from the will . . . , done on purpose." I looked again into her dark blue eyes. I wanted to ask her whether she had ever done anything wrong, whether she had ever been cruel to someone who had done her no harm. I believed that all violence did not come from men. I wanted her to tell me how she was responsible—for her work, for her life—but it was not my place to judge her: I would have to save those questions for myself.

We were both tired. Our visit was over. When I took her hand to say goodbye, I was so surprised that I said straight out, "Your hand is so warm!" Actually it was hot. Jean Rhys's strong fingers burned into my palm.

Down from
Monte Verde Vecchio

The dollar was strong in 1978. John and I had rented an apartment in Rome for most of June and the beginning of July on the Via Nicola Fabrizi in the Monte Verde Vecchio, an elegant quarter that looked down on Trastevere. Roberta and Ivo, our old friends from Boston University, were in Rome, Ivo on a research grant. They had found the apartment for us through Bobby Falcon, an American writer and new friend. It was our second trip to Rome. We were both more relaxed than we had been during our first stay: in 1966 I hadn't yet learned how to travel, and John was shocked by the theatrical baroque and the gaudiness of the Counter-Reformation churches. He said that they were too rich for his Irish soul. He had been brought up Catholic in Boston. "Irish Catholicism is Calvinistic," he would say. "This place looks like a circus. There's too much of everything." At the catacombs of Callisto our guide had been an Irishman in his late thirties. He was sandy-haired and blue eyed, and wore a black suit like a priest. He had a kind of formal charm that seemed familiar. "He's like the young Irish undertakers in Arlington," John said. "He's not quite a priest, sort of a ghoul, just loves it. We *would* find him here—underground."

Now, twelve years later, we had different problems: David, our nine-year-old son, had come with us. We were a tight threesome. Our larger families had dwindled, our friends scattered. At first I worried about David's health. He had been sick with a severe ear infection before we left. Delirious from the high fever, he had woken up screaming that he was being electrocuted and had begged us "to turn down the volume of the snow." He saw dogs crouched in the corner of his room; they were trying to swallow him, he said. Frightened, we bathed him hourly with alcohol and gave him penicillin, which he eagerly swallowed, having already learned about its benefits in a science lesson. I remembered my own mother caring for me when I was ill. She must have heard me in the night. I felt her cool hand on my forehead. I was so glad for the touch. "Joe, she's burning up with fever," she called to my father. They bathed me with a facecloth dipped in warm water and alcohol.

When we left for Italy, David was still thin, and there were shadows under his eyes, but he soon put on weight in Rome. I would take him to Giolitti's for an afternoon ice cream. Giolitti's was Roberta's discovery. When she described her finds, her tone had none of the snobby best-of-this, best-of-that point of view. She was just delighted and grateful. She had a passion for the small pleasures of life and would eventually discover she had talent for the larger ones. The first time I took Dave to Giolitti's he ordered a "Copa Olimpica," a huge sundae topped with whipped cream and long sweet wafers. On our next visit, he asked for a cone. I didn't understand his moderation; I had been a child who lusted for banana splits. For dinner he loved to eat fettuccine with butter and Parmesan cheese, followed by a plate of fresh green beans in lemon and oil. His favorite dessert was strawberries and cream. "Fragole," he would call out, smiling into the waiter's attentive face. After one long dinner with a group of our friends, he had, while we were finishing our coffee, walked around the table and, with graceful flourishes, drawn from his pockets a chocolate for each of the guests. Our friends were delighted with David; they were afraid that all American children might be like the "savage" boy they had seen at breakfast on the roof terrace of the Hotel Portoghese; that one, they told us, had buzzed all of them with his toy plane, shrieked at the "poor pigeons," and then, when forced back to his table, kicked his sister and then his mother, an art historian with "the mildest of expressions." They had never seen David tormenting his teacher. He would whip a ball up the aisle of his classroom when her back was turned. Like my father Joe, the roughneck with a palate, David had always disliked school. I watched him showing off his new style in Rome, wondering what shape his next metamorphosis would take and where these new manners had come from. Perhaps he was copying the dashing waiters at the Vecchia Roma. He insisted on wearing his pale blue suit—bought for a family wedding—to dinner. John would tie his tie for him but went without one himself. Both of us felt like David's retainers. I don't think he's worn a suit since.

Having quickly adjusted to the late Italian dinner hour, he would sleep late in the morning. John and I could count on an hour or two by ourselves. The three of us were together almost all of the time, and John and I felt the lack of privacy. Each morning while David slept, we'd fix a breakfast tray in the dark back kitchen: bread, fruit, cheese, butter, strawberry jam, and a pot of strong Twinings English Breakfast Tea. We had switched to tea; the price of Italian coffee shocked us. As Americans we believed that we had a right to cheap coffee. We'd have a long breakfast on the large bright terrace amid the pots of oleander and basil. The voices of the nuns from the adjacent convent would float up from the garden where they sat in a circle, sewing and laughing.

When David got up, he would not come rushing in, as he had done when he was a little boy. Sometimes I would find him sitting up in the heavy Empire sleigh bed staring out the window, taking in the view and himself with what seemed like timeless calm.

He would still do this at twenty—rest in himself; after he'd showered, he would sit on the couch in the Academy Street living room and look out at the quiet early-morning street. His combed-back dark hair still wet from the shower would leave drops on his slender neck; his strong legs would stick out from under his too-small bathrobe. From just below the knees David's legs are covered with thick black hair, which ends in shaggy points just above the bare white ankle bones. His chest and arms are almost hairless, and his beard is very light, so this thick leg hair always looks like a newly sprouting pelt—a metamorphosis in progress. I wouldn't usually come downstairs until after David had left the house, and I seldom saw him there on the couch. When I did, I would always jump with surprise. He seemed not to hear me, yet I would back away from the door, feeling that my accidental glimpse of his private reverie was an intrusion, though like many parents I was happy to see that he did have a soul of his own.

Of course, you might say, don't we all? There were times when I wasn't sure, when I was afraid that I had so harmed him by my will to control that he—wild and driven to say no to me and to his father—would not find himself.

When he was thirteen, he told us that he was going to come and go as he pleased—no curfews. We said no. No matter what John and I knew about adolescence, David's rebellion took us by surprise. We had to live out furies that seemed god-given— nasty unreasonable gods. I was unnerved, not as my father had been, by the threat of sex, but by the threat of violence. John and I would go out with the dog early Sunday morning and find newly planted maple trees snapped off at the trunk. We'd walk through Robbins park and find that someone had kicked the porch of the Robbins house into jagged splinters. Teenage boys drove their cars into Spy Pond. On Sunday mornings the hedges and tree strips would glitter with broken beer bottles. Gangs of teenagers tore through the town, restless, searching for release. They would drive their cars into street signs, bending the steel poles into the ground. They broke into schools; they broke into cars.

Like my father, I found that I could not let go. "The Fight," a poem I wrote during that time, catches some of the passion of our battle:

> I grabbed my son's shoulders
> to keep him from running.
> He turned in my grip, skin
> slippery, hard as bone. I
> yelled; the sound stopped
> him. Blood flushing up through his
> neck and face as if a strong
> light were turned on him,
> he stood in front of me,
> bare chest, hard tits,
> waist a lace of muscle.
> His shorts were pulled down
> slightly below his navel
> where my blood once pumped
> into him. His legs were
> hairy as a satyr's. "I
> won't let go," I spat. "No,
> no," he yelled, hunching
> his shoulders against my
> wild hands. I ran to lock
> the nearest door, but when
> I came back, calling, "David,
> David," I saw that he had
> slipped out without a sound.

He would climb out the window of his second-floor room and let himself down from the roof, a drop of fifteen feet. On one night John went after him, drove up to the park where the kids hung out, chased him into the woods, tackled him, and carried him back to the car. David seemed relieved. He stopped sneaking out. The three of us agreed on a curfew.

One Sunday afternoon during our stay in Monte Verde Vecchio, we took David up to the Gianicolo hill, which was near our apartment. Pale gray violet-bottomed clouds were rolling in across the western sky. Here and there the low sun broke through and sent down dull gold rays. The light was thick with a kind of held-in glittery dust you see in sun-showers, but the rain never came.

Families strolled about with their children. Cheap gauzy scarves, and flimsy fake gold chains swung from the souvenir booths. You could buy little wafery cones filled with whipped cream. There were violent Punch and Judy shows: wack, wack, shriek, shriek. Some of the watching children screamed and laughed, others stood silent and wide-eyed. The puppets and the small theaters were painted in jam-colored reds and purples.

As you looked up the slope of the hill, you saw groups passing back and forth, forming, swirling. The breeze picked up; the children's hair lifted; the pastel and the white Sunday skirts of the little girls lifted. They led their stolid parents through the dusky light—airy kites pulling dark heavy shapes. But even these parents were being undone by the wind. They swayed. I felt the pull of generations. We all seemed so small, whirled together, delighted, and a little sad.

On our mornings in the Monte Verde Vecchio, John's eyes were clear. At home, he had been drinking heavily—straight gin—but now felt that, perhaps, like an Italian, he could safely drink wine. His plan worked for a while, but he was eating more than usual. He would make fun of himself, "I bit so hard into that chicken leg, I bit my own finger." He held up his hand, small and sensitively bony for such a large man. There was a small cut. He had broken the skin.

For as long as I had known him, he had been powerless over his appetites. There was no possibility of moderation. After smoking three packs of Lucky Strikes a day, he had given them up when he saw his father die early of high blood pressure. That was in 1965 when John was twenty-six. We had flown to Eagle Lake in remote northern Maine, a canoe strapped to the pontoons of the plane. John brought only one pack with him. Those soon went. When we came across the camp of fishermen out on the lake for whitefish, John rummaged around their tent and found his last three cigarettes. He never went back to them.

John started drinking hard liquor again in Rome. He began with *gelato affogato*, ice cream "drowned" in Scotch, and then went on to after-dinner Sambuca. He wasn't getting drunk, though; it took a fifth of gin to do that. Like certain drinkers, he seemed magically invulnerable to alcohol, as if addiction were a kind of gift. His extreme habits had seemed part of his charm, his vitality. For years, he drank the way he could ride out a storm; he was usually the only man walking on the deck of the tossing ship. His friends and I had all loved his energy. We gave him presents of huge heavy-bottomed crystal glasses, enormous breakfast cups, voluminous suitcases. When he put on weight, we'd say, "He can carry it." (After John finally stopped drinking, he went down to 180 pounds, the weight he had been when we all first knew him. We had forgotten that except for his broad chest he was long and slender.) Just recently, feeling wiped out after we had canoed for almost five hours on Lake Aziscohos in Maine, he said to me, "You know, I'm not made of iron." We had needed him to be our strongman, we wanted to believe that there was one among us who could do anything he wanted, have as much as he wanted and still get away with it. In fact, after John sobered up, some of his old friends wouldn't see him anymore. They wanted what they wanted: a hero.

After one long evening of eating and drinking, our friend Roberta, standing over John, who was seated, had taken a handful of his thick black hair; his head tilted back as she pulled and felt. "You'll never lose your hair," she said with confidence. I smiled in agreement. John would never age, we all seemed to be saying, and perhaps we would never die.

From the terrace of our apartment in the Monte Verde Vecchio John and I would look out across Trastevere to the soft outlines of the city. We could see the startlingly modern outline of the dome of the Pantheon. Rome seemed to unfold in waves, for all its size, light and floating in the morning air.

We were always walking down into it. On Sundays we'd turn off our street on to a cobbled passage, which descended in easy shallow flights of stone steps into Trastevere. The narrow alley-like street at the base of the steps was lined with stables and workshops. I'd look in to see a horse calmly chewing its feed. Loud voices and the humid peppery smell of the day's ministra came from the rooms above and mingled with the odor of manure. I saw a stocky man in his undershirt standing at the door of a stable. His arms and shoulders bulged like a boxer's, and his still-hard stomach rounded over his wide belt. He crossed his arms against his broad chest and stared past me.

At the end of the street a dramatically scrawled sign in purple and red announced the headquarters of the Centro Italiano Femminile Artisti e Proffessionisti. The sign was already becoming historical by virtue of its surroundings. The narrow street opened to the Piazza di Santo Egidio. Farther on, we'd pass the Church of Santa Maria in Trastevere, the saints in gold mosaics gleaming from the recess of its porch, and work our way toward the Tiber, crossing at the Ponte Garibaldi. On our right was the boat-shaped Isola Tiberina, like a walled city. For some reason we never went on to the island. Although I knew it was the site of a busy hospital, and I could see crowds of people carrying flowers on their way to visit patients, the island seemed as remote and secret to us as a fairy-tale castle. Directly in front of us was the ugly Synagogue of Rome, looking like a lumpy tea cozy.

In back of the synagogue were the twisting streets of the old ghetto, and the broken debris from the Teatro di Marcello. The scale here was small, the broken columns graceful, again the stones improbably light-looking. A temple pediment was held together by large metal staples, which made the ruins seem even more fragile. On one of these walks an emaciated white cat came out of the ruins and rubbed against my leg. I had no food to give her. She arched her back as she rubbed against my leg. She was starving.

We walked on to the small Piazza Campitelli, which looked like a narrow high-walled palace gallery that had had its ceiling blown off. Bright sunlight poured down from a hot blue sky; the palaces and the church were splendid and filthy. The dirt was ancient, black as the stone embankment of a corrupted river. We would always have our Sunday dinner outside under a large canvas umbrella at the Vecchia Roma, which wasn't fashionable then.

As I sat in the warm shade forking up *rigatoni al forno*, I felt that my walk, whose beginning was signaled by the closing of the apartment shutters against the sun, which would, as predictably as the church bell's ringing, burn into the front room, my walk down from the green hill, across river, past island, into ghetto, added up to something: its own shape. I could move my feet from scene to scene, from story to story. I was also finding my way again, as I had when I was a child noticing streets, and corners, and crossings. An elemental pleasure was being restored to me: first I did, and then I did, and then I did. The pleasure was narrative. The meaning might be revealed—or not.

Bobby Falcon, the American writer who had found the apartment for us, had been living in Rome for more than twenty years and was now planning to leave. He said that when he walked out of his apartment on the Corso one morning and saw a soldier on the roof opposite carrying a machine gun, he knew it was time to go home. His decision to come to Rome in the first place had been just as sudden. "I was on the subway in New York," he told us. "When we stopped at Washington Square, and the doors opened, I said to myself, 'I'm going to Rome.' I bought my ticket the next day."

He was soon well known. Falcon acted in films and made a lot of money writing music for films. He soon knew everyone. He would talk about the high-flying days after the war when the Princess Caetani, who had founded the magazine *Botteghe Oscure*, would have her dinner invitations delivered by a liveried footman. Falcon never ran out of stories, and his charm never wore thin. Short, stocky, fair, he walked with a light step. His thick-cream skin was rosy. As he talked, his glasses with their lime-jello green rims caught the light and flashed their whimsical joke: I am not important; life is absurd.

One night, he cooked dinner for all of us. He placed David opposite him at the far end of the table. "You two sit here," he said to me and John, "Virginia and Leonard there," he teased, putting Roberta and Ivo across from us. "The literary couple," I responded, smiling at Falcon like a clever student—he had meant Virginia and Leonard Woolf. I was surprised to see his cool, appraising eyes, his placid face suddenly grim. Roberta giggled nervously. Falcon knew something I didn't. Roberta was often tense, but I thought it was temperament. After their divorce, Ivo wrote about Roberta's "dark intense intellectual beauty." By that time, she was going to nude beaches, stretching out her shapely legs in the hot sand while Ivo was still comparing her to Susan Sontag. "It's the physical type which still attracts me, plus the promise of big brains, deep thoughts, and a passionate involvement with life." But not the life of the body. When Roberta discovered that she had a body that could feel sexual pleasure, their marriage was over. But back then in Rome she wanted us to believe that she was happy, and I took her at her word. She had never talked to Falcon about her unhappiness; he had guessed.

Falcon lifted his short narrow tube of iced vodka. That season's fashionable after-dinner drink was an iced immaculate spike to the brain. It made the glasses of Sambuca stuck in our hands feel suddenly too big, suddenly too dark—like crude syrup. His apartment was elegantly bare. A scroll-backed settee upholstered in pale pink silk curved against a bare wall like a screen. Next to it, a silvery art deco torch lamp.

"I'm going," he said, "as soon as I can arrange a way to bring my cats back with me. I don't care if I have to sail home. I'll get a private cabin. They can stay with me. I'm not stowing them in a plane with the cargo." (He eventually did sail home, he and the cats in a private cabin.)

We left him at his apartment. Roberta and Ivo went home. Wanting a coffee, we walked up the Corso toward the Piazza del Popolo. Every fifty feet was a soldier with a machine gun. We just kept walking. As we got closer to the piazza, we saw more and more soldiers, but we didn't turn around; we were still headed toward a café and coffee. The huge, dipping space of the Piazza del Popolo beyond the matching domes of the churches, which looked like two massive gateposts without the gate, was filled with trucks and armed soldiers. There had been a bomb scare. The cafés were packed. Young men in pale pants and white shirts, sweaters loosely tied around their shoulders like scarves, were laughing and talking. The soldiers set up a roadblock and began stopping cars.

The square was brightly lit; there was a theatrical glare. We stood in the shadow. You couldn't get into a café. Standing in the Piazza del Popolo, John and I seemed like peasants in history, blinking from the shadows. But we weren't like the peasants in Auden's "Musée des Beaux Arts." They turn away from the disaster quite "leisurely." We didn't have that grace, and this was only a possible disaster. We saw; we were shocked; we were quiet in the dark. We bumbled, as we bumbled with our own lives. It would be a while before the recognition of our helplessness would be a freedom. We sensed that fate would do with us what it wanted.

That summer our chic friends in Rome nicknamed us "The

Holy Family." They were living abroad on grants, writing, free of children. Much later I would learn that they had problems of their own, but that spring in Rome their scholarly and literary purpose did seem superior to our messy family life. We weren't like Roberta and Ivo or like Bobby Falcon, whose swift intuitions sent him into fateful motion. By the time we got home to America, John would be back to a fifth of gin a day. He'd wake up terrified from his first blackouts. I began to go to Al-Anon meetings. When I heard the First Step, "We admitted that we were powerless over alcohol and that our lives had become unmanageable," I understood what I had sensed in Rome. Addiction was our fate. I would also find out that I had a drug of choice—sugar, enormous quantities of sweet stuff. My father used to eat ice cream by the soupbowlfull; I ate it by the half gallon. I hit my bottom when I found myself drinking straight maple syrup— the same color as bourbon—by the tumblerful. I joined Overeaters Anonymous. Six months after our return, John stopped drinking.

Sometimes in the mornings, when John would take David to see one of the great sights, St. Peter's or the Colosseum, I would leave the apartment, turn left on Nicola Fabrizi, and walk to the Villa Sciarra. There would be a few people on the benches, children playing. I loved to look down the long paths clogged with yellow oleander leaves. It was June, but dry leaves kept dropping and dropping, confusing my idea of the seasons, a perpetual shedding.

The narrow leaves dried quickly into stiff curls, which gave off a faint dry sound in the wind. Leaves fell at the same time that the pollen dropped. I think it was pollen. The stuff looked like gold dust. Someone said it came in on the wind from Africa. Showers of gold coated the cars, blew in across the pavement, disappeared in the shade where I sat with my notebook, writing little.

On Sundays the wedding parties came, one after the other, like a slow parade. The brides would have their veils back and their long skirts bunched under their arms; the little couple— ring bearer, in a stiff pastel suit, the flower girl in a high-waisted dress usually stuck with rosettes, stuck with something—would already be tired. The deep rose or green shades of the brides- maids' dresses would stand out against the bride's whiteness. The bridesmaids clutched their bunched bouquets in front of their stomachs like basketballs. For a second everyone would look sullen, then they would laugh and smile, the happiest people on earth.

The little couple would revive, stand up straight. Soft-faced yet cunning, they signified both innocence, which is freedom from time, and the inevitability of marriage: children would be- come bride and groom; the world marched in couples. Couples aged and died: the wedding pair flanked by aging parents, some- times a wizened grandmother or grandfather, widow or widower, obviously part of a broken couple. They were all on their way to have their portraits taken in the bright June light.

In one of his poems, Mandelstam calls Rome the city of wed- dings—a literal description.

It was also the city of death. Aldo Moro had been assassinated near the church of Il Jesu. On our walks we'd come across piles of memorial pink, purple, and white flowers, some fresh, others wilting, shrinking down on the hot street like spinach in a pot. All over Rome were these flowers heaped over bloodstains. I rel- ished the stew of flowers. Rome reduced and ate history. Rome changed linear historical time into cyclical time: winter, spring, summer, fall. I had never been in such a vast city that was still natural. The ruins were full of cats like temple preserves in India, dens of energy, torpor, fecundity, death.

At noon the city began shutting down, grate after grate, shut- ter after shutter would come down with a wavelike rhythm that rolled slowly through the streets to reverse itself in the late afternoon when Rome woke again. The streets smelled of dark oily coffee beans. Fruits and vegetables of the season were on every menu—strawberries in June, so you ate strawberries until they were gone, and then there would be something else. Buy a chicken and you found, not a tiny wilted sprig, but a huge plumy stem of rosemary folded into its cavity. Walk into any church: burning spears of gladiolas rising from the altar into the violet light.

In a church near the Piazza Navona is a larger-than-life-size statue of a woman. The Church has called her the Virgin, but she looks like the Roman Ceres. She is seated; a band encircles her smooth brow, binds her loosely coiled hair. She wears a toga. There is no infant Jesus in sight. At the base of the statue, the pressure of hands has worn the marble to a slippery gorgeous finish more subtle than any jeweler's polish could have done. A huge wheel of flaming candles hangs near the "Virgin's" head, blazing in daylight. The church is bright without the candles. So what! More light.

The flowers sunk down on the bloodstains, the stiff yellow leaves swirled around the bride's feet on the path of the Villa Sciarra.

By the time I started back to the apartment, the morning coolness had evaporated. It was hot and bright. I'd step off the dazzling street into the apartment's cool courtyard, which smelled of fresh water. The portiere would be watering the unspectacular pots of dark green palms. A heavy two o'clock quiet would fill the courtyard. The apartments, with their half-shuttered windows stacked above me, seemed to be as full as casks of aging wine. The small wood-paneled double-doored elevator, slightly larger than an American phone booth, took me up to the fourth floor.

I'd unlock the big carved wooden door with the odd foreign tube-shaped key and immediately step into the deeper coolness of the long wide hall. The cold from the wet-mud-colored marble would come up through my thin-soled sandals.

The walls were painted a lighter shade of terra-cotta. The large bunch of dried rue hanging from the wall near the door gave out its strong unclouded scent, a little like oregano but without the bitter heaviness of that herb—sweeter. On one side of the hall was a long chest of old walnut, its finish cracked and oiled. I'd put down my notebook and take off my sandals to feel the delicious coolness. I'd put my extra change in the shallow copper dish under the lamp shaped like a water jug, adding it to the change that was always there—our landlady's habit, which I picked up—so there would always be spare change for the bus or whatever.

Next to the door was a coatstand and a vase that contained umbrellas. There was also a small straight-backed chair where I would sit to take off my shoes. Sometimes before going out, I would sit in that chair for a moment to think. The chair was perfectly placed. Did it take thousands of years of civilization to know how to place a chair? I asked myself. I would sit in the perfect chair. Before setting out on my walk, I felt casually blessed for the journey; coming back, I felt welcomed. Putting my things on the chest—map, notebook, change, scarf—on my return was like laying a table for the next meal.

In the apartment on the Via Nicola Fabrizi, I would look down the long hall toward the west-facing windows. The lowered shutters tempered the light to a cooled glow. I would take off my clothes, put on the thin robe I'd brought from the States and the cheap terry cloth travel slippers. In a little while John and David would be back. Our family problems would seem both more important and less important. I had gone out and come back, and I would go out again. I'd be eaten.

Cupid
on the Train

Ten years after our stay in Monte Verde Vecchio we were taking the train from Rome north to Spoleto. The express soon cleared the outskirts and began to climb. Most of the windows were open, and the curtains flapped and flapped even though they were tied back against the walls, but I didn't mind the noise. John and I were happy with the draft: the weather was so hot. I found myself checking out the passengers for the one person who inevitably has to shut windows. After fifteen minutes, no one had even fidgeted. Surprisingly we all seemed to be in agreement about the position of the windows.

Up and up we went; the train roared through winding tunnels. We climbed so quickly that my ears popped. Pressure built in the tight tunnels, which went on and on and then suddenly opened to steep green hills patched with olive orchards and vineyards. The distant hill towns looked at first like the dry stone outcroppings that surrounded them. Despite the terrible dryness of that August—there had been a heat wave across southern Europe that had literally cooked people to death in Greece—there was a deep wild stream running next to the track before it wound off into a valley and disappeared from sight.

I pointed to the view; John nodded. We had given up trying

to talk; there was too much noise. I found a headband in my purse and put it on to keep the wind from blowing my hair into my eyes. The car rocked as it climbed. An Italian sat across the aisle from us; he looked to be in his fifties. His hair was cut close to his shapely, powerful head. He was staring at us. When John took out our map so we could follow the route, the Italian saw an opening and immediately moved to the seat opposite me. Pointing to the map, he delivered a primitive geography lesson: "Lazio . . . Umbria . . . Umbria . . . Lazio." Apparently we had crossed the border into Umbria. Again he pompously intoned, "Lazio . . . Umbria." We nodded like idiots. John was unusually patient; his Italian was very good.

The stranger was from Foligno in Umbria. "Umbria had many streams, many streams." He then went on to compare Umbria to Tuscany. The chant picked up another word: "Lazio . . . Umbria . . . Toscana."

Our teacher had his thin short-sleeved shirt unbuttoned. A heavy gold cross, a little like a Celtic cross and very much the style for middle-class men, hung against his hairy chest, as if the cross were a part of the seduction as well as a neutralizer. The hair was flecked with gray; his chest was both muscled and soft; his pecs drooped slightly. As I stared at his chest, I thought: men do have breasts. His, aside from the cross, which must have been as heavy as a Tiffany bottle opener, looked as welcoming as plumped ravioli (the recent rage was for *big* ravioli), but his strong tight neck and head, perhaps hardened from soccer playing, seemed dangerous. His graying hair and eyebrows gave his face a faded aspect, yet his slanting, slightly protuberant eyes were sharp, oddly naive and calculating at the same time.

When I got up and moved to the window to get a better view of one of those steeply terraced towns, I immediately felt his strong urging hands on my sweating back. I was very hot, but his hands were even hotter. They seemed to burn through my blouse. He was all kindness, tactful as a waiter.

In one of my few good bits of Italian, I asked him what was good to eat in Umbria. "Tutti, tutti," he replied with gusto. He looked as if he would eat me. As he spoke, he gently but firmly dug his thumb into the corner of his opened mouth—I could see his even white beautiful teeth—and with the rest of the fingers of that hand loosely closed, exuberantly and rhythmically vibrated the thumb into his receptive face. A Frenchman's kissing the tips of his fingers was nothing to this.

He watched me. Under his manipulative scrutiny, I saw myself—flushed face, damp upper lip, heavy gold ring on the middle finger of my left hand. I didn't wear a wedding band.

A pale scholarly-looking man joined the conversation about food. He had brightened at the exclamation "Tutti!" and began questioning the Umbrian about local specialties. The bullet-headed man immediately took a superior tone. As soon as he learned that the pale man was from Rome, he insisted that the cuisine of Rome wasn't as "vigorous" as the cuisine of Umbria.

Tired of his swaggering, I left the group and stood for a while in the narrow passage between the cars. We were going so fast the landscape blurred. I went into the toilet, carefully wiped the seat, and after I had peed, went on sitting with my pants down like a child, glad to be alone for a while. I swayed with the rhythm of the train and stared at everything and nothing. It wasn't reverie or daydream, because I had no thought, no fantasy. The tiny sink went out of focus—just a hair—but did not blur, in fact seemed clearer in outline; the metal rimmed door became sharper and less clear. I felt rested—without all the self-consciousness of "meditation." Maybe this was the true Western way of "sitting." The Way of the Toilet. Perhaps I wasn't spiritually developed. All the men I knew who practiced meditation were always talking about how many hours they had "sat."

When I made my way back, they were still talking. Suddenly they broke into wild laughter—the Italians, John less so. As I sat down, our Umbrian of the strong thumb placed his index finger across his lips in a comic opera gesture, cautioning the others to keep quiet.

In a few minutes we were in Spoleto. As we walked through the station, John told me that the Italian, in recommending yet another restaurant, the best one, had said, "First you eat, then you go upstairs and . . ." At this point, holding his arm next to his side, he rhythmically pumped his fist. That's when they had all laughed. "Then you sleep," he said raising his finger to his mouth.

Few people got off the train at Spoleto. The yearly arts festival was over and the streets were quiet. We checked into the Hotel Charleston in the Piazza Collicola, and found ourselves in a small room with an enormous bed. We negotiated the strip of floor around the bed as if it were the deck of a small sailboat. There wasn't much of a view. Uncharacteristically, we didn't ask to see another room. As soon as we had unpacked and showered, we went out for a walk. The station and the Piazza Garibaldi were below us, and the peak of the city—the cathedral and the Ponte delle Torri—far above. There was no hesitation about which way to go. Spoleto is a hill town; in a hill town you go up. The steep street, which was too narrow for cars, began just a few steps from our hotel, eventually crossed the Corso Mazzini, and rose to the Piazza del Duomo.

I had thought that once we reached the piazza we would be looking up at the church. Instead we climbed and climbed and found ourselves at the narrow end of a tilting rectangular space enclosed by white stone buildings. From that high point, wide flights of stairs lead down toward the cathedral. Like all the buildings that enclosed the piazza, the cathedral was dazzlingly white, the stone sun-bleached and wind-scoured.

Later, around eight, we met some friends who had been coming to Spoleto every summer for the past five years. They had an airy bright top-floor apartment whose high oval windows framed a series of views of the cathedral and the Piazza del Duomo. Chris, an American poet, said he loved Italy because it was the only country he had ever been in where he could take naps without guilt. "I'm in sync here," he said, laughing at himself. He would get up from his siesta and write in the afternoon. "In Vermont, I can only write in the morning," he said. Victoria had started on a series of small collages. She had her worktable set up in a corner of the bedroom, and bright torn bits of photographs, fabric, paper covered the tabletop. The two finished collages were intricate, mazelike. Victoria loved working small. It was new for her.

They suggested a walk and led us up past the cathedral along a wide—wide for Spoleto—road next to the old fort. Suddenly the valley dropped steeply below us on the right. There was a tiny unpretentious café on the left, which seemed like a cave hollowed in the hillside; a few tables and chairs faced the extraordinary view. We walked on in the dusk high over the gorge whose bottom we could not see. The Via del Ponte was closed to cars and motorcycles. Every fifty yards or so there was a bench tucked against the hillside. We rounded a curve and the lit-up Ponte delle Torri came into view. Supported on Gothic arches built over the original Roman aqueduct, the bridge looked like a delicate paper cutout strung from slope to slope; its pilings were hidden almost three hundred feet below. (When we eventually hiked across, we found that the bridge was just wide enough to allow two people to walk side by side.)

As we walked in the dusk with our friends, our conversation slowed and became easy. We could hear the voices of other strollers ahead of us or behind us. By the time we had come to the end of the Via del Ponte, we could barely see each other. Victoria's brilliant yellow eyes, her sharply angled short short hair, and Robert's fine elegant small-mouthed face had faded in the dusk. It was difficult to distinguish who was saying what. I drew close to my friends in the pauses in our conversation. It was as if the place, and then the darkness, had lifted from us the weight of personality and ambition as America never could and had delivered us to intimacy. And we wanted this weight removed; we wanted to work small. We also seemed free of family. A while back John had gone to the funeral of his aunt Mary, his father's sister. His family on both sides had been very large, more than twenty aunts and uncles all together. He had come back from the funeral grieving at the loss, and feeling that everything had dwindled and was coming to an end. His cousins were scattered; he had only one son. But now in Spoleto we became children of the place. He and I had both been born into the hot press of family life, both surrounded by grandparents, aunts, and uncles. They were all dying out. Against that old communal life we had labored to find our identity, and now we were often relieved to see that identity dissolve, metamorphize. We had become migrators.

That night we ate spaghetti and truffles in a restaurant in the Piazza del Duomo. The tables rode the sloping stones just below the steps and looked as if they were about to slide down across the tilting piazza toward the church, but once we were seated, we found the table secure. As we ate, children played with their soccer balls. Too young for a regular game, they kicked the balls against the wall of the gardens next to the church: bam, bam. The sound echoed within the enclosure; the piazza was a kind of courtyard. The children ran wildly with small steps, little figures dwarfed by the cathedral. The piazza was lit up, and the light shone through the children's hair—bubbles of outlined ringlets above obscured faces. At eleven the lights went out, but the children went on playing.

A man roared into the piazza on his motorcycle and stopped just beyond the restaurant tables. He turned off the machine and began shouting about God. The Italians looked at him quietly and then lost interest. "Pazzo," one of them said. Crazy. In the space of the piazza his words thinned out and were lost.

Florid, heavy, long-haired, he reminded me of the man I had seen in the Porta Portese flea market in Rome. That one was much farther gone. His thick black hair was matted, and looked as if it had not been washed or combed for months. The dirt made his hair look dyed. He was "dressed" completely in black. His "clothes" were thick coarse rags that he had bunched and knotted against his body. His calves were covered with black strips wound like puttees. He had decorated himself with "jewelry": on each filthy finger he wore a ring tab from a soda can. His beautiful florid skin showed through the filth. Around his neck he had a chromium wheelcap rim, the elaborate kind you see on a Lincoln or a Cadillac. His large matted head rose from the center of the stiff metal ruff. Curled on the rim just under his chin was a gray kitten with a delicate head and large eyes. It looked at first like a dead fur tail, the kind that women used to wear. Actually, the kitten *was* a kind of decoration. I couldn't imagine how the crazy man could stand to be bound up, confined, and wrapped in fur on such a hot day. I watched him buy a porchetta sandwich from a polite man with a thoughtful sad expression. A little while later I saw him again on the Viale di Trastevere, sitting on a curb, the shiny rim still around his neck. He had spread out the roast pork sandwich on the road next to the curb, and both he and the kitten were eating from the same greasy paper.

The next morning in Spoleto I passed up breakfast in the hotel dining room. A tall Frenchman, to whom I had given the obvious nickname of de Gaulle, was holding forth to his large family about the quality of the rolls. The crust was not quite right. He should try an American roll, I thought, one of those "bulkie" rolls that comes packaged in plastic and feels like a soggy sponge. Later on in the week, I heard his big voice at a restaurant: he was asking whether the ham was from Parma.

My awe of the French, and my belief in their capacity for joie de vivre, had left me after I had once watched a French couple try to have a picnic. The setting couldn't have been more perfect; we had been looking for a cool place to have lunch after visiting Cortona. Just outside the city, I pointed John up a steep road. We came through a narrow gate in a high wall—just room for one car to pass—and into an empty piazza bordered by a railing. There was shade from the thick oak trees and a good strong breeze. At the edge of the piazza was a locked church and above the church a crumbling fortress. The long alley at the side of the church led to a convent wall, beyond which were terraced vegetable gardens kept by the nuns. A plaque told us that this was the Convent of Saint Margaret, founded in the fourteenth century. The high side windows of the convent were shuttered. It was quiet. The nuns must have been taking their siesta.

We found an old carriageway that took us into deeper shade and had our lunch of bread and cheese and fruit. A few yards away was the French couple. I glanced at them, wondering what they would be eating, imagining that they would have better food than ours. The man was trying to uncork a bottle of wine. He inserted the corkscrew and worked on the bottle for at least ten minutes, all along complaining to the woman. She sympathized with him. She fussily wrapped and unwrapped and rewrapped their lunch. He broke the cork and tried to push it back into the bottle. The cork must have stuck. He then smashed the neck of the bottle against the railing, making a jagged mess. They could not drink the wine. With both hands he pointed to the wine stain on the front of his pants. There were a few yellow jackets buzzing around. Both the man and the woman began frantically batting the air. After an hour of fussing—they didn't eat—they dumped their broken bottle and food into the trash can and left.

When I looked at the guidebook, I found out that we had eaten our lunch at an ancient site—this took no talent in Italy. The fortress was built from Etruscan rubble that had once been a temple to Mars; in the shady grove, Saint Margaret had healed the sick. The breezy spot had been long discovered.

In the Café Collicola near our hotel in Spoleto, I ordered my morning caffè latte. The proprietress was joking with a customer. "Tell me what you want," she said. "I'm your mother. I'll give you anything you want." He was older than she was.

That's a sell I haven't heard before, I thought. The stand-up coffee drinkers were talking at the bar. "My Darling Clementine"
was playing on the café radio. My glass had cooled enough to
drink from, and the milky coffee was rich. On the wide railing
of the café terrace was a row of huge terra-cotta pots filled with
geraniums. I looked at the bright red flowers and thought how I
was already taking this casual beauty for granted. Nuns passed in
summer white. Two Arabs ordered coffee; they were discussing
a letter one of them was about to send. They kept passing it back
and forth; the bright morning light shone through the thin blue
paper. At the next table two elderly women were eating cornetti
and coffee. They were waiting for their car to be washed at the
small garage below the café. A pleasant way to have one's car
washed, I thought. An hour had gone by. I ordered a latte mac-
chiato—milk "spotted" with a few drops of coffee—and sipped
it as I wrote postcards. Then I used the toilet in a small tiled back
room of the café. Above the clean basin was an electrical outlet
for a shaver. Some of the café customers must have shaved here.
There were towels and plenty of toilet paper, and on a high shelf
near a high window was a small pot of geraniums.

I slipped my notebook inside my bag and walked up, this
time turning left on the Corso Mazzini. The cobblestoned street,
which rose less steeply than the route we had taken on our first
walk, led to a small terrace of a park laid with clean, wheat-
colored gravel and bordered with blue hydrangeas. The park
seemed to hang in violet air. I could see that there were steps
that led up to the north side of the Piazza del Duomo, but I decided to spend some time in the park. Below the terrace, Spoleto's
pale orange and gold buildings made the hillside look like a stylized orchard. A young couple was murmuring and kissing on the
bench behind me.

On these walks in Spoleto I would think of Ivo, now dead
of cancer. In the three years before he died he had broken out

of academe. Finally recovered from the breakup with Roberta, he had played the stock market with a nervy intense brilliance, bought three old houses, and began restoring them. Ivo had been with us on our two previous trips to Italy. In 1966, on my first trip, I had followed him down some of Rome's narrow alleylike streets. His overlong slender arms would be close to his sides; as always, he would hunch his shoulders as if against some cold breeze, even in August. His thin white shirt would rest smoothly against his torso, which had the square-shouldered flatness of those teenage champion swimmers who look like Cycladic idols. Ivo was a subtle guide. He would suddenly take my arm and gently pull me toward him. We would have come off the dark narrow street, which gave no warning of the sight ahead, into the sunstruck Piazza Navona, or the Piazza della Rotondo in front of the Pantheon, or the tiny square of the Church of Santa Maria della Pace—all of which I was seeing for the first time. His blue eyes would be serene as he watched my amazed face.

It was also through Ivo that I felt a little of what we used to discuss as undergraduates—agape, spiritual love. Ivo was staying with us in Maine, and he and I were preparing a meal of mussels in wine sauce. I was scrubbing the mussels; he was sitting at the long kitchen table, cutting up garlic. The kitchen was badly equipped: no large chopping knife. Ivo was patiently peeling the many cloves needed and chopping them almost to a paste with a tiny knife. He seemed to have all the time in the world. We chatted as we worked and were comfortable in the long pauses. Every once in a while I would turn from the sink and watch Ivo. I felt I was seeing him for the first time, seeing him in himself, not as I wanted him to be or imagined him to be. He was absorbed, contained, graceful, happy in himself, unaware that I was watching him with acutely free attention.

At about eleven, I walked down to meet John in Spoleto's Piazza del Mercato. He was drinking coffee—no more morning pick-me-ups to stop the jitters—and had the newspaper spread out in front of him. I ordered mineral water and read the upside-down headlines—mostly about the heat wave. "Someone stopped me for directions," John said. "I meant to say that I was *sorry* that I didn't know; instead I told them, 'I am very *happy* that I don't know.'" In Rome he had pointed to a peach and said, "I'd like that fish." John was delighted with these lapses in his good Italian. On the train he had asked if a seat were a "book," mixing up the words for "free" and "book." (A friend told us about a Pole in America who could not get "geezer" and "gizzard" straight.)

"Where shall we go for lunch?" John asked, smiling. "You are having a good time," I replied. He looked up, taking off his glasses. His hazel eyes widened; they looked smoky. He used to be so careful—in some ways—afraid about spending money, afraid of having a good time.

John's family history had trained him to believe that disaster would follow pleasure. His father was a gambler. When he had a few bucks, he'd blow everything on vacations; in October there'd be no money to heat the house. He'd treat himself to cashmere overcoats, buy diamond watches for his wife at Christmas, which she would always return. He still thought of himself as a rich man's son. His father, John's grandfather, had made a fortune in the futures market. Potatoes, turnips, grapes—at one point he had owned every grape in America. The son of farmers, he never invested in the stock market: it was too abstract. On Friday nights he would bring home suitcases full of money to the Winter Street house in Arlington. After dinner they would pull down the shades, and the children would count the money. Often there would be more than fifty thousand dollars. The Lanes liked the feel of the actual money in their hands. John's father would always talk about those Friday nights. Just last week I saw John's aunt Louise. She told me she never went back to the old house. "I like to remember it as it was," she said wistfully.

The Lanes had lived well. The floors of the two parlors of the Greek revival house were covered in pale blue and cream Chinese rugs. The long-legged children played tennis on their own private courts. When they went to Sunday morning mass, they saw orphans being paraded up and down the aisles so that parishioners could take their pick. Few would be chosen. Then they'd go home, the twelve children, grateful for Sunday dinner. The family's prime beef was stored in a walk-in icebox. If it were midsummer they would eat nothing but corn and tomatoes and blueberry shortcake. There was never any liquor in the house. The Lanes were temperance and had helped make Arlington dry, which it remained until the eighties.

The children called their father "the Boss." John's uncle Joseph told me that "the old man could never be wrong. We couldn't fight him."

By the thirties the money was gone. John's grandfather had left his wife and two unmarried daughters in the Winter Street house and gone back to live in Boston where he had started out in business when he came over from Ireland. He took an apartment in the market, in one of the old granite buildings. "He lived right above a stall," John had told me, "right over vegetables. The place looked like a stable." He joined the L Street Brownies, a Boston group whose yearly ritual is a New Year's Day swim in Boston Harbor. "The old man was always rubbing himself with alcohol," John said. "He'd give himself enemas with spinach water. He'd cook up a pile of spinach and drain off the water. Told us kids it was good for his health."

John's father, unlike some of his brothers who went to good schools like Princeton and Yale, became a waiter in one of the Boston hotels. He would gamble away his paycheck on the numbers and always seemed to feel that money would arrive from somewhere, in suitcases perhaps. At his rare appearances at Sunday dinner, he would look at his wife and complain, "Old woman," he would say, "this roast is as hard as your heart." She

would glare at him, "I can't give you filet on what you give me."
There were always arguments about money. Late at night, after
his mother and father had fought and his father had torn out
of the house yet another time, John's mother would fix a pot of
strong coffee, and she and John would sit up talking. The mid-
night coffee became a ritual. "We'd be jumping out of our skins,"
John said. She would be wrapped in her blue chenille bathrobe,
her straight black hair braided into a long rope, her white skin
paler than usual. She would empty the contents of her heavy
black pocketbook onto the table of the breakfast nook, which she
had painted herself. She was an expert with oil paint. There were
no brush marks in the pale gray surface. The red-and-white-
checked curtains were crisp as always. She'd empty her wallet
and count the few bills; then she'd shake out the change purse,
hoping for fifty-cent pieces.

The stalls of the market next to the café in Spoleto were
loaded. One woman was selling gigantic tight-petaled sunflow-
ers as big as the wheel of a child's bicycle. Her thick, stark white
hair was cut to her ears and stood out around her broad tanned
face. Her slanting eyes gave her a Mongolian look. She reminded
me of my grandmother Molly. She had broad shoulders and a
strong neck. When she got up to weigh vegetables in her hand
scale, I could see that she had some arthritis; she rocked a little.
She was selling small hard eggplants with faint white streaks;
green, yellow, and red peppers; dead ripe tomatoes that had lost
their shine and others not quite ripe with streaks of yellow near
the stem and shiny tight skins. The potatoes were magnificent;
like chipped prehistoric flints, they seemed designed to fit in
human hands. In between customers, she would take bites from
her porchetta sandwich, which she held in both hands.

As John and I sat talking, an old Italian woman carrying an
empty shopping bag stopped in front of him, bent down, and
patted his bare legs, "My husband used to have beautiful legs like

that," she said. Her wrinkled face was tanned and handsome; she had heavy gold loops stuck in her ears. Together we appreciated my husband's legs.

John was wearing shorts—JIMMY'Z—that he had bought in California where he often traveled on business; he produced videos for a corporation in Cambridge. He had his own neighborhood there on the beach outside Los Angeles. He'd eat crabs on the fish pier at Redondo Beach, cycle for hours on the bike path that ran along the beach, stop for coffee at a café crowded with Russian immigrants. In California he'd wear lavender shirts, and go to Alcoholics Anonymous meetings on the beach.

At home he worked out at a health club where he had won the masters trophy and lifted the highest weight in any class. "There's going to come a point where I'm not going to get any better, where I can just hope to hold my own," he would say. But he could shrug his shoulders at the prospect of his future decay because he was still in good shape. Yet when he was tired, the ghost look of his former drinking days would play over his face—a flicker of ruin.

After a workout, he loved to relax in the steam, this man who had trouble resting. One day at work a fork lift had rolled off the landing stage and hit him in the head, stunning him. "Oh, this is nice," he had found himself saying. He hadn't been that woozy since he stopped drinking. "It's almost as good as booze," he would say about the steam.

The Italian heat and the slow pace of the days in Spoleto relaxed him. In the middle of the day we ate slowly, course after course—wide flat noodles in an intense sauce made from the meat of wild boar; grilled trout; red peppers, skinned, tamed, and sweetened in a pool of green olive oil; a bowl of melting peaches a beat away from rottenness; I would drink grappa, or perhaps amaro, sweet and bitter, to sip slowly. Was this why our grandparents and parents had labored? So that we could finally relax? We'd make love after lunch and sleep. All during that trip we found ourselves listening to the man on the train. Often on our way to a meal, we'd dig our thumbs into the corner of our mouths and mimic the bullet-headed Umbrian's gesture. "Lazio, Umbria . . . Umbria, Lazio . . ." It turned out that we had been powerless to resist him.

Trees of Home

The wind began at night. The sound of open casement windows banging violently against the bedroom wall woke me, and I went through Il Colombaio, a converted farmhouse rented to us by an American couple, locking doors and closing windows and shutters. Immediately the air became stuffy. I could feel pressure building in the sealed room as if we were climbing; the bedsheets turned gritty.

The windows rattled, and at one point, the hall casement burst open, crashing against the solid plaster wall. I hadn't shot the bolt all the way. Amazing—the glass hadn't shattered.

There were four of us staying at Il Colombaio. John was usually up first; in fact, he was often back from his walk before I got up. Sometimes there would be a bowl of blackberries waiting for me on the kitchen counter. John liked to return with breakfast gifts. On one stay in a dreary motel back home, he had gone out early and stumbled on a farmers' market set up in a parking lot of a Pittsfield mall. He spread out a towel on the bed and laid out his finds: tiny local plums, a basket of blueberries, a wedge of sharp cheddar, some hard rolls. If we were in California, he'd have strawberries. He'd then make coffee with a beat-up kettle he carried along on his trips. He would always bring back the local newspaper, and together we would read the real estate ads.

At Il Colombaio, Lew, Patsy, and I would straggle one by one to the big white sunken kitchen. At each arrival, you could hear the coffee pot clatter on the stove and then the hiss of espresso. We'd each carry a breakfast tray out to the terrace, but that morning after the weather had changed, it was too windy to eat outside.

I stood in the clear space near the back door, facing the ring of cypress trees, which silently bent in the wind. The wind was so strong it was difficult to keep my eyes open—like being under water. The wind did not rise and fall. I listened for breaks in the roar: there were none; it just pressed on, flattening my hair to my head—again like water.

All the previous week, the weather had been very hot. Lew, who had taken a midday walk through the terraced olive groves a few days before, had found himself saying after an hour, "I could die out here," a pronouncement that did not go with his appearance: he would wear on his walks a khaki-colored hat that was decorated just above the visor with small Disney-sweet pastel pictures of Bambi and Thumper.

The wind was cooling things down. We waited for the rain to begin. Swollen clouds with wispy curling edges moved above the low hills. Over the black swaying plumes of the cypress trees, the sky was dull gray and silver.

I walked down the narrow gravel driveway past a hollow filled with cactus and then out to the wider road, turning left at the fork. I'd do this every morning after breakfast. Near a large storybook farmhouse where an Englishwoman was making a beautiful life—all her animals would have been chosen for the ark—were two enormous cypresses. The dense trees barely moved in the wind, which was now at my back.

Just ahead, in a dip in the road, were dry flattened apples fallen from a few hard-to-reach trees at the far edge of the English- woman's orchard. Masses of butterflies would usually rise from the winy fruit as I passed. Today there were no butterflies. I picked up some fallen apples, stuffed them into my pockets, and went on. The road curved and narrowed as it came to its end.

Below, across a field, was another farmhouse of the same dry light orange brick as Il Colombaio. One morning I had seen a fox here. It had shot across the road in front of me into a narrow run through the high grass. I had never seen the trail until I saw the fox use it. He reached the edge of the field and stood watching me for an instant. His sensitive pointed ears stood up straight. His eyes were very bright. I felt happy. From then on, every time I passed the field, I would pick out the fox trail: a dark unmistakable line. How had I missed it?

Where the road ended, the hills dropped steeply into a narrow valley and then rose again. There were usually fires on the distant hills, moving pickets of flame, pushing black smoke before them. The farmers had been burning their fields in the early mornings but not today; the wind was too strong. To the left, the hills were white, that strange bleached chalky soil that you see in some parts of Tuscany, great deep-plowed clods of limestone like massive clinkers shaken out of a giant furnace.

One morning John had come with me. That time we had turned right at the fork and then left into a narrow dirt road that cut through steep vineyards. At the crest of the hill was an empty farmhouse. The roof tiles were broken, the stairs caved in. John, finding the one window that wasn't boarded up, gave me a boost so I could see in. The room was long and low, roofed with timbers. There were no cracks in the thick plaster walls. The floor was littered with paper and dirt, broken bits of crockery. We had immediately begun planning how we would fix up the house, how we would plant the garden, what animals we would have. We wondered how much it would cost; we wondered whether the well still worked, whether there was water. I had seen a desperate English tourist buying up mineral water in the village grocery. She and her husband had arrived at their vacation villa to find that the well had run dry.

John loved to look in the windows of unoccupied houses. When we had been staying at his cousin's camp, a small log cabin without electricity and running water on Lake Aziscohos in Maine, he would take me to the widely scattered cabins on the lake. Most of them were not being used. He had already examined their construction, design, and heating arrangements. He would usually glimpse one room and then imagine the rest of the house. He would begin improving on the design, refining, expanding, choosing the best points for his own imaginary house. Since our son, Dave, was skiing, John thought of building in ski country. But then he would conclude, as he always did, by saying that we already had a house, and it was better to come and go and not be attached to another place. Besides, Dave was traveling with his friends, trying different slopes.

Our house in Arlington had not needed rebuilding; we had done most of our work in the garden, constructing brick paths, edging a long border with large stones that John hauled home from construction sites. Now we added a plant here and there, or we moved plants; there was really not much to do. Perhaps that's why for years John needed to carry on this running, constantly changing plan for a second house. In the past few months he's been working on a log cabin. Just the other day, he came out of the bathroom fresh from his morning shave. Still groggy, I huddled over my tea and the *New York Times*. John had already been up for hours; I shrank from his early-morning cheer. "I've solved the problem," he said. "About how to hoist the logs. You could build the cabin around a tree and use the tree to winch up the logs." "Then what?" I asked, noncommittally playing my part. "Cut the tree down." "That's how Ulysses built a bedroom for himself and Penelope. Around an olive tree." "You see," John laughed. He was still at what he called the Iron Age stage, trying to work out each problem by himself; when he had gone as far as he could go on his own, he would finally look at books and plans and then begin improving on those plans, brooding over them in the same way he brooded over his shoes. He had large hard-to-fit feet and was always adding pads and supports. He had made friends with the "Swamies," as he called them, a group of white-turbaned shoe-selling members of an Indian sect who had opened the Golden Temple shoe store in Harvard Square. His search for the perfect shoe was one form of his quest for the ideal. Ever since I had known him, he had been searching for the perfect watchband, hat, gloves. He made endless adaptations to his clothes, trying to erase the boundaries between himself and the world. I thought of my husband as a mender of the Fall when Adam and Eve were forced to cover themselves with awkward clothing. John loved to discuss his feet with the head spiritual entrepreneur. The way of the foot.

After our stay on Aziscohos, he had decided that we could do without running water and electricity. There we had hauled up water from the lake. John thought that his log cabin should have a well but no indoor plumbing. His cousin's cabin had lamps that ran off a large propane tank. I found I could read by the weak greenish light. John had brought his tapes and a Walkman. He had become interested in opera, another metamorphosis.

Family life wasn't fixed. Though I found myself becoming like my parents when I brought up my own son—the same mixture of fear and generosity—I also learned that family life could also be a kind of alchemy. There always seemed to be something new—not just my looking at things from a new angle. John would sit on the couch, the new large foam-edged earphones covering his close-to-the-head oval-shaped ears. One night he listened to *Madama Butterfly*, while I read Jane Austen's *Emma*, a novel about a woman who thought she knew how things worked, who believed she knew about the human heart. She was usually wrong. The muffled sound of the opera would sometimes escape. Sometimes John would whisper the words, for instance, "Non son più quella! . . . l'occhio riguardò nel lontan troppo fiso." (I am not the same any more! . . . these eyes have gazed too long into the distance.) How can he take it? I would ask myself. I couldn't stand to listen to opera, especially with earphones. The experience of that beautiful sound, that pure feeling pouring into my ears, into the soft hollows inside the hard skull bones, the plates of the bones sending the sound deeper into defenseless tissue, was horrible. Unlike John I needed some kind of foil, some kind of screen: the sight of the beefy tenor, the sweating soprano, my son David as a young boy, mimicking the soprano by singing out "seaweed" in a piercing falsetto, the creak of the stage boards, the cough from the audience. I was shocked by John's capacity to take the naked sound. Seaweed, I wanted to shout.

On one broiling late afternoon on our way back to Il Colombaio after a tiring trip to see the Il Sodomo frescoes in the cloister at Monte Oliveto Maggiore, I had noticed a flock of white sheep climbing one of these bleached hills—white moving over spectral white. From where we were at the foot of the hill, the sheep looked flat, like white birds pressed against a cliff with wings half-folded. They dragged a small black tattered shadow between their back legs. Without those shadows as markers, I'm not sure I would have seen them. "Look at that hawk," John said. The spot grew larger. "I'm sure it's a hawk." I seldom could pick out birds—or any other animals, while John, who never noticed a smudge on a wall, could always spot a bird, or an animal, or an insect. Canoeing through water plants on Spy Pond in Arlington, he would whisper, "Look, a muskrat." He had spotted— among all that grass—the wiry tail sticking up above the water. How does he do it? I wondered. He's so blind.

In a few minutes we were in a valley on a narrow road filled with sheep. These were cropped close across the back and shoulders. Their horns curled close to their heads like perfectly fitting cloches. There was no strain in their sturdy necks; their short spines expressively widened into head bulbs—a soft line from tail to head tip—the Yoga ideal. We inched along, the animals close on either side. Their underbellies showed, bare, black, wet-

looking. Their thick, fusty smell filled the car. Suddenly I didn't
feel tired. The animals rested me; I could rest in them.

Across the valley near Il Colombaio, the fields were
empty. I headed back from my morning walk. Sheets and towels,
hanging in what used to be the hay shed, bellied in the wind and
at intervals slowly dragged like stage curtains. They were still
damp. The wind seemed to be letting up. Under the heavy clouds,
the light was lurid, streaked. Occasionally a sun-smothered glare
would break through, and little broken pools of shadow would
appear under the ruthlessly pruned olive trees. Soon the wind
picked up again with even more force. I let the sheets hang.

Still in his bathrobe, Lew sat in the shuttered living room
hunched over his book about Bernard Berenson; Patsy, the pro-
file of her face like a quarter moon under her piled-up heavy hair,
was writing in her notebook, postcards—Il Sodomo's elegant
self-portrait, the wide big-eyed marquetry cat from the choir
stall of Monte Olivieto—spread out in front of her. She had been
reading *The Charterhouse of Parma*. When we noticed how the
farmers in Montisi constantly cultivated the ground underneath
the olive trees, Patsy had told us about the nobleman in the novel
who looks forward to returning home and turning over the earth
under the trees of his family estate. She moved her raised hands
in a raking motion. "This apparently is very important to the
Italians," she said in the tenderly ironic way she conveyed an
idea. John had retreated upstairs; he was reading a biography of
Mussolini. On the hall table was a sign we had made quoting the
preposterous rule the novelist Anita Brookner had heard from
her grandmother: "A gentleman never wears his slippers outside
his bedroom."

I went out again. A few drops fell like water being flung off the
fingertips. I could see lightning far off in the distance. There was
a muffled sound of thunder, but the thunder and lightning did

not seem to go together. The thunder stopped; the blue streaks shot through the sky—dry and silent. It was as if someone had turned off the sound. "Have you noticed how the cypresses move but don't make a sound?" Lew had asked me.

Lew offered to cook dinner. Later that day he came back from the village butcher with a chunk of smoky bacon. While the pasta boiled, he covered the curled rendered bits with beaten eggs and cheese, threw on coarsely ground black pepper, and served the pasta carbonara in a huge heated platter. Patsy had on large red hair clips to match her long dark red jacket. She poured me a glass of Montepulciano red. I was drunk in a minute. The wine had a terrific kick. We ate and laughed. The nuggets of fatty meat gave the unctuous sauce bite. The wind was still blowing.

The conversation turned to jobs. John said that he believed that he had never been very good at anything. Lew looked up quickly, "And you're the only one here who's earning a real living." Lew was a writer. "You actually work a full week." He talked about his former job as an alcoholism counselor. They had shown a film about the effects of alcohol to the patients on the detox ward. One of the drunks stared at the picture of an enlarged blackened liver and whispered, "I'll never eat liver again."

The small black cat, who daily deserted the Englishwoman's perfect house for Il Colombaio, stepped in proudly with a mouse clamped in her sharp dainty mouth; its tiny legs dangled. The cat ate quickly, making soft crunching noises as we finished off the wine.

That night I woke with cramps—a period coming—and lay awake until morning, listening to the foreign wind. The silent lightning, which blued the walls, still frightened me. The wind tore across the hill, and whistled through the trees, but no rain fell. I felt sad listening to the foreign wind and found myself thinking of Rilke's great poem of autumn:

Already the ripening barberries are red
and the old asters hardly breathe in their beds.
The man who is not rich now as summer goes
will wait and wait and never be himself.

Then, as always, I got impatient with Rilke. No, I thought. Better
to feel the loss, better to feel poor and helpless before the wind.
That too didn't sound right. Oh, come on, you're talking to
Rilke in the middle of the night in Tuscany? What's really going
on with you? The sadness was real and deep, a hot ache under
my breastbone. The wind went on, and I thought of home—
hungrily. I was homesick. I missed the green trees. Whenever I
flew over Arlington on the way into Logan, I was amazed by the
trees. You couldn't see the houses. We lived in a forest of old
trees: oak, sycamore, beech, ash, chestnut, pine, spruce, hem-
lock. I wanted to be under those trees. I wanted to be home in
America. I wanted to feel the cool shade and watch the jagged
leaves, windblown, split the shadows into spangles. I wanted to
hear the north wind zing through the spruce trees. I wanted the
weather to change. (When my back had finally healed after an
injury so that I could drive again, I came over the Winches-
ter hills. I hadn't driven for a year. The green-black pines were
frosted with a light coat of snow, which was already melting.
The trees were as alive as animals, the deep shag of the branches
parted like fur. I looked straight into the green and cried.)

Could I go as far as Thoreau, who believed that the great
American landscape—more rugged and more beautiful than anything in Europe—would produce greater people? "Else . . . why
was America discovered?" he sincerely asked in his essay "Walking." "[O]ur hearts," he wrote, "shall even correspond in breadth
and depth and grandeur to our inland seas." A patriotism for
poets: the heart as an enclosed sea, the correspondence between
the inner body and the outer world of nature; but this outer

world, the American interior was, in Thoreau's metaphoric language, firmly bounded, a contained openness that could change, which would not stagnate, an image of the soul—the only patriotism I could believe in.

I had to admit that something in me—I was shy about calling it my heart—did correspond to America or at least to the trees of home. There in Montisi I understood that I was far more deeply rooted to home than I had ever imagined. And New England was my home. Before this I believed that I was only truly at home in two places: Jersey and Italy. A friend of mine who was involved in Jewish studies talked about how she now understood that her life here was just a pause in the long Diaspora. I couldn't say that for myself. America, no matter how fouled her inland seas, had fed me culture and wildness. Home was not an *idea*; home came with specific earth, with colors, scent, and weather, and also with spiritual and social problems. Like the Italian who came home to his olive tree in Italy—not Greece or France—I had to come home to America. Unlike Thoreau, that devoted son who never wrote about being a son, I had to write about family.

I missed my son, Dave. When he was about three, and we were living in the old house in Framingham, he loved to go out the back door by himself, especially to play in the snow. It was one easy shallow step from inside to outside. "I wish you could tie a long long rope around my waist," Dave said, "and I could go out far far, and if you wanted me, you could just pull a little, and I would come back." I once thought that the story was about his need, but it was about both of us. For so long I had felt the weight of that rope, heard the sounds of his coming and going. I was still listening for him. I called him from the small grocery store in Montisi. The connection was poor, and his voice came across muffled and strange. After the call, I missed him even more.

We were getting along now; the wild fury that had driven

him in adolescence, and had made me feel that I was turning into a wall for him to thud against, seemed to be leaving him. He still wasn't talking much, but he and I were treating each other with a sweet courtesy that seemed medieval. We needed to do simple things for each other. I had become a sort of Lady Mother. Once in a while, if I were up early enough, I'd leave a lunch in a bag on the kitchen counter. "Thanks," Dave would call up the stairs, and take off for work in his blue four-wheel-drive Pathfinder, which he had just bought. (His car payments were enormous.) Occasionally I would iron a shirt for him. In return, he would compliment me on my garden, open a tight jar. Gracefully kneeling at my feet, he changed a flat tire for me— Dave never seemed to make a clumsy movement.

He had left school at sixteen and got his high school equivalency diploma. He worked part time as a cashier in a high-volume variety store and part-time as a cook. He soon went on to a computer manufacturing business where he worked at a variety of service jobs.

"I'm going," Dave would call out at the door as he was leaving for work. He would come home in the dark from his long secret day. I would have arrived home first. I would have put down my schoolbooks. (I was teaching again at the state college in Framingham.) I would have taken an apple or a cup of tea upstairs to my room. I would be reading alone in a quiet house, just as I had when I was a schoolgirl waiting for my family to come home. "Hello? Hello?" Dave would call out as he walked in the door. I would always jump at the sound of that "Hello?" My father had come home with the same question. Dave's voice had the same timbre as my father's. My life had been easier than my father's; my life was easier than my son's. Dave never talked about work. I wondered whether he, like my father, was ashamed.

When Dave was eighteen, two of his closest friends were at the scene of a violent murder that shocked and frightened all of us. It seemed that all our fear, ignited by those Sunday morning scenes of destruction—smashed fences, windows, broken trees—had been borne out. The Saturday night of the murder had started with a bunch of teenagers, including Dave and his girlfriend, Sandy, drinking beer at Spy Pond in Arlington. Some of the group had gone on to Cambridge and gotten totally smashed, drinking zombies at a bar known for serving minors. Dave and Sandy had skipped the bar and gone home to her house. I was on my way back from Paris that night. John's brother, Peter, who had been staying with Dave, picked me up at the airport. I came home tired and was in bed by eight. The next morning I found that Dave had not come home; I called Sandy's house. "She snuck him in again," her mother told me. At about eleven that morning, Jay Moran, an Arlington detective, came to the door. A boy had been stabbed in the driveway of the Masonic temple just across the street from our house. "Had I heard anything?" he wanted to know. "Where was David last night?" he asked. I told him. The boy died later that day.

He and a group of friends were headed to a party in Medford, an adjoining town. They had been drinking pitchers of piña colada before they started off in two cars. The boy who would soon be dead was driving alone, the others in a second car. They turned onto Academy Street. The boys in the first car, realizing that they had gone wrong, turned around in the driveway of the Masonic temple and headed back down to Massachusetts Avenue. The boy driving alone then pulled into the driveway also to turn around but found himself facing a group of boys, the gang just back from the bar in Cambridge, among them Dave's friends Robin Quick and Stanley Reightman. The gang in the driveway and the boy in the car challenged each other, shouting taunts and insults, one witness said. The boy got out of his car and went for Shaun Boucher with karate kicks—later it came out that he had a black belt. Shaun pulled out a double-bladed butterfly knife and stabbed him over and over again. The wounded boy somehow got back into the car, drove down to Massachusetts Avenue, and crashed into the mailbox in front of the town hall. In the hospital his body, gray from loss of blood, had swelled so much that his parents could not recognize him.

The boys who had witnessed the murder kept quiet for nearly a month, then cracked. Robin Quick, who had gone to grammar school with Dave, led the police to the knife; they had buried it in a field near Spy Pond. Shaun was given a life sentence without parole.

That fall Dave and Sandy stayed close to home. At Halloween the four of us sat at the newspaper-covered dining room table, carving jack-o'-lanterns. Sandy's honey blonde hair flew about her face as she worked, pursing her delicate mouth. I found myself noticing her hands—small of back with tapered fingers. Dave's jack-o'-lantern had a fierce, angry face with close-together eyes; mine was sloppy and leering; John's grinning; and Sandy's angelic. The three of us stared in amazement at the angel face. Sandy's retreat to innocence worried me.

Years later, Dave told me and John that, the day after the murder, he had found out that Robin and Stan had been at the scene. For weeks he was afraid that one of them was the murderer. No one was talking about Shaun. As it turned out, Robin and Stanley didn't know that Shaun had a knife. All they saw was a scuffle. Then Shaun called out, "I stabbed him." They didn't believe Shaun until they saw the bloody knife. Robin grabbed the knife and ran to the house of a friend.

"Just think what that was like," Dave said, "Robin washing the blood off the knife in Joe Green's kitchen, standing there, watching the blood flow down the drain." Dave was pale. The three of us were sitting on the porch. The oaks and maples were in full leaf, and the wind made a shushing sound through the branches. Under his black-stroked eyebrows, Dave's dark eyes deepened.

By that time, Dave was in college—America was still a country for second chances. He and Robin and another friend had moved into a light-flooded apartment on the Mystic River Parkway overlooking the Mystic River in tree-thick Arlington.

I slept late in the farmhouse in Montisi. When I got up, I could hear John making coffee in the kitchen below. Patsy and Lew were still asleep. The foreign wind was still blowing. I opened the shutters and looked out to the terraces of olive trees set in the shallow hills like hard embroidery. I was hungry. I wanted my fruit and coffee.

In the afternoon, we drove to Montepulciano to look at the Tempietto, San Biagio. The dome rose at the end of a cypress-lined drive. The church was set on a flat grassy field. There was only a shallow step up from the grass into the church, and although the travertine walls were thick, they did not block out the sound of the wind. Unlike many churches, San Biagio's was connected to the outside; the bare, steeply mounting dome seemed—even from the inside, even as it contained its own atmosphere, its inner sea—to be rising into air. The travertine seemed honeycombed with air.

Near the entrance was a painting of the crucifixion. Two brightly made-up women with dark-dyed lustrous hair came in; one was dressed in sky blue—bag, shoes, scarf, everything—the other in red. They knelt happily before the sad scene, praying quickly. The woman in red stood up and tossed loud smacking kisses at Jesus off the backs of her fingers.

The small door, which was cut in the immense closed door— it could have admitted an elephant—was half-open. Since the church was set so low, the view from the small door was a band of grass under a thin, thin strip of sky. The colors were smoky in the yellowish light—the kind of light you see just before a tornado. The wind whirled around the church like a comet. The low banks of candles near the open door guttered, burning down furiously, lopsidedly, but they did not go out. The whitish flames fattened. I watched the candles drip clear drops. The wind was loud; again the green seemed to smolder, about to burst into flame, but you could see each blade of grass, each detail. I sat with my back against the stone wall; I felt lifted and held, in the moment a believer, while the foreign wind went on.

In a few days I would be home.